Pathways to the Divine

"John Kralovec's *Pathways to the Divine* is a beautifully written and moving story which captures the heart and soul of the ancient Maya in a truly unique and memorable way. The writing is rich and dynamic and includes exquisite descriptions of the author's experiences. While grounded in historical fact and the latest archeological findings, John's profound spiritual insights add a new dimension to academic research. Stories such as Pakal's death and the author's encounter with Ix-Chel at both Tikal and Coba, are fantastically powerful."

— Joy Parker, co-author, *Maya Cosmos:*
Three Thousand Years on the Shaman's Path

"This book is a highly original, engaging, and authentic metaphysical document of a genuine spiritual seeker's journey of a lifetime ... John reveals the incredibly sophisticated spiritual technology of the Maya, Lakota, Anasazi and other indigenous cultures of North America. Even better, he so wholly absorbed me into the mystical visions that he exquisitely described that I lost all sense of self and time and I had my own mystical experiences along with his. It's been a very long time since a book has transported me this way. More than ever in this chaotic world, we need spiritual instructors to guide and inspire us on our own paths to God. Through his book, John has beautifully shared so much of value that he personally discovered and that he learned from others, both in this world and from the higher spiritual realms. In doing so he has become a spiritual guide and inspirational teacher for us. *Pathways to the Divine* is a powerful and important achievement."

— Walter Robert Dominguez, Producer-Director,
Weaving the Past: Journey of Discovery

"John Kralovec has written an extraordinary book that offers a rare glimpse into the spiritual realm of the ancient Maya. No anthropological work can come close to capturing the true grandeur of the culture the way *Pathways to the Divine* does. Kralovec cites many academic works in this well-researched book, but his own spiritual adventures are what make it such a fascinating read. Anthropologists and archeologists can only interpret based on their own life experience, so they're really stuck in what current Maya elders call "a materialistic view." Yet the ancient Maya come alive through Kralovec's shamanic experiences and rich descriptions. For readers who want to know if there's more to life than our 9-5 jobs, TV news and celebrity gossip, Kralovec affirms that the answer is a resounding "yes." And it can be found in deep spiritual work, having an adventurous spirit and belief in the unseen realms."

    — Molly Larkin, co-author,
        The Wind Is My Mother: The Life and Teachings
        of a Native American Shaman

"John Kralovec has shown a remarkable transformation in the past three decades, grasping the essence of both Lakota and Maya spirituality. Now, he is on a journey to serve others and one of those ways is through this inspired work, *Pathways to the Divine*. His message, and those of indigenous teachers everywhere, is vitally needed today."

    — Doug Alderson, author,
        Seminole Freedom; The Vision Keepers:
        Walking for Native Americans and the Earth

PATHWAYS TO THE DIVINE

One Man's Journey Through the
Shamanic Realm of the Ancient Maya

OTTO JOHN KRALOVEC III

SUMMIT PRESS

SUMMIT PRESS

PO Box 235 • Granville, Ohio 43023

First Edition

ISBN: 978-0-9983533-0-2

Library of Congress Control Number: 2016918718

Printed in the United States of America

Otto John Kralovec III

PathwaysToTheDivine.org

FB: Otto John Kralovec

T: @pathwaysdivine

Cover Design by Lászió Kiss, Super Massive Studio

Book Design and Illustrations by Herkelrath Design

Back Cover photograph courtesy of

Grupo Megamedia, Archivo del Diario de Yucatán

DEDICATION

*To my wife, Julie, and my sons, Nick and Chris,
for their continual encouragement, support,
and understanding while I missed so much family time
for this endeavor. I'm particularly grateful for
their belief in me and this project and their
willingness to help me pursue my
spiritual passions wherever they led.*

CONTENTS

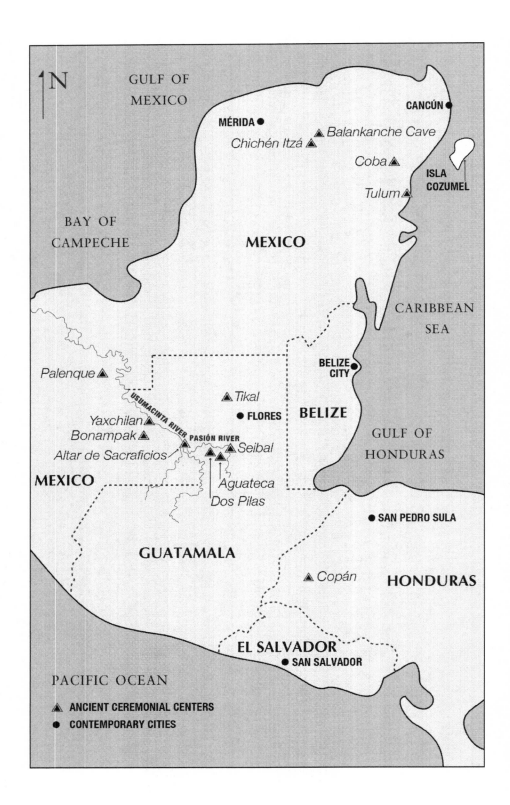

THE MAYA

The ancient Maya civilization began on the Yucatan Peninsula in Mexico three thousand years ago as small self-sufficient farming settlements began evolving into large civic centers. It would become one of the world's greatest, rivaling those of ancient Egypt, China, Persia, and Greece. Scholars have compared the political landscape of the Maya of the Classic period (250–909 CE) to that of Renaissance Italy or Classical Greece, with multiple city-state kingdoms such as Chichen Itza that grew from isolated cities into regional powerhouses dominating politics, trade, and culture.

The Maya were highly literate with an elegant, sophisticated writing system and they distinguished themselves as gifted artists by creating stunning sculpture, pottery, and murals. They were master architects admired for their spectacular, awe-inspiring pyramids, temples, and ceremonial centers, and they excelled at astronomy and mathematics. The Maya were accomplished statesmen and women, noted military tacticians, and fierce warriors. By the time their achievements reached their peak around 1000 CE, their extraordinary cities were located throughout Mexico, Guatemala, Belize, and Honduras, with complex long-distance trade routes including those to Native North Americans living in present-day Arizona and New Mexico, twenty-five hundred miles to the north.

Just after its peak, the Maya's magnificent empire began a mysterious decline. Scholars still debate the cause but many have come to believe it was the result of a combination of factors that included overpopulation, environmental degradation, and prolonged drought. The arrival of Columbus in the Americas was the death knell for native cultures and the Maya were among the first to be targeted for eradication. At the beginning of the Spanish Conquest in the early 1500s, although their empire had been in decline for five hundred years and major cities had been abandoned, the Maya were still a dominant presence with a population conservatively estimated to have been at least eight million. Within the next seventy-five years, over 90 percent of the population was decimated. Small pox, measles, and other European diseases were the primary factors, but many died fighting the invaders.

As the Spanish *conquistadors* took control of the Maya lands and natural resources, Franciscan friars began their equally brutal and ruthless efforts to convert the Maya to Christianity and eliminate the native culture. Historians from the period recorded the widespread destruction of pyramids, temples, and shrines. They also observed that when the Maya resisted conversion to Christianity, the Franciscans tortured and imprisoned their spiritual leaders and burned their books and sacred texts. Of the Maya who survived the holocaust, some were held as slaves, others intermarried, and the remainder fled to remote mountain and jungle areas to survive on subsistence farming, hunting, and fishing. By the 1600s, the Maya had lost everything—their ancestral lands, their magnificent culture, most of their kinsmen, and their freedom.

Miraculously, the Maya managed to survive. Some cultural and social traditions were maintained clandestinely while their spiritual beliefs and some ceremonies were hidden and practiced in secret. Although they have continued to suffer horrific persecution, deprivation, and marginalization over the last five hundred years, their population has grown from a few hundred thousand at the time of the Spanish Conquest to over seven million today. Scholars have recently been able to decipher their hieroglyphics and resurrect their ancient culture. Pyramids, temples, and ceremonial centers have been rescued from the voracious tropical rainforest and restored meticulously. And their astounding spiritual wisdom, the only surviving written record of ancient shamanic practice, is finally reemerging, destined to take its place alongside the other great world religions.

Over my thirty-year journey with the Maya, I discovered that the pyramids and temples remaining today in the physical world are a reflection of their towering spiritual genius and spectacular shamanic insights. The true legacy of the ancient Maya is a stunning holistic and integrated spiritual worldview that provides an ancient path for us to remember who we are, why we're here, and how to live a life of balance and harmony in the twenty-first century. A path that can also lead to Awakening.

Note on terminology: A brief section, beginning on page 373, titled "Terminology," provides readers with an overview of Mayan, American Indian and other key terms used in this book.

PROLOGUE:
IN THE PRESENCE OF THE DIVINE

*Hunab-Ku...the only living and true god [of the Maya]. He had
no form because they said that he could not be represented as he
was incorporeal.*[1] — Diccionario de Moltul

*We should understand well that all things are the works of the
Great Spirit. We should know that He is within all things.*[2]
— Black Elk

PINE RIDGE INDIAN RESERVATION
SOUTH DAKOTA – 2000

Sitting on the ground with a buffalo hide wrapped around my body,
I watched the sun descend softly over the South Dakota Badlands.
A warm June breeze rustled the leaves in the trees and ran through
the tall prairie grasses; the noises of small animals in the brush and
birds singing drifted in the stillness of the evening. I was grateful
to be back in South Dakota, grateful to have returned to the Pine
Ridge Indian Reservation, and grateful to experience another

hanblechya (vision quest). Every summer for the past seven years I had left my home in suburban Philadelphia and traveled to the reservation, home of the Oglala Lakota (Sioux) Indians, to see friends and participate in traditional Plains Indian spiritual ceremonies.

It was hard for me to believe that the previous week I had been in a suit and tie, concluding a three-day strategic planning retreat for the board of directors of a prestigious New England-based healthcare system. Most of my friends and business associates knew me as a respected professional, busy with a growing family and active in community affairs. They knew me through my involvement in church, my participation in my sons' Cub and Boy Scout activities, my volunteer participation with several social service organizations, my four-year elected term to our local school board, and my membership in the Rotary Club. My wife, Julie, was a successful professional fundraiser and our two sons were attending local private schools. But only a few very close friends knew of my fascination with indigenous spiritual traditions and my years of participation in ceremonies.

Over the years I had come to cherish my time on the reservation each summer. I never liked leaving Julie and our young sons, Nick and Chris, behind during these pilgrimages, but Julie and I had decided these trips were spiritual retreats for me and not suited for a family vacation. I appreciated my family's understanding and support. Being on the reservation provided a rare opportunity to set aside my career and family responsibilities, step out of my urban, twentieth century lifestyle, and experience the spiritual wisdom of the Plains Indians—an interest of mine since childhood.

Watching the brilliant yellows, oranges, reds, and purples of the prairie sunset, I reflected on the long and surprising spiritual journey I had taken over the last twenty years. My experiences had started at a workshop in shamanism with Michael Harner at the Esalen Institute in Big Sur, California, and progressed from there to include early vision quests with Indian elders in Arizona, California, Colorado, New Mexico, and Utah. I had traveled on spiritual pilgrimages to sites sacred to the Maya Indians in Mexico and Guatemala. And through my friend and mentor, Thomas Mails—a Lutheran minister, nationally-acclaimed artist, and prolific writer on North American Indian history, culture, and spiritual practices—I had found my way to the Pine Ridge Indian Reservation. Although all of these experiences had been quite different, I was intrigued by the similarities between the North American and Maya Indian spiritual traditions.

As the sun started to disappear behind the distant hills, my thoughts drifted back to my visit to this sacred site the previous summer. At that time I had made a commitment to prepare myself for what now seemed like a presumptuous, audacious, and totally unrealistic undertaking. For the past twenty years I had heard stories of direct experiences of "Spirit" (God) from the North American Indian and Maya elders with whom I had studied. Through my ceremonies and vision quests I had encountered divine energies but somehow the thought had never occurred to me, until the previous year, that it might be possible for me to have the same direct experience I had heard about.

In 1985, during my first journey to ancient Maya ceremonial sites in Mexico, I had experienced divine energies for the first time. At Balankanche cave, near Chichen Itza, I had my initial encounter with Ix-Mucane, the Sacred Earth Mother of the Maya. Deep inside the cave, sitting on the dirt floor of a sacred grotto, an entirely new dimension of consciousness opened for me and for the first time I was able to directly experience my "higher self" or "true self"—that aspect of me closest to the Divine. I found myself inside the womb of the Mother, sitting at the center of the universe, resting in a sacred state of being, in the presence of the Universal Soul. I felt myself connected to a source of self-realization and inner strength I had never experienced before, a *knowing* that I was more than just a physical body.

One week later, while doing a ceremony at the ancient Maya center of Palenque, I had an out-of-body experience while journeying to the highest spiritual realms of the Upper World. There I experienced glorious, Divine, cosmic energy and found myself at the place of original Divine creation, where spiritual essence precedes physical manifestation—a place that was described to me as "the place of all knowingness, of calmness and serenity, of clarity, insight, and wisdom; the place of the fulfillment of the spirit and freedom from that which you are not; the place that is the Source and the destination; the place that is the beginning and end of time, the beginning and end of life, the place of heavenly peace."

As dramatic and life-changing as those initial experiences with the ancient Maya had been, factors in my life had shifted dramatically by 1990, making trips to the sacred sites of the ancient Maya next to impossible. My first son, Nicholas, was born in July of that year and my professional responsibilities as a senior executive in a rapidly growing start-up consulting firm were almost all-consuming. International travel was complicated in those days due to lack of sophistication of computer and cell phone technology; staying connected in remote areas of Mexico was impossible. Also, in the mid-nineties, armed conflict between Mexican government troops and rebel Zapatista forces fighting for the rights of the indigenous Maya had broken out in the regions I had previously visited. Casualties among government troops, Zapatistas, and innocent villagers were mounting at alarming rates and tourists faced enormous risks as well. Travel into those regions was out of the question for me.

In 1990 I danced and "pierced" in a Plains Indian-style Sun Dance in Oregon and at that time decided that rather than attempting to return to Mexico to visit ancient ceremonial sites, I would spend some vacation time each summer on the Pine Ridge Indian Reservation participating in *inipi* (sweat lodge), *yuwipi* (healing), and *hanblechya* (vision quest) ceremonies. Although I missed the intensity of my experiences at ancient Maya sites, I found that my hanblechya experiences were as powerful in their own way and that my spiritual journey was still rich and transformative. So even though my earlier experience in Mexico had given me a foundation for this particular quest, my earlier time on the reservation had prepared me as well.

Now another ten years had passed, and I had spent the previous year preparing to go beyond my previous experiences and, hopefully, encounter the Divine directly. I had learned that letting go of emotional and spiritual blocks was essential to keeping me open and receptive to presence of the Divine[3] and I prepared as I had been taught by the Plains Indian elders, through purification ceremonies and prayer.[4] Each month I performed a Plains Indian-style pipe ceremony asking Wakan Tanka and the spirits for guidance and help in succeeding in my quest to encounter the Divine. Four times during the year, on the fall and spring equinoxes and the winter and summer solstices, I participated in sweat lodge purification ceremonies. I also prepared four hundred and five prayer ties[5] and as each tie was made I offered a prayer for some aspect of my vision quest. These were the same types of preparations I had completed in previous years, but this time I had focused intently on meeting the Divine.

Watching the sun sink below the horizon with the buffalo hide wrapped around me, I started to feel my heart sinking as well. I was struck by the fact that rather than feeling empowered or excited I was feeling resigned and foolish. I wanted an experience of the Divine that was real and tangible—not just a vague feeling but something concrete and dramatic. I was hoping for a booming voice in the sky, a burning bush, thunder and lightning, something—anything—that would be real for me. But now I realized I had only a vague idea of what I hoped to experience, and it struck me that my thoughts on an encounter with God were based mostly on Bible stories I had read or first heard about in Sunday school. My deepest wish now seemed to be a complete impossibility.

The hardness of the earth and the sharpness of the pebbles beneath my legs brought my attention back to the reality of my situation. I was thousands of miles away from home, in the wilderness, naked except for swimming trunks and a buffalo hide robe, participating in a ceremony I hoped would help me realize an elusive dream. I was seeking a vision, and I reminded myself to let things unfold in their own way and accept whatever experience I was meant to have. The fragrant odor of South Dakota sage helped me relax; the weight and warmth of the hide around my shoulders was reassuring. Taking a deep breath, I let myself settle into my experience and began to feel the joy I always felt on a vision quest in South Dakota.

Closing my eyes, I began singing the traditional four directions song, vision quest songs, and other Plains Indian prayer songs I had learned from elders many years earlier. Although I sang them in the Lakota language, the words and melodies had become so familiar that the songs and chants came effortlessly.

The songs helped me feel connected to this ancient rite. For thousands—possibly tens of thousands—of years, visions had been sought alone in the wilderness, without food or water, away from any distractions. Although originally I had encountered the vision quest experience through my studies with North American and Maya Indian elders, I had come to learn that this practice also existed in early Christian and Jewish traditions. Recalling Old and New Testament references to solitary pilgrimages into the desert wilderness helped me bridge the gap between my early Christian upbringing and my current experience. My feelings of connectedness to this ancient Christian and indigenous quest tradition helped me cast away my doubts and misgivings.

As the last light of the sun began to fade I started to pray in the traditional Plains Indian manner, sending my voice to Wakan Tanka—the Great Spirit or Sacred Mystery Power. I prayed to the spirit beings, my spirit guides and helpers to pity me, help me, and heal me. I prayed for my mind and heart to be opened to the presence of Spirit/God. I gave thanks for the ancestors and for the traditions they had preserved and handed down to me. I gave thanks for my life and the many blessings I had received. I gave thanks for those who are yet to come and who will continue these traditions in the future. I gave thanks for my family, friends, and community and offered my prayers for their happiness, health, and well-being.

As I finished my first round of prayers I felt calm, centered, and open to the beauty of this sacred place. It was dark now and the stars shone brilliantly in the sky. My questing site was miles from the nearest small town and I was able to settle into the solitude devoid of the lights and urban sounds that are a constant distraction in my normal life. I started to reflect again on my search for a direct experience of God and wondered what God would be like if He were to appear. Would He indeed be like the God of the Old or New Testament? Or here, in the spiritual heartland of the Plains Indians, would He appear as a different God—Wakan Tanka, the Great Spirit? Or Hunab-Ku, the supreme creator deity, the Divine One of the Maya? If God appeared as Wakan Tanka or Hunab-Ku, I had no idea what to expect; indigenous cultures never created images of God because they believed He was incorporeal and had no physical form.

Suddenly I was overcome with the feeling that something was wrong, that something didn't feel right. This realization caused a wave of fear to shoot through my body. It took me a moment to realize what was so frightening. The air was completely still, with not even the slightest trace of a breeze. And there were no sounds of any kind—no more wildlife rustling in the brush, or birds singing in the trees, no humming or chirping of insects. It was absolutely still and quiet in a way I had never experienced in twenty years of being in nature for spiritual ceremonies. It felt as if all motion had stopped and I was sitting suspended in time and space. And then the most amazing thing began happening.

Everything around me seemed to be coming to life in a totally new and different way. An overwhelming and awe-inspiring sense of sacredness was intensifying as if everything around me was taking on another dimension infused with a pulsing, radiant aliveness I had never experienced before. I recalled the Indian elders' descriptions of everything being alive and filled with Spirit—rocks, trees, animals, and all living beings. I remembered their guidance about opening to the presence of Spirit in ceremonies and allowing Spirit to be fully present in and through all things. Memories of my encounters with the Sacred at Maya ceremonial sites—the cave at Balankanche, the ocean temple at Tulum, the pyramids at Coba, Palenque, and Yaxchilan—came flooding back.

Suddenly I realized that the experience I had been seeking was now unfolding before me. I had encountered sacred time and space on many, many occasions over the previous fifteen years. I had been led deeper and deeper into the heart of the sacred mysteries and indigenous spiritual practices in North America, Mexico, and Guatemala. I had journeyed into the Lower World and Upper World and traveled through the Dreamtime of the Maya. I had been allowed to experience higher spiritual realms and expanded states of consciousness. And now it seemed as if all those experiences had been leading me to this encounter. At the deepest level of my being I was aware that I was having the experience for which I had spent the last year longing and praying.

The intensity of the experience kept building and I was filled with the most extraordinary sense of peace—a deep, deep peace I had heard about in Sunday school that "passeth all understanding." I was also filled with complete unconditional love. The sacredness

I was experiencing—above, below, around, in, and through every-thing—was perfectly balanced masculine and feminine energy; the complete embodiment of the Eastern concept of Yin and Yang. God, the Source of all that exists, the Divine, both male and female, was here with me. Now, for the first time, I completely understood the true essence of the indigenous spiritual experience. Although different peoples have used different terms at different times to describe it, what I was experiencing was the one, all-encompassing Divine reality.

In spite of everything, I felt small doubts begin to creep in. Though powerful, this experience wasn't turning out to be anything like I had imagined it would be. Part of me was thinking I was having the wrong experience, that this wasn't really the way it was supposed to happen. However, another part of me recognized that this was the way it truly was and it couldn't be any other way. For the first time the Indian elders' teachings that the world is alive and filled with Spirit, filled with the Divine, made sense to me. I understood their experience of humankind as a manifestation of Spirit in an earthly body. I understood the Lakota wisdom teaching that living a good life involves knowing Spirit, becoming our "true selves," and following a path with heart.

My mind was racing as I desperately searched for a common thread that would reconcile the Christian teachings of my youth, the spiritual insights I had gained from North American and Maya Indian elders, and the experience I was now having. How could God be fully present in and through the world if He was up in heaven? How could God be both male and female? Was what I was experiencing really what I thought it was? Was this the same experience that indigenous elders, mystics, and spiritual seekers from many different faiths had described to me and written about? At some level I realized the deep and unmistakable truth of my experience, and yet I was struggling to make sense of it all.

And then, as suddenly as it started, my encounter with the Divine faded. I have no idea how long it actually lasted; it might have been a few minutes or it might have been an hour or more. For a short period of time I had been granted the privilege of briefly experiencing a sacred reality that I was convinced was always present, always available to us yet obscured from our everyday consciousness and ordinary awareness. For quite some time I sat in stunned silence, enveloped by darkness, hearing Black Elk's words reverberating deep inside me: "We should understand well that all things are the works of the Great Spirit. We should know that He is within all things."

I spent the remainder of the night at my hanblechya site feeling restless, flooded with powerful and at times conflicted emotions. Unlike the three- and four-day vision quests I had completed during my earlier visits to the reservation, this one was only overnight. For a shorter vision quest like this, the tradition is to stay awake, prayerful, and vigilant throughout the entire night—something I was able to accomplish easily. About mid-morning the next day, the Lakota elder I was visiting, my sponsor on this hanblechya, arrived in his pick-up truck. Still wrapped in the buffalo hide robe, I gathered the ceremonial items I had used and then stepped into his truck for the journey back to his home on the reservation.

We rode in silence, as was the custom immediately following a hanblechya, and shortly before reaching the house we pulled up in front of an inipi (sweat lodge). Performing an inipi ceremony is a tradition that one takes part in immediately before going out to a vision quest site and immediately after returning from one. The lodge was a graceful dome-shaped structure, approximately ten feet in diameter, made of small willow saplings bent and fastened into chest-high arcs. It was completely covered by a canvas tarp with only a small opening for entering and leaving. A few feet from the opening, a large fire pit held red-hot stones glowing on a bed of embers.

Before we entered the lodge, the elder sang a traditional song in Lakota, filled his prayer pipe with tobacco and placed the pipe inside the lodge. I followed him through the small opening, crawling on my hands and knees counter-clockwise around the outside perimeter in the narrow space between the domed wall of the lodge and the three-foot wide pit dug in the center. Although there are typically several people in the lodge for an inipi ceremony, the ceremonies before and after a hanblechya involve only the elder and the person who has been on the vision quest. The two of us sat in silence as the helper outside the lodge brought the blazing-hot stones to the lodge door and we placed them one by one in the interior pit using deer antlers.

When the stones were all in the pit and a bucket of water had been placed inside the lodge opening, a flap of the tarp was pulled over the opening and positioned so that no light could enter our space. It had taken me years to get comfortable in the profound darkness inside an inipi lodge. But the initial shock of the complete and utter darkness accompanying the tarp sealing off the opening was always followed by the soft, and for me, comforting, rosy-red glow of the stones in the fire pit. The lodge was filled with the pungent fragrance of fresh-picked sage placed on the floor just before the ceremony started and the fragrant aroma rising from the cedar leaves we had placed onto the hot stones.

The sound of the elder's sacred spirit-calling Lakota songs reverberated inside the lodge, mingling with the smells and the cedar smoke. Heavy steam rose from the fire pit as he poured water onto the stones from a dipper. Suddenly, the walls of the lodge seemed to disappear and the small, claustrophobic space inside pushed out dramatically in all directions, leaving me with the impression of sitting in the darkness of a wide-open space as expansive as the South Dakota prairie itself. Sweat poured from my body. The sacred songs and primal earthiness of the lodge carried me back in time as the ancient ritual helped me reconnect with ancestral spiritual experiences reaching back a thousand years.

The ancient Lakota songs that had seemed so foreign and unintelligible when I first started on this path were second nature to me now and I sang along with the elder. After we finished the round of spirit-calling songs and the initial round of prayer songs, it was time to pray with the *chanupa*, the prayer pipe. The elder blew puffs of smoke toward each of the four cardinal directions as well as a puff toward the heavens and a puff toward the ground. He prayed in Lakota, some of which I was able to understand and much of which I couldn't. But the intent was clear to me; he was welcoming me back from the spirit realm and offering prayers for my well-being on my continuing spiritual journey.

When the elder finished, he passed the pipe to me, inviting me to add my prayers to his. Usually I would offer many prayers when I was holding the pipe, but this time I felt there was little else I needed to say. He knew exactly what had happened to me on my hanblechya even though we hadn't spoken a word. He had visited me in spirit during the night; he had been by my side during portions of my vigil and had witnessed my encounter with the Divine. The only words I was able to speak were *Pilamaya, Tunka hila* ("Thank you, Grandfather") and *Mitakuye Oyas'in* ("All my relations"). The words unexpectedly brought tears to my eyes and I sat in the darkness of the lodge crying softly as I held the sacred pipe. I realized that my hanblechya experience had shaken me to the core of my being. I was completely exhausted, physically and emotionally, from its intensity and unexpected nature.

When the inipi ceremony finished, we went back to the elder's house and had breakfast. Afterward, we spent time walking around his property talking about current events on the reservation without discussing my hanblechya—we left that conversation in the inipi lodge. Later in the day I took my rental car to a nearby town to buy a week's worth of groceries to leave behind for his family and packed for my return home the next day. That night, we were joined by his relatives and friends, many of whom I had come to know well over the years, as we sat by a fire under an immense South Dakota sky pierced by dazzling stars. This was the part of my trips to South Dakota that was always bittersweet; I was anxious to be home again with my family but disappointed to leave the ceremonies and sacred space.

Coming back to "civilization" had always been challenging for me ever since I started going away on these spiritual quests, but this time it was particularly difficult. I had used my vacation time to come out to South Dakota, and when I returned home I immediately had to go back to work and resume my normal activities in Philadelphia. I didn't say much to anyone about my vision quest. I did share my hanblechya experience with a couple of family members and friends, hoping that talking a little about the encounter would help. But I was still quite troubled that the revelation I had received—the male/female nature of the Divine and the reality that God is present in the world and within all things—contradicted so much of what I had been brought up to believe.

My personal and professional life changed dramatically over the next several years. My mother passed away the summer following my vision quest. That same summer, Julie and I and our young sons, Nick and Chris, moved from Philadelphia to Granville, a small town near Columbus in Central Ohio. I gave up an executive position in a large national management consulting firm so I could start my own consulting practice. With all these changes in my life and the new responsibilities that came with our move and with my new firm, I didn't have much time to reflect on my vision quest and I wasn't able to get back out to the reservation that next summer. I continued my personal spiritual practice, but I was still puzzling over my experience of the Divine and I was still searching.

In September of 2006, six years after my vision quest, I finally had another type of experience that enabled me to accept and integrate my encounter with the Divine. Early that month I spent ten days at St. Benedict's Monastery in the mountains near Snowmass, Colorado, on a Centering Prayer retreat. Toward the end of the retreat I had the extreme good fortune of spending some one-on-one time with Father Thomas Keating. Although we had never met, I was very familiar with Fr. Thomas through his writings and teachings on the Christian contemplative tradition and Centering Prayer. He was also interested in other faith traditions, including Native American, and very supportive of interfaith dialogue. I hoped he could help me better understand my hanblechya experience.

I was very excited about the opportunity to spend time with Fr. Thomas but also very apprehensive. If he could validate my experience on my hanblechya, I knew it would help me resolve the issues with which I had been struggling. At the same time, I was concerned that he might have a different perspective on my encounter that might leave me feeling even more uncertain and confused. We met after lunch in a small room in the Monastery near the chapel and for the next hour we talked about my encounter with God, the Divine. As I recounted my experience, I was struck by his calm presence and his kind gentle eyes. When I finished my story, Fr. Thomas was silent for a moment, and then I heard what I had so hoped to hear and was so afraid I wouldn't.

Fr. Thomas assured me that I had, in fact, had a direct encounter with God. These experiences, he assured me, were not as unusual as one might think; many people have had similar experiences, although they do not often openly discuss them. When I asked about my experience of the dualistic male and female nature of God and the presence of the Divine within all things, he replied that God can appear in many forms, whichever is right for that individual person at that time. Fr. Thomas' words were a great comfort and relief, and I felt the struggle I was having with the apparent contradiction between what I had learned as a child in church and the reality of what was revealed to me as a result of my spirit quest begin to melt away.

Before our time was up, I mentioned to Fr. Thomas that I was thinking about writing a book on my spiritual journey and my time with North American and Maya Indian elders. I asked him what he thought about my including the story of my vision quest and my encounter with the Divine in that book. He was silent for a moment and then shared his concern that including this story might open me up to criticism and that some might not understand or appreciate my experience. He paused and was silent for a moment. Then as he began to speak once more, his face seemed to soften and, with a look of unconditional love and compassion, he told me that on the other hand, sharing this story might actually be helpful to many. I decided then and there that if I ever did write a book, I would share this story.

Fr. Thomas once wrote that "Many paths lead to Source. Some call this Source the Absolute, the One God, the Holy Trinity, Brahman, Great Spirit, Allah, Ultimate Mystery or other names, depending upon the cultural or religious frame of reference."[6] My years of experience with the spiritual traditions of the North American and ancient Maya Indians prepared me for my encounter with the Divine on the Pine Ridge Indian Reservation. The shamanic path I followed is not the only one leading to Source, but it is an extraordinary path with heart through a sacred landscape of stunning richness and beauty.

The stories in this book, stories that span thirty-five years and five countries, present a record of my own personal journey into the realm of the sacred spiritual mysteries of the Maya. It is my sincerest hope that my journey and insights will be a source of discovery, illumination, and healing for all who are seekers of the Ultimate Mystery.

Chapter Notes

1. Roys 1933: 167
2. Brown 1953: xx
3. See Chapter 4, "Good Road Ceremony" and Chapter 6, "Journey with the Celestial Bird".
4. In Thomas Mails' wonderful book on the Lakota Holy Man Frank Fools Crow (*Fools Crow:Wisdom and Power*), Fools Crow describes his method for preparing himself to experience the presence of Wakan Tanka and allowing Him to work through Fools Crow for healing. Fools Crow always began by purifying himself through ritual and then focused on ridding himself of anything that may have impeded his contact with Wakan Tanka including "doubt, guilt, fear, selfishness, wanting to tell Wakan Tanka how and when things ought to be done..." (Mails 1991: 51). I was inspired by Fools Crow to prepare for my encounter with the Divine by similar ritual purification ceremonies and prayers for letting go of personal limitations I had discovered over the years.
5. These are also sometimes referred to as tobacco ties and are made using two-inch square pieces of cloth, folded around a pinch of tobacco and tied in a continuous strand of thin cotton twine.
6. Keating, Fr. Thomas. June, 2010. "Seekers of Ultimate Mystery." *Contemplative Outreach News.* 25 (2). 1-5

INTRODUCTION

We have forgotten who we are. We have forgotten why we're here.
We have forgotten how to live a life of balance and harmony.
— Lady Sak K'uk'

These are the words spoken by the spirit of Lady Sak K'uk' when she appeared to me in 2015 at the ancient Maya ceremonial center of Palenque. Lady Sak K'uk', who lived one thousand four hundred years ago, was a queen of Palenque and mother of Palenque's most famous ruler, Janaab Pakal I ('Radiant Sun Shield'), also known as Pakal the Great. I received this transmission thirty years after my first visit to Palenque, when I had arrived as a seeker, a novice, an initiate. Now I had returned and my spiritual journey had come full circle. I had finally remembered who I was, why I was here, and how to live a life of balance and harmony. The teachings of Maya shamans and my visionary encounters at ancient ceremonial centers over three decades had led me to experiences beyond my wildest dreams. What I'd found was not at all what I had expected, and was more profound than I had ever imagined.

When I started my spiritual search in the early 1980s, I was disillusioned with the traditional approaches to religion I had grown up with. I had only the vague idea that I was looking for "more," hoping to discover a greater sense of meaning and purpose in my life. I was struggling to find *something* but not sure exactly what that something was or where I was going to find it. My childhood fascination with Native American cultures led me to my initial exploration of shamanism, which was followed by in-depth studies and training with indigenous North American Indian elders and later with Maya Indian shamans and priests. Through them I found the "more" I had been seeking—an authentic experience of the sacred and transcendent nature of reality.

I was five years old when I was first touched by the mystery and majesty of the Maya. Sitting on the floor of our family living room, I was looking through an oversized picture book on ancient civilizations and turned to a page with an image that sent chills through my body. The breathtakingly beautiful image was a reproduction of a nineteenth-century lithograph by Frederick Catherwood that had originally appeared in the book *Incidents of Travel in Central America, Chiapas, and Yucatan* by John Lloyd Stephens. Catherwood's drawing depicts a colossal upright stone monument with a sculptured image Stephens referred to as an idol. In his description, Stephens wrote: "The subject of the front [of the monument] is a full-length figure, the face wanting beard, and of a feminine cast, though the dress seems that of a man. On the two sides are rows of hieroglyphics, which probably recite the history of the mysterious personage."[1]

The fantastic image seemed to reach out to me through time and space, calling me and waking what felt like an ancient, forgotten memory. Although Stephens and Catherwood didn't know it at the time, and I didn't know it as a child, the sculpted, larger-than-life image was that of Waxaklajuun Ubaah K'awiil, the eighth century ruler of the ancient Maya city of Copan. When I first started studying with North American Indian elders and spiritual leaders, I was told that sometimes a person chooses a specific spiritual path and sometimes a path chooses a person. For me, the encounter with Catherwood's lithograph sparked a lifelong fascination with the ancient Maya and started me on the spiritual path it now seems I was destined to take.

As a young boy growing up in the suburbs of Chicago, I was immersed in Christian religious traditions. My maternal grandfather was a Baptist minister and my father was raised in the Roman Catholic faith. While I was growing up, as a compromise perhaps, our family attended an Episcopal church. I have fond memories of my early church experiences, and I was particularly drawn to the mysterious accounts of divine intervention and encounters with angels as well as stories of visions, inspired teachings and miracles. But I now realize that my true spiritual journey began not in church but at the Field Museum of Natural History in Chicago. The museum was my gateway to the fabulous realm of the ancient Maya and the spiritual practices of the indigenous cultures of North America.

During my frequent visits to the museum, I found myself captivated by the indigenous worldview represented by the images and artifacts on display. The beautifully detailed models and dioramas of ancient Maya cities brought their civilization to life for me and provided a context for the haunting images that Catherwood captured so magnificently in his drawings. In the North American Indian section of the museum, displays of sacred objects and ceremonial regalia from the Plains and Pueblo Indian cultures introduced me to their spiritual practices and ceremonial traditions. The mystery of the indigenous ceremonies and the primal authenticity of their rituals were far more moving for me than the experiences I was having in church.

Standing in the dimly lit galleries with these displays of North American Indian cultural artifacts, I felt myself transported into a mysterious, magical world totally unlike the world just outside the museum. My father would read the texts describing the items and displays out loud to me—painted drums, hide rattles, decorated buffalo skulls, fringed ceremonial "Ghost Dance" shirts, Sun Dance eagle-bone whistles, Pueblo Indian ceremonial altars, and depictions of mysterious rituals that occurred in secret underground chambers known as kivas.[2] Although I wasn't able to grasp the significance of everything I was seeing, I turned my imagination loose as I tried to enter these mystical, sacred realms with native priests and holy men leading spiritual initiation ceremonies.

Sometime well before my twelfth birthday, I had a remarkable experience while I was viewing a Pueblo Indian ceremonial altar on display at the museum. The altar was the centerpiece of an annual ceremony performed by priests in underground kivas prior to planting the corn crop. The English translation of the Pueblo Indian name for the ceremony was "to put in order, in proper shape or condition." During this secret ceremony, priests conducted rituals that included prayers, sacred chants, and offerings to prepare the fields for planting. Through the rituals, fields were put in proper spiritual condition, metaphysically protected against destructive forces such as drought, sandstorms, and insects, and then consecrated for the approaching planting season.

The altar in the museum consisted of a large symbolic image of the Sun, created with colored sand on the floor of a kiva. Surrounding the image were a variety of ceremonial objects that included flint spear points, bowls of corn meal, and a *tiponi*—a sacred ear of corn decorated with feathers, turquoise, and shell. I was fascinated by the aura of sacredness that seemed to surround the altar and the fact that unlike the major Christian ceremonies to which I was accustomed, this ceremony took place underground and in seclusion, with a small number of participants. The ritual seemed to have a powerful elemental, primal character and even though I knew nothing about the ceremony itself, I sensed I was in the presence of something holy.

While I gazed at this scene, I lost focus on the individual objects as an image materialized above the center of the altar. I saw an aged Indian grandmother sitting on the earth at the edge of the barren village cornfields, spreading her arms in a protective, nurturing, and caring gesture. The dry, weathered skin on her face was etched with deep lines and creases; a formidable strength and determination shone through her soft, dark brown eyes. Like the ancient stone mesas surrounding her, she seemed rooted to the earth, a manifestation of the sacred Earth Mother. Waves of nourishing healing energy poured forth from her strong, steady hands into the ground. She was stunningly beautiful as she prepared the fields for the gift of life.

I recalled the words from the description of the ceremony on the plaque identifying the exhibit: "to put in order, in proper shape or condition." She was bringing order, balance, and centeredness to the fields. Through her prayers and blessings, she was preparing, consecrating, and purifying the earth before planting began. She was creating harmony and balance within the space that would embrace and nurture the crops. She seemed less concerned with the eventual outcome of the harvest than with the task of creating the ideal spiritual conditions in which the miracle of the germination of the corn would occur. She was sanctifying the space where the corn would grow to give life and sustain her people, who refer to corn as their "Mother."

Slowly the image faded and my awareness returned to the sounds of the crowded exhibit hall. I looked over to my parents and sister hoping to see confirmation that they too had seen what I'd just seen, but it wasn't there and I felt a pang of sadness and a sense of isolation. I knew this was more than an idle daydream; I'd been touched by something mysterious, profound, and sacred. During the next few years I had a few similar experiences with other exhibits at the museum.[3] The Indian ceremonial objects there opened a portal that transported me into the extraordinary realm of indigenous spirituality and started me on a spiritual quest that eventually took me far deeper into these ancient ceremonial practices than I could ever have imagined at that time.

We moved from Chicago to Palo Alto, California when I was twelve. I remained involved with the Episcopal Church, and my interest in indigenous spirituality faded as I became preoccupied with typical adolescent interests. It wasn't until I was in my twenties that my earlier spiritual longings resurfaced. Like many other baby-boomers, I found myself moving away from institutional religion and toward the Human Potential Movement that had started when I was in high school in the 1960s. In college I realized I was on a spiritual quest, although during those years I had no clear idea of what I was looking for other than greater personal awareness and a richer and more authentic spiritual experience than the ones I'd had in church.

I was in my early thirties when I took up the study of shamanism and began training in shamanic visionary techniques of journeying and healing. Shortly after my training started, I began participating in North American Indian ceremonies and spiritual rituals in California and Arizona. During the next four years, I traveled to locations throughout the Southwestern United States to visit sites sacred to the indigenous peoples and to participate in vision quests, purification (sweat lodge) rituals, and other traditional indigenous ceremonies. The shamanic techniques came easily to me and I experienced improved physical health, a greater sense of well-being, and a healing of the emotional wounds from having grown up with an abusive, alcoholic father. It was exciting for me to participate in ceremonies I had learned about as a child and I felt completely at home on this path.

In 1985 I embarked on my first journey to the Maya sites of Chichen Itza, Tulum, Coba, and Palenque with my wife, Julie. In order to prepare for the trip, I read the latest publications on the

Maya that were accessible to non-scholars, but mainly I followed the indigenous practices for preparing for a vision quest or spiritual pilgrimage. I wanted to take everything I had learned from the shamans and medicine men with whom I studied and use this knowledge to approach the ancient ceremonial centers as a spiritual initiation rather than a tourist adventure. Before leaving on the trip I had hoped my experiences in the ruins would be somewhat like those I'd had on vision quests at other sacred sites in North America—deeper emotional healing, greater insight into my spiritual development, a revelatory dream perhaps, or hopefully, contact with the spirit of an ancestor. What I actually experienced, however, was far more remarkable and in some ways more profoundly unsettling than I could have imagined.

These experiences were especially unsettling for me because in a real sense I was living my life in two worlds. Although I had been studying shamanism and North American Indian spiritual traditions for several years, the majority of my time was spent pursuing a career in business. Each time I returned to my normal life from a vision quest or other intense spiritual ceremony, it was an adjustment for me. But my reentry after my first Maya pilgrimage was a real shock. At the ancient Maya ruins, I had traveled deeper into the non-physical spiritual realms than I had ever traveled before and had experienced an amazing world that was almost beyond belief. In retrospect it seems as if my earlier training had been preparing me for this encounter, but at the time, I struggled to come to terms with experiences at odds with my core beliefs about the "normal" world.

Following that first trip, I continued studying with North American Indian elders and participating in vision quests, purification rituals, and prayer ceremonies. Two years later in 1987, I returned again to the realm of the ancient Maya when Julie and I took a fourteen-day trip on the Pasión and Usumacinta rivers to visit spectacular Maya sites in Guatemala and Mexico, including

Tikal, Dos Pilas, and Yaxchilan. I prepared much as I had for the first trip but this time my experiences were quite different. For some reason I still don't understand, I had practically none of the profound, life-altering experiences I'd had on my first trip. I did however, experience a portal opening for me at Yaxchilan into the ancient spiritual realm of the Maya. That portal has remained open for me to this day.

I continued studying with North American Indian elders and participating in indigenous ceremonies. In 1990 after our first son was born, I danced and "pierced" in a traditional Plains Indian Sun Dance and met the Maya Daykeeper and ceremonial leader, Hunbatz Men, while he was traveling in the United States. During the next two decades, my professional business responsibilities increased, our second son was born in 1996, and we moved from Los Angeles to the Philadelphia area. During all of these life changes I struggled to find time to continue my spiritual pursuits. Julie and I rejoined the church with our growing family, despite the fact that at this point in my life I was more interested in studying the historical Jesus, mystical Christianity, and the Gnostic Gospels than traditional Christian doctrine.

Extended travel out of the country would have been very difficult for me during this period, so I stayed closer to home. For six years, I traveled for two weeks each summer to the Pine Ridge Reservation in South Dakota, the home of the Oglala Lakota (Sioux), to participate in traditional pipe, inipi, and hanblechya ceremonies. I also had the good fortune to participate in yuwipi healing ceremonies and experience the summoning of spirits to aid in healing. I often spent time at Pendle Hill, the Quaker retreat center outside Philadelphia, and my spiritual journey also led me to participate in several Centering Prayer retreats, including two ten-day retreats at St. Benedict's Monastery in the spectacular Colorado Rockies.

It wasn't until 2007 that I returned to visit the ancient Maya ceremonial centers. By that time my sons were older and I had started my own management consulting firm, so I had more control over my time and schedule. Since my first trips to the Maya ruins, international cell phone technology had been developed and Internet cafes had sprouted up even in the relatively remote areas near the Maya ceremonial centers. With cell phone and internet access, I could travel and still remain connected to my family and professional responsibilities. During the 2007 trip, I spent three weeks traveling alone in Mexico, Guatemala, and Honduras. I re-visited several sites and traveled to the ancient city of Copan where I saw the actual sculpture of Waxaklajuun Ubaah K'awiil that had so enthralled me as a young boy.

I prepared as I had for my first two trips, only now I understood that I had gone well beyond the initiation stage of my earlier journeys and that my pilgrimage to the sacred sites of the ancient Maya would be more an act of devotion than a quest for knowledge or insight. Even though my spiritual path had been very eclectic over the intervening years, all these experiences had propelled me further into a much deeper understanding of myself, and a greater appreciation for the common spiritual threads transcending different cultural boundaries and traditions. I tried to keep my expectations in check at the outset, remembering my disappointment that my second trip was so different from my first. But this time, my pilgrimage turned out to be, in many ways, even more spectacular and rewarding than the first.

I returned to Mexico again in 2009 and to Mexico and Guatemala in 2010. Each time, my experiences were richer and deeper. Over the years, I've continued to study the latest academic research findings on the ancient Maya and strengthen my ties to the Maya ceremonial community. I've also continued to follow the work of scholars writing about the diversity of early Christian communities and the suppressed biblical texts rejected by the early orthodox Christian authorities. In retrospect, understanding the early church has been extremely important in helping me understand the behavior of the Franciscan friars who encountered the Maya during the Spanish Conquest in the 1500s and worked relentlessly to destroy their spiritual heritage.

My journey deep into the heart of indigenous spiritual traditions and into the farthest reaches of the spiritual realms of the ancient Maya has not been an easy one physically, emotionally, or mentally. The inipi, hanblechya, and Sun Dance ceremonies I've experienced have at times been emotionally gut-wrenching and close to physically unbearable. My solitary all-night prayer vigils in remote Maya ruins deep in the jungle rainforests have sometimes terrified me. And yet, the extraordinarily profound spiritual insights, healings, and revelations I've received have been worth the cost. It's taken me over thirty-five years to make sense of many of my experiences, but now I am able to see clearly the patterns and progression of the journey and to understand the seemingly disparate elements deeply enough to begin to share them with others.

Over the years, my spiritual journey has forced me to confront and reevaluate almost everything I thought I knew about religion, spirituality, and the world as they were described to me in school and in church. I've spent years wrestling with some of the contradictions I've encountered and struggling to understand experiences I've had. The combination of academic insights and practical experience has helped me develop a rich perspective on this spiritual path. I've found answers to most of my original questions about the spirituality of the ancient Maya, although I know that in some ways my exploration has only begun. It is my sincerest hope that others will benefit from my spiritual struggles and breakthroughs and that their journeys will be more fulfilling as a result.

It is now possible to have a much clearer picture of the spiritual worldview and beliefs of the ancient Maya than ever before. In some cases, current research findings correct earlier misconceptions about ancient Maya beliefs. In other cases, contemporary indigenous ceremonial practices aid our understanding of ancient spiritual traditions. The visions and revelatory experiences I describe in this book also provide exciting new insights into the sacred realm of the ancient Maya. To understand the experiences that I recount in the following chapters, it's helpful to understand what we now know about the basic spiritual worldview of the ancient Maya, including their shamanic practices and beliefs about God, deities, visions, prophecy, and revelations.

SHAMANISM

In 1989, based on a stunning breakthrough in deciphering ancient Maya hieroglyphics, scholars determined that shamanic beliefs and practices were at the foundation of ancient Maya spirituality.[4] This breakthrough brought the spiritual world of the ancient Maya into much sharper focus. Ancient stone carvings, images on pottery from antiquity, and hieroglyphic texts revealed a stunning sacred cosmology filled with shamanic power and mystery. Aware that contemporary Maya communities, like other indigenous peoples, had preserved traditional shamanic practices, scholars began "comparing ancient imagery and the archaeological remains of ritual to the practices of modern Maya shamanism"[5] to look for insights into ancient ritual practice.

The word "shaman" is derived from the indigenous cultures of Siberia and has been adopted by anthropologists to refer to men or women—typically visionaries and healers—who are able to access non-physical, unseen spirit realms for assistance in healing, or to gain knowledge and power. Shamanism is the most ancient spiritual practice known to humankind; some anthropologists believe that shamanic practice may date back to the earliest beginnings of human civilization. Shamanic beliefs and practices have been found in indigenous cultures throughout the world including Asia, Australia, Africa, North America, Mexico, and South America. Anthropologist Michael Harner's workshop on shamanic visionary techniques of journeying and healing was my introduction to this ancient, universal understanding of reality.

All shamanic cultures, including the Maya, share a common conception that the universe is composed of three realms of existence. These include our physical world and two non-physical realms—the Lower World and the Upper World. Maya scholars often refer to these as the Middle World, the Underworld and the Overworld respectively. The concept of three realms is not unique to shamanism; growing up in the Christian faith I learned about Heaven and Hell, and later I learned about the astral and causal planes of Eastern mystical spiritual traditions. The unseen spirit realms of the indigenous shamanic peoples are much different from the Christian concept of Heaven and Hell. Nevertheless, descriptions of these realms include surprising similarities.

In the shamanic worldview, our physical world—including the Earth, humans, and animals—coexists with the two other non-physical realms. The Upper World is the invisible realm inhabited by supernatural beings, ancestor spirits, and other non-physical entities. The Middle World corresponds to the earth and physical heavens, including the sky, sun, moon, planets, and constellations. The Lower World, often envisioned as lying below the Earth, is the invisible realm of generative powers and also the dwelling place of other supernatural beings, ancestor spirits, and guardian spirits. Although the non-physical realms remain unseen in ordinary reality, for shamanic cultures they exist in a parallel universe referred to as "non-ordinary" reality.

Shamans are the intermediaries between ordinary and non-ordinary reality and have been trained to travel outside of time to these spirit realms. Shamans use a variety of techniques including drumming, sacred songs, invocations, and prayers to achieve an altered state of consciousness that scholar Mircea Eliade refers to as "shamanic ecstasy." In this state, shamans journey to the unseen realms to perform individual and collective healings and contact ancestor spirits and supernaturals for assistance. Eliade observes that this state "is less a trance than a 'state of inspiration'; the shaman sees and hears spirits; he is carried out of himself because he is journeying in ecstasy through distant regions" and that a shaman is "visionary and inspired."[6]

The shamanic world of the ancient Maya is unparalleled in sophistication, richness, and diversity. The ancient Maya shared the common indigenous view that the natural world is filled with physical places of spiritual power. Mountains, caves, lakes, and other bodies of water could be natural gateways and portals to the unseen realms. The Maya dramatically recreated these natural gateways and places of power through sacred architecture in their ceremonial centers. Pyramids not only represented but actually became sacred mountains; temples and labyrinths were actually sacred caves. All of them were constructed to embody the spiritual power inherent in natural formations, all were imbued with sacred spiritual k'uh energy, and all contained portals to the spiritual realms.

For the ancient Maya (as well as other indigenous, shamanic cultures), the boundaries between the physical and non-physical, between ordinary and non-ordinary reality, were porous and easily transcended. Shamans, visionaries, oracles, and prophets or *chilams* (the term we use today to describe the role of a chilam is "channel" or "trance channel") were held in the highest regard. Ancient Maya rulers were often regarded as the supreme shamans aided by priests and other elites who "could serve as conduits through which supernatural forces were channeled into the human realm. In their function as intercessors, Maya kings, priests, and elites proclaimed their power as shamans."[7]

ONE GOD, MANY DEITIES

The writings of Franciscan friars during the Spanish Conquest in the 1500s reference the Maya concept of a supreme deity referred to as Hunab-Ku. In the sixteenth century *Diccionario de Motul*, ascribed to Fr. Antonio de Ciudad Real, Hunab-Ku is described as "the only living and true god, and he is the greatest of the gods of the people of Yucatan. He had no form because they said he could not be represented as he was incorporeal."[8] The current publications I've studied written by Latin American scholars typically accept the sixteenth century accounts of Hunab-Ku as the supreme deity. More importantly, the contemporary Maya elders I've studied with also refer to Hunab-Ku as the supreme deity.

Many North American scholars, however, do not currently share this perspective. Early twentieth century publications on the ancient Maya by North American scholars routinely contain references to Hunab-Ku, yet in today's publications it is almost impossible to find such references. Some scholars believe the concept of a supreme deity was not indigenous but may have been introduced by the Franciscans. Some believe the concept of a supreme deity is at odds with the general belief by some scholars that the Maya were and are polytheistic. Others may be reluctant to reference Hunab-Ku due to the fact that no specific hieroglyphic symbols or artistic representations specifically relating to Hunab-Ku have been found, even though we know from the Franciscan sources that Hunab-Ku "could not be represented."

Even though contemporary scholars have eliminated references to Hunab-Ku, Maya scholar Robert Sharer has observed that for the ancient Maya, "[an] invisible, sacred quality (k'uh) inhabited all things in the universe—rocks, trees and all human beings."[9] He also found that "the k'uh, or sacredness inherent in all things, whether natural or supernatural in our terms, could be manifest in supernatural beings we label "deities." Inasmuch as all Maya deities are aspects of the same sacred quality, the Maya supernatural realm can be viewed as monotheistic."[10]

I believe this sacred quality, k'uh, inherent in all things, describes the Maya concept of Hunab-Ku, and that I experienced this same transcendent presence during my vision quest on the Pine Ridge Indian Reservation in 2000. For the Maya, as well as the North American indigenous peoples, the world is alive and filled with sacredness. This is not an aliveness that comes from breathing or a beating heart or photosynthesis; this is aliveness that comes from Spirit's actual presence in the world.

My struggle to make sense of my Pine Ridge experience led me to search in unexpected places and to find surprising answers. I rediscovered the writings of the second century Roman Stoic philosopher Epictetus whose panentheistic perspective of God (pervading all creation) was remarkably similar to that of the teachings of the indigenous elders. Epictetus' descriptions provided an important bridge for me between the Greco-Roman traditions I was familiar with and the indigenous worldview.[11] I found the writings of Christian mystics and contemplatives and the work of Fr. Thomas Keating also extremely helpful in allowing me to fully accept what had occurred that night in South Dakota. However, it was the early Christian, Gnostic, and mystical writings discovered at Nag Hammadi, Egypt, that helped me put this experience into a larger context that made sense.

Many of the Nag Hammadi writings contain wisdom teachings about the Divine that are quite different from those I was exposed to growing up in the Church, including writings that encourage individuals to seek a direct experience of God through prayer, fasting, ritual, revelation, and ecstatic trance. Scholar Elaine Pagels references teachings from Nag Hammadi texts, assuring us that "we have a latent capacity within our hearts and minds that links us to the divine—not in our ordinary state of mind but when this hidden capacity awakens."[12]

She also references other writings by the Gnostic theologian Ptolemy who refers to *apolutrosis*, a "second baptism" ceremony that joined an individual with "the previously unknown part of one's being which connects one with the divine."[13]

Pagels' research also highlights the teachings from The Gospel of Thomas, another of the works discovered at Nag Hammadi. In that gospel, Thomas teaches that "God's light shines not only in Jesus but, potentially at least, in everyone" and encourages the hearer "*to seek to know God* through one's own, divinely given capacity."[14] In the Gospel of Thomas, I also found the words that perfectly described my struggle to fully understand my encounter with the Divine in South Dakota: "Jesus said, 'Let the one who seeks not stop seeking until he finds. When he finds, he will be troubled, when he is troubled he will be astonished.'"[15]

I could now see a link between the spiritual practices I had learned from the indigenous North American and Maya Indian peoples and the early Christian, Gnostic, and mystical traditions. All were and are seeking a path to the Source and contact with the numinous transcendent reality. The early Christian practices that included prayer, fasting, and sacred songs used "to prepare [seekers] to receive 'the vision of God,'"[16] had much in common with the indigenous spiritual practices I had been following for the last twenty years.

Another aspect of the conventional view of ancient Maya spirituality I'd been troubled by since I started studying this topic was the characterization of the Maya as polytheistic (worshiping many gods). I had frequently encountered anthropologists, historians, and theologians using that term in a somewhat pejorative manner to differentiate so-called primitive pagan or heathen spiritual practices from the monotheistic traditions considered more advanced and often described using the term "great" (as in "the world's great monotheistic traditions"). As I continued my ceremonial practice with indigenous elders and studied this subject more deeply, I realized that the characterization of the Maya as polytheistic was not accurate and that, in this case, the distinction between monotheism and polytheism was an artificial one.

Most of our knowledge of ancient Maya spirituality comes from the writings of a Franciscan missionary (and later Bishop) Diego de Landa, who was present in the Yucatan during the time of the Spanish Conquest in the mid-1500s. When Friar Diego de Landa arrived in the Yucatan in 1549, Maya civilization was still intact and their ancient culture and spiritual heritage were still preserved. His book, *Relación de las cosas de Yucatan,* records the traditional spiritual practices of the Maya and makes contemptuous reference to Hunab-Ku as well as other Maya gods and goddesses.[17] We also have records of multiple gods and godesses from a few surviving Maya books (codices)[18] written somewhere between five hundred and one thousand years ago, as well as images and inscriptions on ancient pottery and sculpture.

Today, scholars use the term "deities" to describe supernatural beings of the ancient Maya that were formerly referred to as gods and goddesses. Recent research has led scholars to distinguish two additional types of spirit beings: supernaturals and ancestors.[19] Of the three, scholars have found that only deities are associated directly with k'uh, the sacred divine essence, in ancient inscriptions. We now know that based on their association with k'uh, the ancient Maya recognized deities as manifestations of Hunab-Ku; their distinct attributes are meant to reflect the unique expressions of the Divine essence in creation. In this sense, the Maya share some similarities with the Hindu perspective that the multiple deities recognized in their spiritual traditions are all aspects of the same Supreme Being, the single Divine essence.

Although the distinction between monotheism and polytheism has been reinforced by the Church and many scholars over the centuries, I was fascinated to learn that even in antiquity this distinction was seen by some as an artificial one. The noted Greco-Roman philosopher, historian, and biographer Plutarch, who was also a priest at the shrine of Apollo at Delphi, discussed this in his first century CE essay titled *Isis and Osiris*.[20] According to scholar Luke Timothy Johnson, Plutarch understood that "there are many gods and many religious rituals, but beneath them all there really is only one divine principal that rules the world" and that "underneath the welter of observances that seem to separate people, there really is a common worship of one god."[21]

Through his landmark translation of *The Book of Chilam Balam of Tizimin*, Maya scholar Munro Edmonson discovered that all Maya deities are aspects of Hunab-Ku ("the sole God") and are "unified (*hunab*) in his person."[22] The teachings I've received from indigenous elders and my direct encounters during prayer vigils and vision quests have confirmed for me that ancestor and other supernatural spirits are different from deities, and that ancient Maya deities are in fact a manifestation of the Divine. If we're open to considering that Hunab-Ku is the name the Maya gave to a universally recognized Divine presence in the world, and that the Maya deities were all aspects of the same Divine essence, we will be able to view the spiritual world of the Maya in a new light. We can begin to appreciate the inherent greatness of their spiritual traditions and realize that, though different, their sacred practices were as sophisticated, meaningful, and relevant as any of the world's other Eastern and Western spiritual traditions.

VISIONS, REVELATIONS, AND PROPHECY

To fully understand the spiritual worldview of the ancient Maya and other indigenous peoples, it's important to recognize the central role of both visions and prophecy. For indigenous peoples, visions are a spiritual or mystical experience of seeing a supernatural event. They are not ordinary dreams or daydreams; they are often sought through vision quest ceremonies involving careful preparation, purification, solitude, fasting, and prayer. Many indigenous peoples believe that no one can have a vision of his or her own free will; they are gifts from Spirit and the higher realms. Even among those who seek a vision, not all are granted them and those who have one vision are not always guaranteed another. Their importance, however, cannot be denied. Anthropologist Ruth Benedict found that spiritual visions are the "unifying religious fact" of North American Indian tribes.[23]

Although visionary experiences differ among different indigenous peoples, they all share common characteristics. Lakota (Sioux) Indian elder George Sword once described a vision as "a communication from Wakan Tanka or a spirit to one of mankind. It may come at any time or in any manner to anyone." In Sword's account, "it may be communicated in Lakota, or *hanbloglaka* (language of the spirits). Or it may be only by sight or sounds not of a language."[24] Lakota Medicine Man Archie Lame Deer maintains that a vision "is not a dream; it is very real. It hits you sharp and clear like an electric shock." For Lame Deer, visions happen when "you are wide awake" and suddenly experience the tangible presence of someone, a spirit being.[25]

The acceptance of visions and revelations as legitimate and valued elements of the spiritual journey is at the core of indigenous spiritual practice. There is a wealth of documentation of North American Indian practices since the nineteenth century and vision quests are still central to indigenous spiritual practices today. We also have reports of Maya vision quest practices at the time of the Spanish Conquest. In his *General History of the Continent and the Islands of America,* published in the early 1600s, the Spanish historian Antonio de Herrera described a Maya vision quest that follows the same basic format as those I've personally experienced and that others have documented for North American Indian tribes. Although Herrera mistakenly referred to ancestor and guardian spirits as "devils," he wrote: "the Indian repaired to the river, wood, hill, or most obscure place where he called upon the devils by such names as he thought fit, talked to the rivers, rocks or woods, said he went to weep that he might have the same as his predecessors had."[26]

Herrera continued to observe that "In that melancholy fit he fell asleep, and either in a dream or waking, saw [a guardian spirit]."[27] The vision quest Herrera described was intended to help the seeker contact a guardian spirit or *nagual*, and his statement "that he might have what his predecessors had" refers to other seekers who had received a personal tutelary spirit as the result of a vision quest. Although Herrera describes a vision quest that occurred over four hundred years ago, it's clear from his description that vision quests had occurred before the one he described. Given the primal role of vision quests in indigenous cultures, they were undoubtedly a common practice for the ancient Maya even though they may have taken a different form in antiquity.

I had the good fortune of experiencing spiritual visions on my very first journey in 1982 to sacred sites at Chaco Canyon in New Mexico and the Navajo Indian reservation in Arizona—experiences I describe in Chapter One. Since that time, I've visited dozens of sacred Maya sites, several on multiple occasions, throughout Mexico, Guatemala, and Honduras. This book recounts the profound, life-changing visionary experiences I had at those sites. At times they occurred spontaneously, without preparation or planning. Other times they happened as a result of careful, deliberate preparation. And many times I prepared myself to be receptive to visionary experiences and none occurred.

Prophecy is the other aspect of ancient Maya spiritual practice that is important to understand in order to have a full grasp of their sacred worldview. Prophecy is often understood as the practice of predicting the future but it actually has a much broader definition and application. Often considered a spiritual gift, prophecy involves the act of receiving communications from a divine, mystical, or supernatural source and then passing that information on to others;

many of the world's religions, including Christianity and Judaism, have strong prophetic traditions. The Maya have also had a strong prophetic tradition and several accounts provide a fascinating insight into this ancient practice, including the writings of Fr. Diego de Landa and the Spanish historian Antonio de Herrera y Tordesillas, as well as the various books of Chilam Balam.

Fr. Diego de Landa encountered the Maya practice of prophecy and referenced it in his book, *Relación de las cosas de Yucatan*. Landa noted that the special class of Maya priests who were prophets were known as *chilams*. In his account, Landa observes that the "the duty of the *chilams* was to give the replies of the gods to the people, and so much respect was shown to them that they carried them on their shoulders."[28] According to scholar Ralph L. Roys, the title "*chilam* meant 'mouthpiece or interpreter of the gods.'"[29] Ralph Roys' writings include portions of the Mayas' *The Book of Chilam Balam of Tizimin,* that records prophecy occurring at the time of the Spanish Conquest and contains this description of a *chilam* in a prophetic state:

> [The chilam] retired to a room in his home where he lay prostrate in a trance while the god or spirit, perched in the ridgepole of the house, spoke to the unconscious chilam below. Then the other priests assembled, probably in the reception hall of the house, and listened to the revelation with their faces bowed down to the floor.[30]

This is a magnificent description of the practice known today as channeling or trance-channeling and it is clear from these accounts that this was a common and highly revered practice. In an early edition of *Relación de las cosas de Yucatan*, Landa also gives another fascinating account of prophecy that routinely occurred at the sacred temple dedicated to the Goddess Ix-Chel on the island of Cozumel. In his description, Landa refers to both an "idol" in the temple (a statue of the Goddess Ix-Chel) and the "demon" within the idol (the supernatural spirit of Ix-Chel) communicating through the prophet, who in this case was a priest Landa refers to as "an old Indian" who was called Ah Kin.

As Landa relates, "Anciently, all this country and the Indians went ordinarily to [Cozumel] to worship [the statue of Ix-Chel] which they had in certain ancient buildings and which they venerated greatly." Landa further observes, "the Indians went to see [Ix-Chel] speak with the said Ah Kin and told him why they came and that which they wished. And the said old Indian, Ah Kin, spoke with [the statue of Ix-Chel] and with the [spirit of Ix-Chel] within the [statue]; he replied to all which was asked and they learned from him all they wished."[31]

The Spanish historian Antonio de Herrera y Tordesillas, writing in the early 1600s, also describes the temples on Cozumel and in a manner similar to Landa's he refers to the oracles as idols. He also rejects the legitimacy of the prophecy of the oracles and suggests priests were deceiving the pilgrims. In his history, Herrera recounts that of all the public temples and personal household shrines ("oratories"), the ones Maya people venerated most, "were the temples on the Island of Cozumel." He also noted that "[pilgrims] who had been there were considered sanctified; and those who did not go sent their offerings. And there were some [oracles] that gave replies. In other places the priests invented them, deceiving the people in order to get the presents from them."[32]

It has taken me quite a while to get comfortable with the concept of visions and prophecy and even longer to accept the visionary experiences I had on vision quests and at sacred Maya sites I visited. Early on, I realized I was struggling because these phenomena were not accepted by either of the two groups that had shaped the way I viewed the world: the scientific community and the Church. The empirical, scientific approach to understanding the world—one I had always appreciated, valued, and shared—seemed completely at odds with this type of mystical experience. Also, within my church community, I never encountered support for the kinds of visionary experiences I was having even though visions and prophecies in the Old and New Testaments are central tenets of Christian faith.

Fortunately, I found the early Christian, Gnostic, and mystical writings provided insights into the world of visions and prophecy that helped me bridge between the worlds of indigenous spirituality and my Judeo-Christian heritage. Many of the Nag Hammadi documents contain references to the central role that visionary and revelatory experiences played in those early faith communities. It was comforting to find that these practices were not only accepted but venerated as an authentic and direct means of attaining higher spiritual awareness.

In addition to New Testament accounts of the visions and revelations of Jesus and his followers, Elaine Pagels recounts that several highly-regarded leaders of early Christian communities "often relied on dreams and revelations."[33] Three early well-known prophets "began traveling from one rural church to another claiming to communicate directly with the Holy Spirit" and "wherever they went the three shared their visions, spoke in ecstasy, and urged others to fast and pray so that they too could receive visions and revelations."[34]

During the formative period of Christianity, certain church fathers grew increasingly concerned that the visions and revelations of some Christian and Gnostic leaders did not support what was emerging as the "orthodox" view of Jesus and God. In studying the Nag Hammadi documents, Pagels found that many of the writings "express the hope of receiving revelation and encourage 'those who seek for God.'"[35] For early church fathers trying to consolidate power and control through the organized church, this type of spiritual practice posed a great threat. It is no surprise, then, that writings encouraging visionary practices and spiritual disciplines designed to lead one to a direct experience of "God within" were declared heretical and banned. In 367 CE the Bishop of Alexandria demanded that the heretical writings be destroyed.

In spite of their rejection by my own root religious tradition, visions, revelations, and prophecy have been a common aspect of spiritual practice throughout the world for millennia. In that respect, indigenous North American and Maya Indians share a common heritage with mystically-inclined adherents of Judaism and Christianity as well as followers of eastern spiritual traditions. Knowing the motivation behind the early Church's attack on mystical practices has helped me accept and appreciate the importance of visions, revelations, and prophecy in indigenous North American and Maya Indian spirituality. Although the ancient Maya had a unique and distinct spiritual worldview, I've learned that by understanding their world, I can much better understand my own.

North American and Maya Indian Ceremonial Practices

My studies with North American Indian spiritual leaders began when I was in my early thirties. In retrospect, my experiences at the Field Museum as a young boy foreshadowed the experiences I would have later as an adult studying with indigenous elders. Although the Maya fascinated me, the spiritual practices of the North American Indians were dramatically and immediately accessible to me from the very beginning—the museum displays conveyed marvelous insights into their extraordinary ceremonial life. The Maya, however, were more remote and less available.

Their hieroglyphics had not yet been translated and the spiritual dimensions of their culture were not at all understood. As a result, the Maya models, dioramas, and pottery on display at the museum were accompanied by only the most superficial archaeological information that did not have the same emotional impact on me as the ritual artifacts and re-creations of esoteric rituals of the Plains and Pueblo Indians.

While my first introduction to indigenous spiritual practices occurred through my studies of shamanism, my first actual participation in indigenous spiritual practices and ceremonies occurred with North American Indian elders. During this time I was living in Los Angeles and had many opportunities to study with elders who visited to teach workshops or conduct ceremonies. I was also relatively close to sites sacred to the indigenous peoples of California, Arizona, and New Mexico and could easily travel to those locations. The ceremonial sites of the ancient Maya in Mexico, Guatemala, and Honduras, on the other hand, were much more challenging to reach and my inability to speak Spanish was a hurdle as well.

When I started studying shamanism in 1981, I had no idea that these timeless practices—common to indigenous peoples throughout the world—were also the foundation of the ancient Maya worldview. My practical experiences with North American Indian shamanism prepared me to understand the spiritual realms of the ancient and contemporary Maya in a way that would have been impossible without that training.

In 1985, shortly before my first trip to their ancient sacred sites, the few writings on the Maya available commercially provided minimal insight into their complex spiritual realm.[36] Later, as dramatic breakthroughs in deciphering Maya hieroglyphics revolutionized our understanding of the spirituality of the ancient Maya, I was increasingly surprised to find similarities with the North American Indian spiritual and ceremonial practices with which I had become so familiar. As I continued to read and study the latest research findings, over the years I became convinced these experiences could shed light on ancient Maya traditions.

It's been surprising to me that I haven't been able to find any significant references by Maya scholars to North American Indian ceremonial practices even though they both share common shamanic practices and visionary perspectives. Many anthropologists believe that every culture is unique and that it is misleading to read too much into similarities between them. For these scholars, the spiritual practices and ritual activities of the North American Indians that are similar to the spiritual practices of the ancient Maya are not helpful in understanding the sacred realm of the ancient Maya. My thirty-five years of experience with North American Indian spiritual practices have convinced me this is not the case and that we can learn much from these similarities.

Through my contact with the Pueblo Indian and Plains Indian peoples, I learned they have similar ceremonial practices for summoning ancestral and supernatural spirits for guidance and healing. During the yuwipi ceremonies in which I've participated on the Pine Ridge Indian Reservation, drumming, sacred songs, and prayers are used to conjure spirits who then aid the medicine man in healing the person who has requested the ceremony. For Pueblo tribes, drumming, sacred songs and prayers are also used to invoke *kachina* and ancestor spirits during ceremonies in underground kivas. The summoning of spirits by the ancient Maya is well documented, and from what I have read it appears that they used timeless, universal methods similar to those common to North American Indian people today.

In 1986, I saw Linda Schele's and Mary Miller's spectacular exhibition "The Blood of Kings: A New Interpretation of Maya Art" at the Cleveland Museum of Art. The entire exhibition was filled with the most extraordinary Maya art I had ever seen. But

I was particularly struck by the ancient Maya practice of blood-letting. Four years later I participated in a Plains Indian-style Sun Dance held at Pilot Rock outside Ashland, Oregon. During the Sun Dance, I was pierced with two small portions of buffalo rib sharpened to a point and pushed through the skin on my chest. In many ways, the Sun Dance is quite different from Maya bloodletting, yet I know that piercing at the Sun Dance helped me understand that Maya ritual in a way that would not have been possible otherwise.

Another cultural connection can be seen in the fact that both the Maya (ancient and contemporary) and the Pueblo peoples in Arizona and New Mexico share a common relationship with *maize* (corn). The Maya refer to themselves as "the people of the maize" and the Hopi Indians believe that "corn is the Mother of the Hopi."[37] Many Maya today still adhere to agricultural and ceremonial practices related to maize that were documented by the Franciscan Friars in the sixteenth century, and that were undoubtedly used by the ancient Maya as well. And interestingly, Pueblo peoples follow traditional ceremonial practices that are in many ways like those of the Maya.

Several of the visionary experiences I've had among the Maya ruins and which I relate in this book, are similar to North American Indian ceremonies I've personally witnessed for summoning spirits and supernaturals. In Chapter Nine: Lady Xook's Sacrifice, I describe the parallels between the Sun Dance and my vision of ancient Maya bloodletting. In Chapter Eleven: Consecration of the Maize, I highlight the similarities I've observed between Pueblo Indian ceremonies and my vision of a maize consecration ceremony at Copan. While others have written solely about Maya practices today, I've included some of my experiences with North American Indian practices because those are the ones with which I've had the most personal experience. In retrospect, it seems fortuitous that these experiences have added unique insights to my understanding of the world of the ancient Maya.

Karen Armstrong, in her book, *The Case for God*, stated that "one of the conditions of enlightenment has always been a willingness to let go of what we thought we knew in order to appreciate truths we had never dreamed of. We may have to unlearn a great deal about religion before we can move on to new insight."[38] It was only after I let go of many childhood beliefs about religion and spirituality, and even the nature of God, that I was able to appreciate truths I had never dreamed of. I had an enormous amount to unlearn before I could move on to new insight. And so it is for all of us. Once we're able to let go of our preconceptions and misconceptions, we can more fully appreciate the inherent greatness of the spiritual traditions of the Maya and realize that, though different, their sacred practices were as sophisticated, meaningful, and relevant as any of the world's other great Eastern and Western spiritual traditions.

It is important to understand that the sacred sites of the ancient Maya are still "alive" and filled with spirit today. The sacred energy—*k'ulel*—left behind by ancestors and supernaturals in the distant past remains embedded in the stones and energy matrices of the old ceremonial structures. The sacred geometry in these sites has preserved portals to the other worlds that are still accessible to us. If we are able to shift our focus away from the purely physical aspects of this magnificent culture to their deeper, richer, metaphysical realms, their spiritual genius will emerge.

This is a time of rediscovery and rebirth—a time for the full story of the ancient Maya to emerge in a way that honors their stunning traditions and exceptional spiritual accomplishments. I believe the revelations I offer in this book are a gift from the higher realms meant to be shared with others. Many portals to the sacred realms and other worlds of the ancient Maya have opened for me during the past thirty years and I've had the privilege of witnessing extraordinary rituals, ceremonies, and supernatural phenomena. I believe we are still at the beginning of our spiritual journey with the Maya. Others who have had similar experiences will undoubtedly make future contributions to our shared knowledge. And I hope that my own personal journeys will continue to allow me to travel deeper into their magical, metaphysical realms. Through these spiritual explorations we will be able to preserve the precious wisdom teachings that have been a gift from the ancestors, and develop a fuller, more meaningful understanding of the Maya peoples and the true significance of their ancient ceremonial centers. If my writing provokes some controversy, I hope the resulting dialogue will lead us ultimately to a more complete understanding of the beauty and grandeur of the Maya civilization.

Chapter Notes

1. Stevens 1841: 137
2. A *kiva* is a ceremonial structure used by indigenous Pueblo Indian peoples in the Southwest for sacred rituals. Ruins of ancient kivas, built over one thousand years ago, are found among abandoned pueblo settlements throughout the Southwest. Kivas are also in active use by the contemporary Hopi and Zuni tribes in Arizona and New Mexico. The kivas found in ancient ruins are typically circular and partially or wholly subterranean; contemporary kivas are typically rectangular and often at least partially above ground. North American kivas function much like the sacred caves and labyrinths of the ancient Maya. They are sacred ceremonial spaces connecting the physical world and realm of spirit. Pueblo kivas have a hole in the floor, called a *sipapu*, which serves as a portal to allow ancestor and supernatural spirits to enter and leave the physical realm through the kivas.
3. The North American Indian exhibits I experienced as a child have all been taken off display and replaced by new exhibits.

Photographs and historical material on the earlier exhibits can be found in the museum's library and reference sources. The museum's Fieldiana Anthropology Publications (early 1900s) also have photographs, drawings and documentation of the North American Indian ceremonial objects, museum displays (including the Powamu altar I saw as a young boy), and ceremonial practices.

4. Schele and Freidel 1990: 45
5. Ibid., 45
6. Eliade 1964: 222–223
7. Foster 2002: 178
8. From the *Diccionario de Motul,* quoted in Roys 1933: 167
9. Sharer and Traxler 2006: 720
10. Ibid., 735
11. A. A. Long's *Epictetus: A Stoic and Socratic Guide to Life* provides an excellent overview of Epictetus' philosophical teaching (as recorded by his student Arrian), which helped me understand the Greco-Roman panentheistic perspective of God-in-the-world and the teachings of North American Indian elders that the world is alive and filled with Spirit.
12. Pagels 2003: 164
13. Ibid., 139
14. Ibid., 34
15. Ibid., 57
16. Ibid., 100
17. Tozzer 1941: 110
18. Maya books, called codices by scholars, were written by Maya scribes on a type of paper made from beaten bark and sometimes deer skin; pages were joined along the edges to form a continuous screen fold. Scribes recorded historical, astronomical, and ritual events using a combination of hieroglyphic writing and images. In their zeal to convert the Maya to Christianity and eliminate their

"pagan" spiritual practices, the Franciscans destroyed the codices whenever they found them, the most dramatic and infamous event being the *auto de fé* (Inquisition) presided over by Fr. Diego de Landa in 1562. Scholars estimate that hundreds, perhaps a thousand, codices were destroyed, with only a few surviving to this day.

19. Houston and Inomata 2009: 193–95
20. *Moralia*, Volume V.
21. Johnson 2002: 125. In *Isis and Osiris*, Plutarch writes, "Nor should we think of the gods as different gods among different peoples, nor as barbarian gods and Greek gods or as southern and northern gods, but just as the sun and the moon and the heavens and the earth and the sea are common to all, but are called by different names by different peoples, so for that one rationality that keeps all these things in order and the one Providence that watches over them and the ancillary powers that are set over all there have arisen among different peoples in accordance with their customs different honors and appellations (Loeb Classic Library pp. 155–157)."
22. Edmonson 1982: 44
23. Benedict 1923: 40
24. Walker 1991: 79
25. Lame Deer and Erdoes 1972: 65
26. Benedict 1923: 35
27. Ibid., 35
28. Tozzer 1941: 112
29. Roys 1933: 3
30. Ibid., 182
31. Tozzer 1941: 109
32. Herrera in Tozzer 1941: 219
33. Pagels 2003: 86
34. Ibid., 84

35. Ibid., 97
36. My studies of the ancient Maya began with Michael D. Coe's *The Maya*, Charles Gallencamp's *Maya: The Riddle and Rediscovery of a Lost Civilization*, William Gates' translation of *Yucatan Before and After the Conquest* by Friar Diego de Landa, Robert J. Sharer's *The Ancient Maya*, Victor Perera and Robert D. Bruce's *The Last Lords of Palenque: The Lancandon Mayas of the Mexican Rain Forest*, and Dennis Tedlock's translation of *Popol Vuh*.
37. Mora 1982: 17
38. Armstrong 2009: xviii

INITIATION

INITIAL JOURNEY

When the doors of the kiva are open, all may enter; many will dishonor us, some will enter asleep and remain asleep, some will enter and be transformed. — Hopi Indian elder

CASA RINCONADA
CHACO CANYON, NEW MEXICO – 1982

I felt something extraordinary was about to happen as we drove past the moonlit ruins of the ancient Anasazi Indian civilization located in Chaco Canyon in New Mexico. The dust from the old dirt road[1] that ran through the center of the ancient grouping of sandstone buildings was seeping into our van and rising up to obscure the faint outlines of the abandoned, thousand-year-old pueblo ruins. We were headed to Casa Rinconada, an ancient circular ceremonial structure, the predecessor of the contemporary kivas that were the site of the sacred Hopi and Zuni Indian rituals I had learned about at the Field Museum as a boy. Casa Rinconada was the spiritual centerpiece of the magnificent Anasazi culture that had flourished at Chaco between 850 and 1250 CE.

Our group of eighteen was already a week into a ten-day pilgrimage sponsored by the Ojai Foundation to visit sites sacred to the Indians of the Southwest. This journey—my first direct encounter with ancient and contemporary Indian communities and ceremonial practices—had been everything I had hoped it would be. We had seen kachina[2] dances on the isolated mesa-top villages of the Hopi Indians in Arizona, trekked through the spectacular Canyon de Chelly, and visited other sacred sites of particular spiritual significance to the indigenous peoples of the Southwest. This night we planned to initiate our stay in Chaco Canyon with a ceremony inside Casa Rinconada, the largest and most dramatic of all the ancient kivas.

It was a relatively smooth, short drive to the site from the park campground where we were staying, nothing like the seemingly endless washboard dirt road we had endured to reach the park. The route our three vans followed to Casa Rinconada ran along the bottom of the canyon between massive sandstone mesas and magnificent ancient Anasazi structures. The most imposing and accessible buildings we passed had been constructed sometime between 900 and 1150 CE but abandoned in the 1200s as a result of prolonged drought. Although I had never visited Chaco Canyon before, I had read about the spectacular ruins and it was exciting to be on the verge of experiencing them in person. The stars were brilliant in the clear desert air; the light from an almost full moon cast shadows that gave the ruins an otherworldly look and feel. The periodic howl of coyotes on the mesa tops in the distance seemed to beckon us to another world and into another reality.

As we drove through the night, my thoughts drifted to the strange sequence of events that had led me to these ancient ruins in a remote part of eastern New Mexico. A little over a year earlier I had been living in San Diego, California and was planning to drive up to Berkeley to attend my brother's graduation from the

UC Berkeley Law School. I had wanted to stop and visit Esalen Institute in Big Sur on the way. To do so, I had to attend a workshop, so I registered for the workshop scheduled for the weekend of my visit—Dr. Michael Harner's introductory workshop on shamanism. I purchased a copy of the book Michael had recently published, *The Way of the Shaman*, to prepare for the event.

Reading Michael's book, I rediscovered a world I hadn't thought much about since we had moved to California from Chicago when I was twelve years old. Memories from the Field Museum came flooding back and I found myself reentering the world of indigenous spirituality that had captivated me as a young boy. Suddenly, this enchanting, miraculous spiritual realm that had seemed so remote and almost dreamlike to me as a child started to seem much more real and accessible. I realized it was a world that I could not only come to understand but also actually enter, a world that might reveal secrets I had longed to know since my childhood. As I read Michael's book, I became increasingly hopeful that this might be the first step for me on an astonishing spiritual journey.

In addition to learning more about the shamanic beliefs of the indigenous North American Indian cultures, I was anxious to learn specific shamanic tools for healing and accessing the other non-physical realms. My experiences at the Field Museum had convinced me there were spiritual mysteries beyond my youthful comprehension. I was sure there was more to existence than just the physical world I experienced every day, but the only idea of alternative realities I had at the time was based on the concepts of Heaven and Hell I had been exposed to in church and through literature. I hoped that the workshop would help me open the door to these other spiritual realms and introduce me to the ancient, universal shamanic way of perceiving and being in the world.

During the workshop, Michael introduced us to the concepts of the Lower World, the Upper World, and shamanic states of consciousness. Through the use of drums, rattles, and visualization techniques he instructed us to enter a light trance state, somewhat like deep meditation, for the purpose of "journeying" to the Lower and Upper Worlds in non-ordinary reality. We learned how to work with spirit guides, tutelary spirits, and power animals. We also learned the techniques a shaman uses to interact with helping spirits to perform spiritual healing, to remove spiritual blockages, to retrieve lost souls, and to receive spiritual guidance to help others and ourselves. And then we journeyed, over and over again, into the hidden spirit realms to perform shamanic healing.

Whether because of my temperament, innate ability, or early experiences at the Field Museum, I found I was able to easily journey to both the Lower World and the Upper World. From our very first journey with Michael, my experiences were intense and deeply moving. In the Lower World I encountered spirit guides and tutelary animal spirits; in the Upper World, numinous spiritual beings appeared as glowing orbs of radiant light. I found that both the Lower and Upper Worlds were as rich and complex as our physical realm, embodying some of the attributes of our physical world, yet with dramatically different energies. The paranormal realms of the spirits were filled with magnificent mysteries and hidden spiritual powers.

The fascinating ceremonial artifacts I had seen at the Field Museum suddenly took on a whole new meaning as I was learning how to actually enter the world of indigenous spirituality. I began to understand how those sacred ritual objects were used in spiritual practice. The discoveries were thrilling, and each new journey brought with it a deeper sense of wholeness and personal healing. I did struggle with the fact that the shamanic realm I was encountering was so different from the Heavenly world that had been described to me in school and church since childhood. Yet, for me, this was as authentic and real as anything I had ever experienced.

As I continued attending workshops with Michael, one of the shamanic healing techniques we practiced most frequently was soul retrieval. Indigenous shamanic cultures believe that whenever someone suffers a traumatic event (for example any kind of sexual, physical, or emotional abuse, being in an accident, etc.) they may experience a partial loss of their soul—the spiritual essence that remains with us throughout life. In Western psychology we refer to this as "disassociation," but shamanic cultures believe part of the soul flees the physical body in order to survive the experience and is then trapped in non-ordinary reality. During shamanic soul retrieval, working in pairs or small groups, one of us would journey into non-ordinary reality where we were taught how to locate the missing part of another's soul and then return to ordinary reality where the returned soul essence was reunited with the person who experienced the trauma. Through this process, we repeatedly witnessed physical and emotional healing, sometimes with startling, dramatic results.

We were also trained in shamanic techniques for guiding souls from the physical world into the afterlife at the time of death. This practice, known as "psychopomp" (from the Greek *psuchopompos* for "guide of souls"), is not unique to shamanism and I had a vague memory of reading about ancient Greek psychopomps in my Introduction to Western Civilization class in college. With Michael we learned how to locate a newly-departed soul in non-ordinary reality and help it reunite with deceased relatives and loved ones or connect with helping spirits. I was particularly fascinated by this process at the time, but I had no idea that four years later I would be asked by the spirits at the ancient Maya site of Palenque to serve as a psychopomp to release old souls still trapped in the ruins.

I developed close relationships with many I worked with during my shamanic training and through them I was introduced to the Ojai Foundation in Ojai, California. At the time, the foundation was led by anthropologist Dr. Joan Halifax and offered a variety of programs and workshops featuring indigenous spiritual leaders. I learned that the foundation was sponsoring a trip to visit sacred Indian sites in Arizona and New Mexico and I knew immediately this was something I wanted—needed—to do. And now I had arrived in Chaco Canyon, the next stop on a shamanic path. I was about to enter the sacred realm of the ancient Anasazi Indians, pursuing a childhood dream and hoping to find personal healing and solace.

As I looked out the window at the crumbling, decaying structures along the side of the road, I felt a surge of anxiety that had been with me off and on for the entire trip. As excited as I was about this journey, I couldn't escape the worry I felt about the recent turn of events in my life. For a moment I was overcome with the hopeless feeling that my life back in Los Angeles seemed to be crumbling like the ancient ruins before me. It had not been a good year for me even though I had a lot to be grateful for. I was struggling to deal with problems in my career, finances, and relationships and I was feeling rather lost and uncertain.

I had recently moved to Los Angeles to take a new job with a large, prestigious management consulting firm. This had been a significant step up for me in my career. I had an office on the twenty-second floor of one of the most desirable downtown office buildings, a red BMW, and a great apartment in Westwood near the UCLA campus. But my father had died nine months earlier, I was still struggling to pay off his enormous medical bills, my first wife and I were in the middle of divorce proceedings, I was about to lose the house my wife and I had owned, and I was having second thoughts about my new job. For some time, I'd been dreading answering the phone because I was sure there would be more bad news on the other end of the line.

The jolt of the van coming to an abrupt stop brought my mind back to Chaco Canyon and I was glad to get some distance from troubled thoughts about my life back home. We had parked on the side of the road near a narrow dirt trail that led up to the grand kiva. I was almost one thousand miles from Los Angeles entering a one-thousand-year-old ceremonial structure and I was profoundly grateful to be there at that moment. As doors were closing for me in the life I had known, I was hoping that new doors might begin to open. While I waited my turn to leave the van, I began preparing myself emotionally and mentally for my first time inside an ancient kiva and my first chance to use the shamanic tools I had learned from Michael in an authentic ceremonial setting.

After leaving the vans, our group walked in silence, single file, on the short dirt trail that led to Casa Rinconada. My first view of the massive kiva literally took my breath away. Bathed in soft, radiant moonlight, it was the most stunning structure I had ever seen; its ancient masonry sandstone walls seemed to pulse in the crisp night air of the desert, radiating energy as if imbued with a sacred aliveness. I knew that for indigenous cultures, kivas were portals to the Lower World and vehicles for transcending the boundaries of the physical universe. As I approached Casa Rinconada there was no doubt in my mind that I was about to enter this other world. I found myself humbled and filled with awe at being in this ancient ceremonial setting.

Casa Rinconada is an imposing cylindrical structure—sixty feet in diameter and fifteen feet high—built with hand-hewn sandstone blocks. It emerges from a massive mound of earth with approximately half of the structure below ground level and the remainder visible above ground. When it was built originally, the kiva was covered with a roof made of logs and branches supported by massive wooden pillars two feet in diameter. The roof and supporting pillars had rotted away hundreds of years earlier; now the sacred ceremonial space inside the kiva was completely open to the elements. To-night, the chamber was flooded with moonlight and filled with the aura of the countless Anasazi ancestors who had come to the kiva to pray, to heal, and to be healed.

By the time I finally reached the entrance to the kiva, all random thoughts seemed to have left my consciousness and I was absolutely riveted by my surroundings. Everything in my field of vision seemed to be coming into sharper focus. The smell of sage and creosote was particularly pungent, I could feel my heart beating faster, and I was acutely aware of my every breath. The trail ended at a large above-ground masonry antechamber that protruded from the northern side of the kiva's main wall. The antechamber had been constructed with a large hole in the floor that opened to a flight of narrow, steep stone steps angling downward. The steps ended at a large subterranean doorway opening onto a passage into the kiva's interior.

As I waited my turn to descend the steps in the antechamber, I closed my eyes for a moment to say a silent prayer. When I opened them I experienced something that both startled and terrified me. Looking down, I saw that my physical body appeared to have been completely transformed into a body quite unlike mine. I was much shorter, much more muscular, and darker skinned; I had a body that would have belonged to one of the indigenous ancestors coming to this kiva for a ceremony a thousand years ago. I was totally unprepared for the vividness of this experience which filled me with both excitement and intense fear. I stared at my hands and arms in shock and disbelief. Then, not knowing what else to do, I took a deep breath and descended the stairs leading to the kiva chamber.

At the bottom of the stone stairway, I ducked down to pass through the low opening into the interior of the kiva and caught my first glimpse of the sacred chamber in the dazzling moonlight.

Entering the subterranean kiva involved a process of going down and then up again. The opening to the interior had been built below the actual floor level of the chamber so that one had to first descend the stairs and then pass through the short doorway before re-ascending by means of a long, narrow, masonry-lined ramp that inclined upward to the floor of the kiva. My descent to the passageway opening was like the shamanic descents to the Lower World I had seen in my mind's eye many times before, only this time the physical act of descending heightened the experience dramatically.

As I emerged from beneath the kiva wall and walked up the ramp, I experienced myself entering an enchanted, dreamlike, liminal state. Time slowed and everything around me appeared in crystalline clarity and bold relief. I was still struggling to discern whether I was a twentieth-century seeker or an ancient Anasazi ancestor returning for ceremony.

When I arrived at the end of the ramp I noticed that others in our group who entered ahead of me had taken a seat on a stone bench built by ancient stone masons against the perimeter of the ceremonial chamber, and I followed their lead. I leaned back against the ancient masonry of the kiva wall and tried to blend with the energy of the sacred space. Although the desert night air was cool, the sandstone blocks of the wall felt warm against my back. The moonlight seemed to soften the hard stone features of the chamber. I felt as if I'd been transported to a timeless, mystical space. Closing my eyes, I drifted through this other dimension, feeling the power and presence of the kiva moving through me.

Being inside the kiva was both profoundly moving and very disorienting. I was finally present in an ancient, sacred ceremonial place—one that had been used for hundreds of years by the ancestors of today's Pueblo Indians. I was a complete outsider and yet I felt truly at home in a way I had never experienced before. I sensed that a door was about to open for me into the ancient, timeless, sacred world of indigenous spirituality—a world unlike anything for which my Midwestern upbringing had prepared me. This was something that held the possibility of fundamentally changing my life and my perceptions of the world.

Once our entire group had arrived in the kiva and had a chance to settle into the experience, we were instructed to move together to the center of the chamber and spend some time meditating in silence. Sitting crossed legged on the ground, I closed my eyes and used the shamanic journeying techniques I had learned. I felt my breath deepening and my mind quieting as I became more aware of my surroundings and the energy of the kiva. As I let myself go deeper into my experience, I felt the energy of the sacred chamber moving through me. Somewhere in the distance I heard the soft sounds of a drum beating rhythmically, leading me on a journey through sacred time and space. Everything around me seemed to soften and the kiva walls seemed less solid, more porous and permeable.

As I sat in silence with my eyes closed, I experienced what seemed to be an intense flash of light. I had the startling impression that the floor of the kiva was dissolving, and I found myself falling through space, traveling deeper into the Lower World. The walls of the kiva seemed to have vanished, and I experienced the unlimited timelessness and spaciousness of this non-physical world in non-ordinary reality. The experience was similar to the earlier shamanic journeying I had done, but this time the sense of movement was much more vivid and intense as I traveled deeper through the ancient portal within the kiva. Then, suddenly, the sensation of falling ended and I felt that I had reached a very, very old and very, very sacred place.

I was overcome with a sense of inner peace and deep connectedness. This was entirely different from my existence in Los

Angeles, yet, at the same time, somehow familiar and welcoming. I had found my way into an ancient, timeless world that seemed more real and authentic than much of what I experienced in my ordinary life. Most significantly, it was as if I were rediscovering a part of my life that had been missing—maybe forgotten or abandoned or both. I felt a wholeness I had not experienced before and experienced healing on a very deep and profound level. I was filled with gratitude for the gift of this experience.

I'm not sure exactly how long I remained in this transcendent state—it might have been ten or fifteen minutes or maybe longer—but at some point I sensed something was calling me back to the physical world inside the kiva. As moving as my experience had been, I'd had enough and was ready to return to the physical world. Taking a deep breath, I experienced myself moving once again through time and space, but this time out of non-ordinary reality and back to the present. As I sat with my eyes closed and waited for my awareness to fully return to the chamber, I relished the hardness of the kiva's earthen floor, the tang of the cool night air, and the intense pungent odor of sage and creosote bushes in the surrounding desert.

Opening my eyes and looking up, I marveled at the pulsing of the brilliant stars suspended in the darkest sky I had ever seen. The moon was still moving through the heavens and had shifted during our silent meditation, casting completely different shadow patterns inside the ceremonial chamber. Glancing at my body in the moonlight I was relieved to find that I looked "normal" once again, but something quickly changed that relief into fear. I had been told by Indian elders that the indigenous peoples have always believed in life after death; those who have left their physical bodies are not gone from us but exist in the spirit realm. As I sat in the kiva, my senses heightened by my recent journey, I had the distinct feeling we were not alone; I felt we had been joined by Anasazi ancestors.

Out of the corner of my eye, I began to glimpse move-ment in the shadows against the wall of the kiva. My fear inten-sified as three male spirit beings emerged from the shadows and moved toward the circle our group made in the moonlight. The thought raced through my mind that the journey I had just taken had somehow opened the door for their manifestation. In a way I didn't understand at the time, the veil between the worlds of matter and spirit had fallen away for me and the two worlds had become one. I was grateful that the spirits of the indigenous ancestors had led me unexpectedly into their realm—a place as real as any I had experienced, a place I seemed to have been searching for since I was a young boy—but now I realized they had followed me back.

As they approached us, the spirits appeared to me in strik-ingly solid physical forms—they looked like contemporary Pueblo Indians "dressed" in clothing that might have been worn by the ancient Anasazi. Even though I knew they had no physical sub-stance, it seemed as if I could have reached out and touched them as they moved behind me, out of my field of vision. Filled with fear and barely breathing, I sat as still as I could, hoping the spirits were welcoming and not malevolent. I sensed them coming to a stop and sitting a few feet behind me. My fear subsided somewhat when they seemed to simply continue sitting with us in silence in the moonlight. As I glanced at everyone's faces in the group, I real-ized the only other person aware of their presence was one of our leaders; he was looking directly at them.

Speaking softly, almost reverently, we each took turns shar-ing our experiences out loud with the entire group. Most had en-joyed a tranquil meditative time while a few of us had journeyed to the spirit world. Neither the leader nor I mentioned the pres-ence of the ancestor spirits. We then said prayers for the well-being of the ancestors of Chaco Canyon and expressed our gratitude for the privilege of being in this sacred place. Then slowly, reluctantly, we all stood and moved back toward the doorway that led under the wall of the kiva. As before, we walked single-file, retracing our path up the narrow stone steps, through the antechamber, and back down the trail to the vans. No one spoke in the van as we made the short trip back to the campground; everyone seemed to have been deeply moved by the experience. We sat in silence, driving past the ancient stone structures that seemed to be glowing in the moonlight.

I couldn't get to sleep that night because I couldn't shake the uneasiness I was feeling about the encounter with the ancestor spirits, even though the three spirits had stayed behind in the kiva. My first spirit encounter in Indian Country had been a little too real. Eventually, I decided to take my sleeping bag out of my tent and sleep in one of the vans. I had no way of knowing at the time but this was just the first of many spirit encounters I would have at sacred ceremonial sites, particularly those of the Maya. I was comforted somewhat by recalling shamanic insights Michael had shared during my training, and that he later recounted in an interview:

> When you start shamanic journeying, if you're the kind of person the spirits feel compassion for and want to help, you're going to get lots of teachings you never asked for and never expected. Because once you go through those doors—whatever those doors are—the spirits will teach you according to your preparation, and your life will change. Even one journey may start changing your life.[3]

Over the years I became increasingly comfortable with these types of experiences and I learned that spirits do indeed bring gifts of insight, wisdom, and healing. This first experience at Casa Rinconada had been an extraordinary gift.

We broke camp the next morning, spent a short time visiting other areas of the ruins, and then left Chaco Canyon to head for Rough Rock, Arizona, on the Navajo Indian Reservation. I was relieved to be leaving the ancestor spirits from the kiva behind. Arrangements had been made for us to spend the little time remaining on the trip with a Navajo family who had graciously consented to let us spend a couple of nights in their *hogan*, a traditional Navajo log structure. Members of our group were also given the opportunity to spend the last night of the trip on a traditional vision quest—an overnight spiritual vigil, alone, in a remote area not far from the hogan. Although I had some trepidation, I had heard about vision quests and was eager to have this experience.

In order to prepare, we each went off alone from the hogan, on foot, to find a questing site that felt right to us. When I found my site—on top of a mesa a couple of miles from the hogan—I followed the instructions I had been given and prepared a circle approximately six feet in diameter using large stones to mark its boundaries. I then returned to the hogan to wait until dusk. We were told to dress warmly because the temperature in the desert dropped significantly overnight, and to take a sleeping bag or blanket for extra warmth. We were instructed to try and stay awake all night and not, under any circumstances, to leave our circle of stones. We were to simply be there; aware, alert, and open to whatever experience presented itself.

After an early dinner, I grabbed my sleeping bag and some fresh sage I had collected earlier in the day and started walking west toward the mesa and my site. I was so lost in my thoughts that I really didn't notice much about my surroundings. I was still feeling uneasy about the spirit encounter at Casa Rinconada and I was anxious about being out alone overnight in the remote semi-wilderness. I kept reminding myself that statistically I was much safer out here than on one of the almost weekly plane flights

I was taking on business, or driving on the Los Angeles freeways, or walking the streets of downtown L.A. late at night after a long day at the office. But that didn't really help. I was still feeling fearful.

The site I had picked out was on top of a mesa that rose about eighty feet above the desert floor; to reach the top I had to climb a relatively steep grade of boulders and loose rocks. The area looked much different at dusk than it had when I first saw it the day before. I soon realized I couldn't find the exact route I had taken earlier, and once on top of the mesa, I couldn't find the site I had prepared. I was annoyed at myself and getting increasingly anxious—daylight was fading quickly and I felt completely unprepared and vulnerable. I heard a small band of coyotes howling in the distance and, although I was pretty sure they wouldn't come too close, their presence still frightened me.

I rushed to collect stones, hastily built a new circle, and sat down inside. Taking a large sprig of fresh sage out of my pocket, I lit it and smudged myself—drawing the fragrant smoke from the sage over and around my head and shoulders with the cupped palm of my hand. Shaking the sprig gently to keep it lit and smoking, I passed it slowly over all the stones that formed my vision quest circle. I then offered the smoke of the sage to each of the four cardinal directions, then above to the sky and below to the earth. The sage had a wonderfully calming effect on me. I took a deep breath and said a silent prayer, asking for strength, courage, and guidance.

My mind started to settle down and for the first time since leaving the hogan I began to be fully aware of my surroundings. I loved the desert—the crisp evening air was exhilarating, the pungent odor of sage was refreshing, the solitude was glorious, and the vast expanse of desert around me was liberating. My thoughts seemed to drift randomly to various aspects of my life, and I found myself unexpectedly thinking about my maternal grandfather. He was a Baptist minister and one of the finest men I had ever known.

He died when I was quite young and I hadn't thought about him in years, but now I vividly remembered his gentle demeanor, his kindly presence, and the soft, approving looks he always gave me. I found myself musing about what he would think about this Indian adventure of mine and whether or not, given his deep Christian beliefs, he would approve.

I looked up toward the horizon at the magnificent desert sunset. Although there was still a little light, the sun was below the mesa tops in the distance. Suddenly, to my astonishment, I saw my grandfather just outside my vision quest circle, looking down at me. I stared in disbelief. He seemed so real and present that I felt I could almost reach out and touch him. He was surrounded by an aura of radiant white light, gazing at me with that familiar, wonderfully gentle and loving look on his face. While I was sitting there dumbstruck, he nodded and smiled at me. Although I didn't hear him say a word, I could tell from his countenance that he was happy for me and completely approved of the journey I was taking.

As suddenly as he had appeared, he vanished. The experience was so real that I would have bet my life that he had actually been there, but it was also so improbable based on everything I had been taught. My mind flashed back to my encounter with the spirits at Casa Rinconada and it occurred to me that as the door to the spirit realm opened for me inside the kiva, I was given the ability to be aware of my grandfather's presence. However, this encounter had seemed more real and was much more intense and personal than the one in the kiva. As I struggled to make sense of it all, I was completely certain of one thing—I had my grandfather's unconditional love and complete support and approval for my spiritual journey. This vision was his gift to me.

I spent the rest of the night deep in thought about my life in Los Angeles. For the first time in quite a while I felt some of my burdens lifting. The magnificently clear sky, dazzling stars, and crisp desert air helped me clear my head so that I could see the pieces of my life in sharper focus. As the hours passed, I felt increasingly confident that things would somehow work themselves out and that I would find the answers I needed. While I wasn't feeling great, I was feeling better and certainly more hopeful then I had in a long time. My world seemed to have opened up to allow other possibilities to emerge. I was also more at peace with my spirit encounter at Casa Rinconada.

During the night I pulled my sleeping bag up around my shoulders to keep warm, and periodically burned a sprig of sage. I couldn't have slept even if I had wanted to. Every coyote howl, every noise in the brush, every creak of a branch sent a jolt of adrenalin through my body. But I didn't feel threatened the way I had earlier and, while I wasn't really enjoying my experience alone in the desert, I felt good about what I was doing. I appreciated the solitude and was grateful for the absence of distractions. This was the first time I'd had an opportunity to be truly alone with myself in a long time. While I wished the circumstances in my life were different, in my solitude I had a clearer perspective and the challenges I was facing seemed more manageable.

Sometime during the middle of the night I sensed the energy around me starting to shift. It felt as if the earth were opening to the coming of a new day; the hardness and sharpness of the night seemed to give way to a softer, gentler, more receptive energy. Everything started coming back to life, waking up in anticipation of the sunrise. I was reminded of an experience I'd had at sunrise earlier in the trip, on a mesa top at a Hopi Indian village. I was standing outside a contemporary Hopi kiva listening to the sounds of drumming and chanting by Hopi priests, ceremonial leaders, and kachina dancers inside the kiva. They were performing a ceremony to spiritually prepare their fields for the planting of corn. When I looked out into the distance to the fields below the mesa where the corn crop was to be planted, I saw waves of energy rising from the earth to meet the sky. At the same time, waves of energy from the sky were descending to meet the earth. It seemed as if the forces of heaven and earth were in perfect alignment and equilibrium—blending and merging to form one perfectly integrated energy field. The whole scene shimmered and pulsed in the first light of day. My thoughts drifted back to my childhood vision of the Grandmother over the Hopi altar in the Field Museum, preparing the fields for planting. As dawn approached the mesa top, I suddenly and fully understood the significance of that vision.

Now as I sat in my vision quest circle I could actually feel the generative, sustaining energy of the earth moving around and through me. I was perfectly content to just sit with this experience as I watched the first rays of the sun break over the horizon—for the first time in many, many years I was at peace. I sat for a long time savoring the experience until the sun fully emerged from behind the distant mountains, signaling the time for me to return to the hogan. I burned more sage and offered prayers of thanks to my grandfather, the indigenous ancestors, and the native peoples of this area. I gave thanks for my experiences on my vision quest and prayed for the health, happiness, and well-being of my family, friends, and those who were with me on this trip.

After climbing down the face of the mesa, I found my way back to the narrow dirt trail that led through the chaparral to the hogan. I walked slowly, mindfully, this time taking in every detail I possibly could—the pungent odor of sage and creosote bushes, the soft, subtle colors of the desert cactus and plants, small lizards darting between rocks, and an occasional snake in the underbrush. I could see my boots sinking ever so slightly into the dusty surface of the trail and small puffs of dust coming off the Vibram soles. My body felt healed and rejuvenated, light and refreshed. I relished every step back to the hogan.

The hardest parts of this trip for me were the flight from Phoenix back to Los Angeles and reentry into my life back home. I had had my first contact with spirits at an ancient ceremonial site and my first experience with what indigenous cultures characteristically describe as a "vision." But these experiences were clearly outside the mainstream of the world I knew in Los Angeles and would have been completely discounted or even ridiculed by some of my friends, professional colleagues, and clients if I had chosen to tell them. On the other hand, I had touched something that seemed so real, authentic, and profound that I knew this was the spiritual path I had been looking for—it was leading me to focus on things beyond my career. My life outside of work was becoming richer and more meaningful and, as a result, I was feeling more resilient and balanced, and better able to cope with career pressures and challenges.

I was certain that the journey I had started would lead me even deeper into the world of indigenous spirituality. The door had opened for me and there was no turning back. My continuing involvement with the Ojai Foundation helped me move deeper into the sacred world of the North American Indians. Through them, I began developing relationships with contemporary North American Indian elders and spiritual leaders that allowed me to participate more deeply in authentic spiritual ceremonial practice.

During the next two years I had the opportunity to attend other workshops with Michael Harner in Berkeley and Marin County. Through these experiences I became increasingly adept at shamanic techniques and was able to deepen my understanding of the trans-dimensional space outside our physical realm. The unique qualities of the Upper World and Lower World became much more familiar and I learned to discern the specific energies of each; my encounters with spirit beings became more vivid and their spiritual guidance easier for me to understand. My transitions in and out of the spirit realms in non-ordinary reality also required less effort and I began to appreciate the interrelatedness and continuity between the physical and non-physical spheres of existence.

Also during this time, friends introduced me to Marcellus "Bear Heart" Williams, a full-blood spiritual leader of the Muskogee-Creek Nation who had been trained in the traditional ways of his tribe.[4] Bear Heart was the subject of the book *The Wind is My Mother*, co-authored by Molly Larkin and published in 1996. Under Bear Heart's guidance I completed several traditional vision quests, participated in many inipi ceremonies, and attended four Native American Church ceremonies. I spent as much time as I could with him during his frequent visits to Los Angeles and traveled with him to South Dakota and Colorado. With Bear Heart, I had the extraordinary good fortune to actually live the Native American spiritual pathways that had captivated me as a young boy.

In 1985, while I was studying with Bear Heart, I decided to make a pilgrimage to visit the sacred ceremonial sites of the ancient Maya Indians in Central Mexico and the Yucatan Peninsula. I didn't know any Maya elders at the time and wasn't aware of their approach to preparing for such a journey, but Bear Heart helped me prepare by following traditional Plains Indian practices. Through my previous journeying and spirit encounters in sacred time and space, I knew this would be a major spiritual undertaking and that the power and intensity of the ancient ceremonial centers might easily eclipse anything I had yet experienced.

My intention for my pilgrimage was to visit the Maya sites in a humble and respectful manner. I wanted to honor and pray for the ancestors whose traditions had captivated me as a child and for the contemporary Maya who are the guardians of those traditions today. I wasn't expecting anything specific, other than being able to experience firsthand the grandeur and majesty of the ancient ceremonial centers. I had learned from my earlier vision quests that I needed to simply remain open and receptive to whatever was in store for me, and that what I would experience would be exactly what I needed to experience at the time.

In the year preceding my trip, I completed four inipi purification ceremonies during the winter and summer solstices and the fall and spring equinoxes. Every month I set time aside for a prayer ceremony to reaffirm my intention for the pilgrimage, to offer prayers honoring the Maya ancestors, and to pray that I would be able to connect with the spiritual energy of the sites during my pilgrimage. As Bear Heart taught me, I also prepared four hundred and five prayer ties (sometimes referred to as tobacco ties), forming each tie by wrapping a small, two-inch square of cotton cloth around a pinch of tobacco, and then tying all four hundred and five packets on a continuous length of lightweight cotton twine. Each tie held a specific, individual prayer related to some aspect of my upcoming journey.

My wife Julie and I planned our trip around the sites that interested me most in Central Mexico and the Yucatan Peninsula. Bear Heart instructed me that spiritual preparation for this type of journey was even more important than physical preparation, so by the time of our departure I had certainly spent more time with my vision quest preparations than with travel plans, shots, and packing. I had no idea what was in store for me but I felt ready for anything; I was confident I was as prepared as I could possibly be. I was in an open and respectful state of mind and certain I would be guided and watched over by the spirit realm.

Chapter Notes

1. The dirt road we traveled that night was paved several years later by the Park Service due to increasing traffic and concerns over the preservation of the ruins. At the time of my initial visit

to Chaco Canyon and several subsequent visits, access to Casa Rinconada was completely unrestricted. The Park Service later placed a fence around the entire kiva to prevent public access and preclude damage to the ancient masonry structure.

2. Kachina is the term generally used to refer to supernatural forces and spirit beings recognized by the North American Pueblo Indian peoples. The spiritual world of the Pueblo peoples includes hundreds of different kachina spirits representing a variety of natural forces (thunder, rain, wind, and celestial bodies), ancestors, and supernatural "deities." Kachinas are represented by small carved, painted, and decorated wooden figures (kachina "dolls"), and in community ceremonies by masked dancers in regalia, representing supernatural powers and beings. Those who dance in kachina ceremonies have historically been referred to by anthropologists as "impersonating" kachina spirits, but after my experiences at kachina dances, I believe that dancers are actually channeling kachina spirits, bringing them into the physical realm from the spirit realm. Kachina spirits are summoned during secret ceremonies performed inside kivas and enter the physical ream though circular portals called *sipapus* built into kiva floors.

3. Interview with Michael Harner by Bonnie Corrigan, "Shamanic Healing: We Are Not Alone," *Shamanism*, Spring/Summer 1997, Vol 10, No 1

4. Bear Heart passed away in 2008. He was an extraordinary mentor and a wise and compassionate guide. Like my grandfather, he was one of the men I admired most in my life. I will always be grateful for the time I had with him.

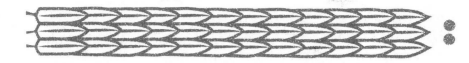

THE WORLD TREE

The Cave at Balankanche
Yucatan, Mexico – 1985

It was late afternoon, and the brilliant sun over the Yucatan Peninsula was just beginning its descent in the west while the moon, barely visible in the daylight, rose in the east. As I stood near the base of the Castillo pyramid in the center of the Main Plaza at Chichen Itza, I took a slow, deep breath of moist tropical air and reminded myself that I was finally here, the place I had dreamed of visiting since I was a young boy. The weathered stone masonry of the magnificent ancient ceremonial structures around me stood out in stunning relief against the lush rainforest.

At almost midnight the day before, Julie and I had boarded a plane in Los Angeles to begin an exhausting sixteen-hour journey that included a trip through customs in Mexico City, a long layover and connecting flight to Cancun, and a two-and-a-half-hour ride in a rental car to our hotel at the edge of the ruins. But now, gazing at some of the most famous architecture of the ancient Maya, the weariness vanished, replaced by awe and excitement. We had traveled over one thousand miles and were now surrounded by fabulous ancient pyramids and temples built over one thousand years ago, in a magical jungle setting filled with parrots, toucans, black spiny-tailed iguanas, butterflies, and kinkajous.

Because we had arrived so late, we were disappointed to have only a brief time at the ruins before the park closed, but the fact that our hotel was a short walk away and had spectacular views of the ruined ceremonial structures took some of the disappointment away. Back at the hotel, we had dinner on the patio in the midst of flowering tropical gardens and soaring royal palms. During our meal we marveled at the moonlit ruins in the distance and talked about our plans for the next few days. The next day-and-a-half would be spent at Chichen Itza, and then we would visit the nearby cave at Balankanche. After that, we planned on driving to Playa del Carmen and taking a ferry to the island of Cozumel for two days, before going on to the ruins at Tulum and Coba.

I had a hard time sleeping that night and couldn't stop thinking about all the incredible things we had planned. Chichen Itza was turning out to be everything I had hoped it would be, and I was excited about seeing more. We got up early the next morning and, after a quick breakfast, went directly to the ruins. The ancient ceremonial structures had a magical, organic spiritual presence similar to Chaco Canyon, but the sheer size of the site and the beautifully designed and constructed monumental architecture created an imposing setting unlike anything I had experienced before. The majestic El Castillo pyramid with the dramatic Temple of K'uk'ulkan positioned at its top, the Temple of the Warriors' massive trunked pyramid and large colonnade with remnants of massive stone pillars, and the Great Ball Court, the largest in Mesoamerica, were all breathtaking.

Chichen Itza was founded around 800 CE during the Classic period. Although the city initially achieved dominance through military conquest, it quickly grew to be the preeminent commercial and political power for the next two hundred years. In its heyday, Chichen Itza was the most cosmopolitan of all the Maya capitals and controlled the largest and most populous state in Maya history. By 1100 CE, however, the city fell through conquest, and archaeological evidence from that time points to widespread destruction and sacking of the capital. By the time the Spanish arrived in the 1500s, Chichen Itza had been largely abandoned and only a small settlement remained, although many of the spectacular ruined buildings and ceremonial structures were still standing.

I hadn't planned to do any shamanic journeying at Chichen Itza or any type of vision quest or prayer ceremony; I simply wanted to experience the grandeur of the site. But toward the end of the afternoon something startling and unexpected happened. On my way to visit the building known as the Observatory, I passed an unassuming ruined structure and happened to glance inside. There, in broad daylight and in vivid relief, I saw a male ancestor spirit—a spectral presence with the classic Maya facial features, dressed in a plain white tunic.

Apparently sensing my presence, he turned his head to face me. Our eyes met, both of us incredulous: I was shocked to see him and he seemed equally shocked that someone from the physical realm had actually been able to see him. I glanced away briefly and when I looked back, he had vanished. On the ground where he had been standing was a large iguana that quickly scurried off into the underbrush outside the structure. The encounter seemed as real as the one with my grandfather on my first vision quest in Arizona, but this one was much more unsettling. It was broad daylight and I hadn't been involved in a ceremony or shamanic journey. I didn't know what to make of it all, so at the time I dismissed it as the result of an overactive imagination or stress from the long trip.

Julie and I spent most of the next day further exploring the ruins, and then drove four miles to the cave at Balankanche. For the Maya and other indigenous peoples, the natural world was imbued with sacredness; caves, along with mountains, were places of immense spiritual power and served as important and prestigious pilgrimage centers and shrines. To the ancient and contemporary Maya, caves are portals to the Lower World, a realm of both potential danger and fertility. The ancient Maya believed caves were the natural wombs from which human beings emerged during creation. Caves, as portals enabling access to ancestors, spirits, and divine beings, continue to be regarded as sacred places.

Although caves, both naturally occurring ones and many beautifully-designed, meticulously-constructed cave-like structures, were the religious heart of many ancient Maya sites, it took archaeologists and anthropologists many years to understand their religious significance. Even though the books written by John Lloyd Stephens and illustrated by Frederick Catherwood, published in the mid-1800s, included many descriptions and illustrations of caves they found near or in Maya sites, scholars didn't start a serious systematic study of Maya caves until the early 1980s. Archaeologists now believe the Balankanche cave was first used as a ceremonial site in the Late Preclassic period (300 BCE to 250 CE), and pottery artifacts indicate that the cave was used most frequently from the end of the Classic to the beginning of the Early Postclassic period, about 850–1100 CE.

When we reached Balankanche, Julie and I turned off the main highway into a small semi-deserted parking area covered with crushed limestone, parked our rental car, and walked a short distance toward the cave. Its opening was somewhat below ground level at the base of a large, gently sloped, crater-like depression. The entire area in front of the cave's opening was covered with the same limestone as the parking lot.[1] This rather small and unimpressive entrance to the cave was guarded by an old, rusted, heavy iron gate with a large padlock, beside a dilapidated ticket booth. We joined another couple and their son inside a small thatch shelter at the edge of the site.

As we waited to enter the cave, I recalled the writings of Maya archaeologist E. W. Andrews IV, who first visited Balankanche in the 1930s. At that time, the area in front of the cave's opening was occupied by a large rectangular plaza surrounded by a quadrangle of well-preserved platforms (up to nine feet high) that supported stone buildings with vaulted ceilings, presumably ceremonial structures. A massive circular dry-masonry wall, six feet high, six feet wide, and one hundred fourteen feet across— about twice the size of Casa Rinconada in Chaco Canyon—occupied the center of the plaza.[2] The dramatic grouping of ceremonial architecture led scholars to believe that Balankanche had been a sacred place where the city's elite conducted important rituals.

When Andrews visited the site again in 1954, the original buildings had been ravaged by looters and stone robbers. During his visit in 1959, he noted that the desecration of the site had continued; local construction crews had removed the remaining stone except for the circular wall and had recycled it by using it in the highway being built nearby.[3] Now, in 1985, even the stone wall was gone, possibly ground into the crushed stone that surrounded the site and parking area. It was a profound disappointment to me that the ceremonial architecture around the cave's entrance had completely vanished. I thought I would never be able to fully experience or appreciate the original grandeur of Balankanche.

I tried to imagine how the site had looked originally; the ancient stone and masonry structures that once stood there must have created an imposing and dramatic presence guarding the mouth of the cave. I wondered if the massive walled circular structure had been anything like the Casa Rinconada kiva, with a similar ceremonial function. Chichen Itza was at its zenith at almost exactly the time of Chaco Canyon; so it is likely that both structures were in use at the same time. Archaeologists had discovered ceremonial and trade items from Mesoamerica at Chaco Canyon, and I wondered if cross-cultural exposure to sacred architecture and spiritual practices had occurred as well.

Our guide finally arrived, unlocked the massive padlock, and opened the gate leading into the cave. Fortunately, Julie and I, along with the other couple and their son, were the only ones who had arrived for the tour. My plan was to lag far enough behind the group to have a more private experience, and to spend some time alone if possible. I had not had any direct contact with contemporary Maya elders prior to this trip and had no idea what to expect inside the cave. Gazing at the entrance, my thoughts returned to Casa Rinconada, the unsettling spirit encounters I'd had there, and my unnerving experience with the Maya ancestor spirit the day before. I hoped I would be safe and able to handle whatever I encountered here.

As Julie and the other family disappeared into the mouth of the cave, I moved toward the entrance, imagining myself in the ancient plaza, inside the original massive kiva-like structure. I stopped, faced the cave's entrance, and opened a small packet of copal, resin incense the Maya use for ceremonial purposes, which I had brought with me from Los Angeles. Lighting the copal I smudged myself, using my cupped palm to pass the smoke from the incense over my body, and savored its sweet pungent fragrance. As the smoke from the copal enveloped me and drifted out on the gentle breeze, I felt the smudging clear and cleanse the energy field around me and my disappointment and anxiety lifted.

My earlier ceremonial experiences had taught me that this was the moment to allow myself to open to the presence of the sacred; this was the time when the veil between the physical world and the realm of spirit would begin to dissolve. I became acutely aware of feeling grounded, focused, and filled with a sense of well-being. I felt the hot sun on my back and the warm, moist air flowing in and out of my lungs. The sounds of crickets and frogs and the rustle of leaves in the brush were calming and reassuring. In a few moments I would descend into the darkness of the fabled Maya Lower World (known as Xibalba in ancient Maya mythology) and I was hoping for a transformative experience. But for the moment I was relishing the expansive feeling of being fully alive in the present.

I closed my eyes, knelt, and placed my palms flat against the ground. I prayed silently to Hunab-Ku for the health and well-being of the Maya ancestor spirits at Balankanche. I prayed also for the guidance and blessings of the spirits of this sacred place. I asked that this experience be a source of personal healing and provide insights that would take me further along my journey of self-knowledge and spiritual growth. I also asked for help to journey to the Lower World humbly and respectfully and to be in harmony and balance with my surroundings. Finally, I prayed to be open to experiencing the power and sacredness of Balankanche and to be kept safe and protected.

I rose slowly, filled with gratitude for the gift of being able to enter this sacred site. Opening my eyes, I looked over to the entrance of the cave and was startled to see that what had appeared only a few minutes earlier as a rough-hewn opening in the limestone wall now seemed to be pulsing with radiant light energy, transformed into a sacred portal that would allow me to pass into another state of being. Taking a few slow, mindful steps, I approached the entrance of the cave, feeling the familiar anxiety and excitement I had come to expect from my other ceremonial experiences. Facing the entrance, I paused, closed my eyes, and reflected on the thousands of Maya who had undoubtedly passed through this portal over the centuries to participate in ceremonies.

When I opened my eyes this time, I was startled by a drastic shift in consciousness not unlike the one I had experienced at Casa Rinconada three years earlier. I was acutely aware of being in the present, but simultaneously I was experiencing myself as a young Maya from the distant past, ready to be initiated into the mysteries of the Xibalba. As if in a lucid dream, I was preparing for my journey by participating in an ancient Maya ritual for cleansing, balancing, and purification. For a few brief moments I was completely disoriented—seemingly lost in time and trapped somewhere between the physical world and the realm of spirit. If it hadn't been for my earlier experience at Casa Rinconada, I would have been too terrified to go on.

As an initiate, my body had been painted with a light coating of clay mixed with blue pigment, a sacred wash that would allow me to move more easily through sacred time and space. My feet were encased in sandals, ones I'd worn in other ceremonies many times before and would wear on many ceremonial journeys to come. I was vaguely aware of family, friends, and other members of the community who had gathered in the ceremonial precinct for an all-night vigil to support my initiation.

As I tried to steady myself and sort out my situation, I felt beads of sweat on my brow and noticed that my heart was beating faster and that my breathing had become a little labored. I looked to the cave's entrance—the portal to the Lower World—and began walking toward it. After a few unsteady steps, I passed into the cave and felt I was experiencing a new dimension of sacred space. Being in the cave felt much different from being inside Casa Rinconada. Both were permeated with a sense of sacredness, but the natural limestone formation here had a rich, organic feel unlike any man-made ceremonial structure I had ever visited. I knew from my readings before the trip that the main tunnel passage I was following would soon connect with several large domed chambers. Underground water flowing through the soft, porous Yucatan limestone had hollowed out this natural formation of interconnected chambers to create a vast subterranean, cathedral-like ceremonial structure.

The tunnel passageway descended steeply from the entrance until it leveled out at approximately thirty feet below ground level. Small artificial lights stationed along the passageway provided meager illumination in the here and now, but I was also keenly aware—with the part of my consciousness that was experiencing this descent as an initiate—that a thousand years ago, this passage had been lit by flickering torchlight.[4] As I continued to follow the path through the cave, I felt a strong connection to the many priests, priestesses, young initiates, and spiritual seekers like myself who had passed through this tunnel on their way to and from the heart of the underground cavern.

Walking mindfully, I noticed that I was feeling more balanced, grounded, and in harmony with the energy of my surroundings. My steps were steady and the disorientation I had felt earlier had vanished. Now, rather than feeling as if I were in two separate worlds, I was experiencing myself moving through sacred time and space in the Lower World. With every step I felt an increased sense of inner peace and contentment at the deepest level of my being. I had a premonition that the path through Balankanche would lead to greater clarity and insight and, ultimately, to my spiritual home. The thought baffled me at the time, but became crystal clear as my journey progressed.

At first, the passageway was open and spacious. Stretching my arms out to the sides, I could not touch the tunnel walls, and the ceiling seemed to be quite high overhead. The artificial lights cast dim, irregular shadows on the rough limestone walls. The air was warm and heavy with moisture and carried a rich, musty odor. As I moved deeper into the cave, I was surprised to find that I was still feeling safe, nurtured, and protected. The caves I visited as a young boy during family vacations in the Midwest always fascinated me, but at times they felt claustrophobic and seemed like hard, cold, sometimes scary, and often inhospitable places.

The passageway snaked downward in twists and turns. As I stepped over rocks that had been dislodged from the walls and ceiling of the passageway and walked around fallen boulders, it occurred to me that the tunnel passageway was in some ways an apt metaphor for my life's journey—irregular, unpredictable, and full of twists, turns, and surprises. In the years since my first Chaco Canyon trip, I had changed jobs, remarried, and bought a home in the Westwood area of Los Angeles near UCLA. I was much happier at work, excited about my new relationship, and feeling much better about everything in general. But my life certainly had not followed the clear, straight trajectory I had imagined it would.

I passed through a large domed chamber and kept moving deeper into the sacred core and timeless essence of this ceremonial space. I was still far enough behind the group to feel completely alone. Suddenly, I thought I heard low, soft drumming coming from a place even deeper within the cave—a gentle, rhythmic, welcoming heartbeat. No one in our party including the tour guide had carried a drum, so I couldn't imagine where the sound was coming from. But the drumbeat didn't alarm me; instead, it felt wonderfully reassuring. My pulse quickened and my excitement increased as I continued toward the sound of the drumming. At this depth in the cave I was moving through semi-darkness, illuminated only periodically by the dim artificial lights.

Next, something completely unexpected occurred that was similar to an experience I'd had on my first vision quest at Rough Rock on the Navajo Reservation. On that quest, sometime in the early predawn darkness, I had felt the earth awakening and coming to life. Now a similar phenomenon seemed to be occurring as Balankanche Cave itself seemed to come alive. The energy that surrounded me inside the cave shifted dramatically as if it were vibrating intensely at a much higher level. I sensed I had encountered a transitional zone within the tunnel passage as I moved deeper into the cave and was about to cross a threshold that would lead me into a deeper, richer spiritual state.

In front of me, the passageway seemed to end at a limestone wall that rose up a short distance. Steps had been carved into the face of the rock wall, and as I looked up, I could see the tunnel continuing into the dark recesses of the cave at the top of the wall. A shock of recognition passed through me. Before the trip, I had read that in 1959 a local tour guide, Humberto Gómez, had unexpectedly discovered that part of the cave had been sealed with a false wall, probably to keep the Spanish conquerors from desecrating the inner chambers. In these chambers, archaeologists had found priceless ancient ceremonial artifacts including intricately-carved incense burners, pottery, and stone implements. I was standing where the false wall had been erected.

The steps in the wall were slippery from the moisture in the cave; a thick rope handhold anchored to the face of the wall provided support. After reaching the top, the limestone passage became considerably narrower. But rather than feeling hesitant, I felt surrounded by love, beauty, and joy. It dawned on me that the energy I was experiencing had a distinctly feminine quality, like the sensation I'd experienced in many of the sweat lodge ceremonies I had attended over the years. Suddenly, the thought occurred to me that I was journeying deep within the womb of the sacred Earth Mother, the womb of the Divine Feminine, and moving toward a place of rebirth and greater self-awareness.

The passageway soon opened up and I found myself entering a much more spacious area. My body felt vibrant, tingling with aliveness. The energy around me continued to shift and a wave of anticipation, longing, and desire washed over me. The sound of the drums beat louder and the sweet, pungent odor of copal filled the limestone chamber. I sensed I was in the presence of unseen ancestors and guides from the non-physical realms accompanying me on this journey, but unlike my experience at Chaco Canyon, I was comforted by these spirit presences. I closed my eyes and paused briefly to take in the feeling of aliveness all around me.

Opening my eyes, I looked around and noticed that this portion of the limestone tunnel passageway was much broader. The ceiling had a smoother, rounded shape, and the walls appeared to be quite smooth as well. The surface of the tunnel floor had changed from rough and irregular rock to what appeared to be compacted mud and sand. A deep feeling of sacredness pervaded the entire area. I could feel my heart beating with greater intensity until it seemed as though my heart and the drums were in unison. I felt I was no longer breathing on my own, as if an invisible sacred breath had taken over the rhythm of my breath.

As I continued to gaze at the passageway I was startled to see the faint outlines of human forms taking shape in the dim light, forms that immediately reminded me of my spirit encounters at Casa Rinconada. They continued to solidify with greater clarity and definition until I suddenly realized I was witnessing an ancient initiation ceremony. The Maya initiate with whom I had connected at the mouth of the cave had been on his way to join this ceremony, to rendezvous with ancestor spirits, teachers, guides, and fellow initiates.

Somehow, I had found myself in the middle of an ancient Maya ceremony that seemed to be occurring simultaneously in the distant past and in the present. Four pairs of individuals were sitting along one side of the path and five along the other. Each pair was spaced equally along the length of the passage with enough room in between to give them some privacy. Each pair consisted of a young initiate and either an ancestor spirit from the supernatural realms or a spiritual mentor who was physically present. The initiates had journeyed thorough the cave, much as I had earlier, and had paused to work with one of the spirits, priests, priestesses, shamans, or elders.

The whole scene reminded me of my many encounters with North American Indian elders or spiritual leaders following a vision quest ceremony. In those situations, the person who had just completed the quest met for a private conversation with the elder or leader who had sponsored them on the quest. They discussed key events that occurred during the quest, dreams or visions they may have had, and any other unusual or paranormal occurrences. Elders then interpreted the dreams and visions, transmitted spiritual wisdom, and provided future guidance and direction.

Although I couldn't hear the specific conversations taking place before me now, it seemed as if the initiates were describing their reasons for journeying into the depths of the sacred grotto. They were sharing their doubts and fears as well as their joys and aspirations. Some seemed to be asking for healing for themselves or others or both. Elders were offering spiritual direction and guidance, sharing ancient wisdom traditions, and transmitting sacred knowledge. The teachings seemed to include ancient prayers, sacred songs, and mystical chants. Everyone there was immersed in a deep, rich experience of the sacred in the holy setting of the cave, watched over by the Divine presence.

I was absolutely riveted by what I saw, and I longed to know exactly what was being said. At the same time, I felt completely disoriented. Time seemed to have become distorted, and physical and non-physical reality seemed to have blended. I still wasn't sure whether I was in the present witnessing an ancient ceremony or in the past living it. I wasn't sure if a portal had opened for me at the entrance to Balankanche and I had been transformed into the young Maya initiate, or if a portal had opened and I, as myself, was being allowed to observe something truly profound. The harder I tried to understand the situation, the more confusing it became. In the end, I decided that the best thing for me to do was to simply breathe and accept things as they unfolded.

Several minutes later, the images began to fade and I found myself alone again. As I continued walking, the passageway seemed to be bathed in radiant light and vibrating energy waves radiating out through the limestone from somewhere deep within the entire sacred space-time continuum itself. I felt myself drawn to the chamber that lay beyond the far end of the passageway. My heartbeat quickened as I was filled with a premonition that the chamber I was about to enter was actually the womb of the sacred Earth Mother, the Divine Feminine.

Standing at the threshold of the large domed chamber, I looked in and saw Julie and the rest of the tour group about to enter a passageway leading off from the far left side. I stepped into the chamber and stopped, marveling at the sight before me. The spectacular circular grotto was about sixty feet in diameter and had a remarkable twenty-five-foot-high vaulted ceiling covered with thousands of glistening stalactites. In the center was a massive, pillar-like column formed naturally of long ropy stalactites and stalagmites. The massive column rose from a mound-like base and continued until it merged with the stalactite-encrusted ceiling. The small, damp stalactites reflected the artificial light in the cave in stunningly beautiful patterns.

From my reading before the trip, I had learned that Balankanche is a Yucatec Maya name meaning "Throne of the Jaguar Priest,"[5] or "Throne of Balam."[6] As I studied the massive center column, I noticed the large, naturally-formed niche that the archaeologists who had discovered this chamber thought might have served as a symbolic throne. Numerous Pre-Columbian ceremonial artifacts were placed around the mounded stone formation at the base of the column in roughly the same position in which they had originally been discovered in 1959. The artifacts included stunning pottery *incensarios* (incense burners) sculpted with the likeness of the Maya rain god Tlaloc, other bowl-shaped censers, and miniature metates (stone bowls used to hold corn being ground) and *manos* (smooth hand-held stones used to grind corn in a metate).[7]

Viewing the massive stone column and priceless Pre-Columbian artifacts in person was in itself a fascinating experience, but I suddenly had an astonishing insight. I remembered from my reading that the Maya believed a sacred World Tree, Wakah-Kan,[8] existed in the Lower World. All the references I was familiar with at that time spoke of Balankanche as the Throne of the Jaguar Priest and as a ceremonial site associated with the Rain God Tlaloc.[9] None had connected Balankanche with the World Tree, but I suddenly realized without a doubt that I was standing before the fabled and sacred Wakah-Kan.

I was stunned by this revelation. Completely unexpectedly, I had found myself in the presence of one of the most sacred of all indigenous spiritual phenomena. This was not simply a curious, random, limestone formation that mimicked an important element of Maya spiritual mythology. I was standing at the symbolic center of the Maya universe,[10] deep in the heart of the Xibalba, at the foot of Wakah-Kan, the pathway that spanned all three realms of existence— the Lower World, the Physical Plane, and the Upper World— and served as the portal to the highest spiritual realms. And all this was located deep within the womb of the Great Mother.

Still attempting to come to terms with my realization, I recalled earlier writings I had encountered about the central role the archetypal World Tree had played in the sacred mythologies of cultures world-wide. Whether referred to as the World Tree, the Cosmic Tree, the *axis mundi*, or the Sacred Tree of Life, mythologies of many early civilizations—including Egypt, India, Scandinavia, North American Indian, and other indigenous Mesoamerican Indian cultures—all recognized its existence and revered its being. I felt humbled to be here in the Lower World of the Maya, experiencing the spiritual archetype and physical presence of a sacred being that embodied knowledge, enlightenment, and transformation.

Although I didn't know it at the time, countless ancient Maya hieroglyphic texts deciphered by Maya scholars in the late twentieth century make clear that the Maya considered Wakah-Kan a sacred living being. This is exactly the feeling I had standing before this amazing Tree of Life. I marveled as I looked up at the chamber's ceiling. The small limestone stalactites surrounding the Tree's trunk had the distinct appearance of organic foliage that appeared to spread up to the heavens above. The chamber was filled with shimmering waves of vibrant energy radiating out from the living core of this sacred being. The limestone trunk seemed to soften and dissolve to reveal a pulsing, organic presence and life force. My intuition told me that understanding the presence of Wakah-Kan within the womb of the Great Mother would lead me to greater self-awareness and a fuller understanding of my true spiritual nature.

I was still standing in front of Wakah-Kan when Julie and the rest of the tour group reentered the chamber. They had just finished visiting another large grotto to the left of the main chamber and were headed back to the entrance of the cave. I spoke with Julie briefly and, in broken Spanish, told the tour guide I wanted to stay a little longer in the main chamber before returning. He agreed and I watched as the group left and headed back down the tunnel. As wonderful as my earlier ceremonial experiences had been in the States, this was by far the most significant journey into sacred time and space I had taken. I had gone much deeper than I had ever gone before and was struggling to take it all in.

I walked slowly around the perimeter of the grotto, continuing to marvel at the massive presence of Wakah-Kan, admiring the priceless ceremonial offerings at its base, and looking for a place to sit down and savor the grotto's energy. Almost directly opposite the entrance to the grotto and behind the Tree, I soon found a spot that felt right. I sat down on the floor by the base of Wakah-Kan, crossed my legs, and leaned back against the limestone wall. A sense of deep peace and sublime sacredness pervaded the entire space. My mind wandered to the bible stories I had heard of the "Holy of Holies," the Hebrew term for the sacred inner sanctuary of the Temple of Jerusalem. This place surely must have held a similar significance for the Maya.

My physical body seemed to be resonating with the same frequency as the Tree. I sensed it as a being of light energy, manifested in stone and yet alive, timeless, ageless, having existed always and continuing to exist forever. I imagined myself blending with this sacred energy, feeling my roots going deep into the ground and my limbs extending like branches to the heavens. In this state I experienced the World Tree actively establishing a perfect balance and equilibrium among the three worlds as it drew forth primordial, cosmic, sacred energy and moved it among them harmoniously.

Sitting there, I felt the essence of life flowing through my physical body. I felt my heart beating with the heartbeat of the Divine and Wakah-Kan; the earlier drumbeats now seemed like heartbeats. I felt my sense of self expanding, my self-imposed limits dissolving. My fears and doubts, worries and anxieties, limitations and short-comings faded as I opened to a deeper awareness of the aspects of myself that were close to the Divine. I was open, aware, receptive, and connected to a source of self-realization and inner strength I had never experienced before. For years I had heard indigenous elders and spiritual leaders speak of our "higher self" or our "true self." At this moment, for the first time, I was living that reality. I was sitting at the center of the universe, resting in a sacred state of being in the presence of the Universal Soul, and in a way I didn't fully understand at the time, simply being there had allowed my higher self to emerge. I felt nurtured, guided, and surrounded by love.

Opening my eyes, I glanced around at my surroundings. The energy seemed to have subsided and I felt much more in touch with my physical body. Suddenly, I had the stunning realization that we emerge from the Divine as a spiritual essence, a soul destined to enter the womb to be born in a physical body. Wakah-Kan is the conduit, the mystical link, between our higher spiritual nature and our everyday self in the physical world. Here at Balankanche I knew that this transformation process took place in the womb of the sacred Earth Mother, the Divine Feminine. Through Her we come into the world from the Source and through Her we can find our way back to the Source.

Still sitting with my back against the wall of the chamber, I imagined looking through the trunk of Wakah-Kan and visualized the passageway from the grotto leading back to the outside world. I imagined seeing my life and the world from the perspective of my higher self, my true self—the aspect of me closest to the Source— resting in the state of grace I had experienced a few moments before. I felt a sense of deep inner peace and excitement about new possi- bilities and new ways of experiencing my life. Suddenly, I knew and understood that I was more than just my physical body and more than my beliefs about myself and my world. A whole new dimension of consciousness opened for me; I knew I could continue my life's journey freer and less encumbered.

I had heard from Indian elders in North America that cer- tain sacred stones possess consciousness and can store information. Here, the limestone walls around me seemed to have captured an- cient events involving the prayers and wisdom teachings of the Maya ancestors. At that moment in the darkness and silence at the heart of the ceremonial grotto, I was struck by the knowledge that through the spiritual genius of the ancient Maya, these ancient traditions had been preserved in this holy place. The esoteric teachings were alive and accessible centuries after Franciscan missionaries had tried to destroy all vestiges of ancient Maya spiritual practice during the

Spanish Conquest in the 1500s. I had just had the extraordinary good fortune to be a recipient of this rare and remarkable gift.

After taking a deep breath, I offered a final brief prayer of thanksgiving and then stood to continue my journey where I had left off. As I was walking counter-clockwise to complete my circling of Wakah-Kan and the sacred Center, an odd sensation came over me. I sensed myself moving not only physically around the World Tree but also simultaneously through time. With each step I felt I was leaving the distant past of the young Maya initiate and moving toward the present. Each step brought me closer, in time and space, to where I had started my journey through this cave.

When I reached the opening to the chamber, I turned and faced Wakah-Kan. I knelt, placed my palms flat on the ground, and bowed my head slightly. I could still feel a profoundly deep heart and soul connection to the energy of the Tree of Life. Standing once again, I turned and continued back down the path that had brought me there.

As I walked, I struggled to reconcile my discovery of Wakah-Kan inside the sacred Womb, deep within the heart of the Lower World, with the Christian teachings from my youth. As a child I had learned that all that existed below us was Hell, the place of suffering and punishment for the wicked after death. What I had discovered at Balankanche was far different. Although my experience in the sacred grotto was completely foreign to what I had been taught about the masculine nature of God, I couldn't deny the reality of my encounter or the profound spiritual truth revealed to me. I had experienced the Divine Feminine and through Her had found a path to my higher self that led to the Source. This realization would fundamentally change my view of the world and the direction of my spiritual journey. For decades I had been searching for "something," but didn't really know what it was or where to find it. I hadn't found it through the church of my upbringing. It wasn't until I studied indigenous spiritual traditions that I felt I was coming close to the deep, authentic spiritual experience I longed for. Now, with this connection with my higher self and the experience of the Divine, the path was becoming clear to me.

I was still lost in thought when suddenly I sensed an ancestor spirit walking beside me. I immediately recalled a similar experience I'd had several years earlier as I was leaving my first vision quest in Arizona, only this time the spirit being seemed vaguely familiar. At that moment, I felt as if I had been joined by a guide or guardian. I wondered if I might have asked for the presence of this being of light in a dream or a long-forgotten childhood prayer. I realized that I was in the presence of an ally who had chosen to help me work with the energies of Balankanche.

Continuing on, I retraced my steps through the antechamber and into the narrow limestone passageway that ended at the top of the limestone wall. I had the distinct impression that the limestone passageway had become a birth canal leading to the outside world from the womb of the Earth Mother; I now felt I was on a journey of rebirth and regeneration, guided by Wakah-Kan's powerful, limitless presence. The moist limestone surrounding me seemed to have a soft, gentle, soothing quality. I paused briefly before beginning my descent and then, one by one, placed my feet on the limestone steps down to the outer passageway, steps worn and smoothed by the feet of thousands before me.

Once on the floor of the larger passageway, I knew that my journey into sacred time and space had ended. I had left the supernatural realm behind and was on my way back to the physical world where I lived my "normal" life. My ally had departed as quickly as he had appeared, but I hoped that someday more would be revealed to me and he would walk beside me again.

Just before I exited the cave, I had a fleeting vision of the young Maya initiate I had experienced earlier being greeted by relatives, friends, and well-wishers as he emerged upon the completion of his initiation. He stood in a shallow basin while the blue clay that had covered his body was carefully washed off with water that had been blessed. The blue wash, now infused with sacred energy, was collected in the basin and saved. In the future, it would be used to paint his own ceremonial objects and to paint personal images on sacred places and power spots. The objects and images would be a constant reminder of his journey through the supernatural realms; they would help keep the portal open for him to explore an expanded state of being and becoming.

Even though it was late afternoon when I exited the cave, the sun seemed unusually bright and my eyes had a hard time adjusting to the light. I turned back to face the entrance of the cave and bowed my head slightly as a gesture of respect. I felt exhilarated but drained and I was actually glad to be back in ordinary reality. Julie was patiently waiting for me at the thatch shelter. The other family had left and our guide was anxious to close and lock the gate for the night. As I glanced back at the opening to the cave and the surrounding area, I was amazed that such an inauspicious setting could conceal one of the most extraordinary sites in the entire Maya realm.

Walking slowly back to the parking lot with Julie, I savored the warm, moist, late-afternoon air and the sunlight as it softly filtered through the trees around me. We opened the door of the rental car and let the hot, stale air escape while I turned to take one last look at the cave. My journey to the Lower World at Balankanche had opened doors to the sacred world of the Maya much as Casa Rinconada had opened doors for me years earlier. I had no idea where this journey was leading but I knew it had led me to the right path and that my life would never be quite the same. I was surprised at how familiar and comfortable this all felt, even though this was as far from my early life in Chicago and my home in Los Angeles as I could possibly get.

I rolled down the windows of the VW Beetle, pulled out into the road, and drove the three miles back to our hotel near the ruins of Chichen Itza. Julie and I walked to the patio lounge to relax and enjoy the sunset. Our waiter encouraged us to try some Xtabentun, a native liquor made from honey from the xtabentun flower, anise, and rum, which the ancient Maya were reputed to have offered to their gods during ceremonies. It seemed strange to have been in the heart of the Maya Xibalba a few hours earlier and now to be having a typical American tourist resort experience. But that was just how these events seemed to be unfolding in my life—a foot in two radically different worlds—and I just did my best to balance them.

Sitting on the patio, my thoughts turned to what an unexpected surprise Balankanche had been. I hadn't thought much about Balankanche when I had planned the trip. The site was only superficially mentioned in guidebooks at the time, and the books I had read before the trip did not even hint at the deep meaning or full impact of the sacred grotto. And I certainly hadn't expected a spontaneous journey into the supernatural realms, including a deep shamanic experience with visions and contact with ancestor spirits. This had been, by far, the most intense experience I'd had at an indigenous sacred site.

We left Chichen Itza early the next morning and drove straight to Playa del Carmen, intentionally avoiding the tourism of Cancun, to catch a morning ferry to the island of Cozumel. I was keeping a journal of my experiences at the ruins we had visited so far, and I spent some of my time during our two-day stay on Cozumel reflecting on my experiences of the similarities and differences between North American Indian and Maya ceremonial practices. When we left Chichen Itza I was still struggling to absorb and understand my experiences at Balankanche, a struggle that continued during our time at Cozumel. But sometime during the ferry trip back to Playa del Carmen I finally decided to let go of trying to figure everything out and just let my understanding unfold.

Chapter Notes:

1. My family and I visited Balankanche again in 2008 on a trip to the Riviera Maya during my sons' spring break. The site had gone through another transition to accommodate the dramatic increase in tourist traffic that had occurred over the years. The crater-like area in front of the cave entrance had been terraced and converted to a botanical garden. The thatch shelter was gone. The small, dilapidated ticket booth that was near the cave entrance on the first visit had been replaced with a modern visitor center situated at the top of the terraced garden at ground level.

2. E. Wyllys Andrews IV 1970: 1, 7

3. Ibid., 1

4. The small lights along the main tunnel passage when I first visited Balankanche have been replaced with large flood lights illuminating the main passage as well as numerous branching side passages and grottos. Today, the main path through the cave is covered in concrete and pavers. Visitors are not allowed to leave this walkway. In addition, a multi-lingual narrative is broadcast through a series of loudspeakers placed throughout the cave's interior, making it impossible to tune into the energies of this sacred cave.

5. E. Wyllys Andrews IV 1970: 11

6. Gallenkamp 1985: 204

7. I didn't know it at the time, but scholars believe Maya priests placed these sacred objects here and sealed the passage to protect this chamber and its precious contents from the Spanish Conquistadors and Franciscan friars. Many of the objects on display in the cave were the "idols" that led the friars to persecute political and religious leaders for refusing to abandon their spiritual traditions. In 1562, the Franciscans initiated the

infamous *auto de fé* (Inquisition) in the town of Mani approximately seventy miles from the site of Balankanche. According
to scholars Scholes and Adams (2: 209-21, esp. 212-214) over
4,500 Maya were tortured and more than 158 died as a direct
result of torture at the hands of the friars; many others committed suicide after being tortured or to avoid torture.

8. Over the years, as academic research has progressed, the
spelling used by scholars for some Maya words and proper
names has evolved. The spelling used here for the ancient
Maya word for the World Tree, Wakah-Kan, follows Schele
and Mathews 1998.

9. Rain gods are believed to live in caves. Rain itself is thought to
be formed in caves.

10. The idea of the "symbolic center of the Maya universe" is widespread throughout Maya culture. No particular place is *the* center
of the universe, but each village had its *own* center of the universe
—its own "navel of the world." This idea seems similar to the
European idea brought forth by St. Augustine that "God is a circle
whose center is everywhere and whose circumference is nowhere."

MORNING STAR RENEWAL

It was mid-morning when I first caught a glimpse of the ocean from inside the ruins of Tulum. The site was even more spectacular than I had imagined from the photographs I had seen. Built on a bluff overlooking the Caribbean, the ancient stone temples and shrines seemed to shimmer in brilliant sunlight. The views of the ocean from the walled ceremonial precinct were magnificent, with clear blue sky dissolving into crystalline, blue-green Caribbean waters at the horizon, and lush tropical vegetation framing dazzling white limestone-sand beaches below. The weather couldn't have been more perfect, 80 degrees with clear skies and a warm tropical breeze and practically no humidity. I loved being near the water here at Tulum; smelling the salty air and hearing the sounds of the ocean and shore birds was intoxicating. Tulum's original name, Zama (City of Dawn) perfectly captured the feeling here of new beginnings.

Julie and I had taken an early ferry from Cozumel to the town of Playa del Carmen and had driven an hour to reach the ruins. We parked in the lot next to the western edge of the ruins,[1] bought our tickets, and entered the ceremonial center through the main passage in the west. Although the area was first settled around 300 BCE and Tulum began developing as a sea port around 770 CE, the sacred architecture surrounding us was built around the time Tulum emerged as a preeminent port and trading center during the Postclassic period, approximately 1200 CE. The temples, monuments, and other structures were not as spectacular as many I had seen, but the multitude of warm colorful shadings on the stone platforms and walls, weathered and softened by the elements, imbued the site with an enchanted quality.

Many years after my trip to Tulum, I learned that for the ancient Maya, Tulum was strongly associated with the Moon Goddess, Ix-Chel, one of the most important figures in the Maya pantheon. Her image adorned many of the temple murals within the ceremonial center. Tulum's Temple of the Frescos and Temple of the Diving God contain multiple images of Ix-Chel with symbolism related to the moon, sun, Venus, and a cosmic umbilical cord.[2] According to scholar Susan Milbrath, "Tulum was dedicated to the cult of the lunar goddess" and "the site may have been a center of pilgrimage for pregnant women who sought assistance of the moon in her aspect as patroness of midwives."[3] Tulum was also part of an extended pilgrimage route that included both Isla Mujeres and Cozumel, the site of Ix-Chel's principal shrine.

Ix-Chel had many attributes for the Maya, who knew her as the Moon Goddess and patroness of procreation, childbirth, medicine, and weaving. She was also referred to as Lady Rainbow when she brought the yearly rains to fertilize the crops. Ix-Chel was especially important to shamans, physicians, and midwives. In his writings, Fr. Diego de Landa noted that the Maya held journeys to her shrine on the island of Cozumel "in the same veneration as we have for pilgrimages to Jerusalem and Rome," and that they visited "to offer presents there, especially to Cozumel, as we do to holy places."[4]

Walking through the ruins, I was immediately struck by the dramatic difference between Chichen Itza and Tulum. Chichen Itza was a massive site; the core ceremonial area covered two square miles and was filled with monumental stone structures including the world-famous Castillo pyramid, grand ceremonial platforms, a magnificent ball court, and the seemingly endless columns in front of the Temple of a Thousand Warriors. Chichen Itza also had a distinctly harsh, aggressive, imposing martial presence. Stone carvings on structures depicted political conquests, war, and the bloody sacrifice of ritual ball games. Although Tulum had a spectacular physical setting, its smaller and more modest structures lacked Chichen Itza's almost overpowering grandeur.

In many ways, Tulum couldn't have been more different from the cave at Balankanche where I had just been. The dark, shadowy subterranean passageways of the ceremonial grotto were a stark contrast to the brilliant sunlight, breathtaking aquamarine hue of the ocean, and the lush, vibrant, tropical foliage at Tulum. Instead of moving through confining limestone tunnels and dense humidity, here we enjoyed gentle sea breezes as we leisurely strolled under a seemingly endless expanse of beautiful blue sky. Tulum had an airy, open, sensual feel and the modest ceremonial structures seemed softer, more graceful, and perfectly matched to this extraordinary Caribbean setting.

Suddenly I had an insight that almost brought me to tears. Three days earlier I had been in the womb of the sacred Earth Mother, deep inside the holy grotto at Balankanche, and had experienced a spiritual awakening. Now, at the pilgrimage site at the City of Dawn, in the presence of the Moon Goddess, I was at the one place in the entire realm of the ancient Maya most closely associated with ceremonial rebirth and renewal. By journeying here, I had unexpectedly and unintentionally continued the process of spiritual rebirth and renewal that I'd begun at Balankanche.

As I explored Tulum, I experienced a gentle, nurturing, healing quality to the energy that was unlike anything I had encountered before. The site itself seemed to be a magnificent reflection of the essence of the Moon Goddess. Her imprint was everywhere, from the extraordinary ocean setting to the lovely, delicate architecture and the ancient masonry walls filled with an incandescent vitality. Ix-Chel's gentle, loving touch seemed to grace every facet of the ancient ceremonial site. Surrounded and enfolded by the presence of the Divine Feminine, I felt whole and at peace. As I explored Tulum's ancient temples and shrines, I came to realize that for me and countless pilgrims before me, Tulum was a place of refuge blessed by Her presence.

Although Tulum is dramatically smaller today, archaeologists believe that at one time the ancient site and settlement covered almost four miles of coastline. The main ceremonial center sits on a thirty-six-foot-high bluff that drops sharply down to a beach and ocean below. The ancient structures along the eastern, ocean-facing side of the site are built up to the edge of the bluff. Tulum's other boundaries are enclosed and protected on three sides by a massive stone masonry wall. Five narrow vaulted passages provide access through the protective wall into the main ceremonial precinct. Outside the great wall, the remains of additional temples, shrines, platforms and altars—as well as caves and *cenotes* (water-filled limestone sinkholes)[5]—can be found near the coastline.

As Julie and I explored the ruins, it was hard for me to believe that this relatively small ceremonial precinct, about the length of four football fields, was all that was left of a once magnificent and thriving port and trading center. In 1518, during the Spanish Conquest, an expedition led by Juan de Grijalva encountered the walled city of Tulum. According to expedition records, Grijalva "perceived a city or town so large, that [the city of] Seville would not have seemed more considerable nor better; one saw there a very large tower; on the shore was a great throng of Indians, who bore two standards which they raised and lowered to signal us to approach them."[6] In the early 1500s, Seville, Spain was an international seaport with a population of sixty thousand.

The ruins were not at all crowded that morning. Julie and I shared the site with only a few dozen other visitors and were able to explore the ruins and go inside all the ceremonial structures without any restrictions. We wandered through the ruins together for a while and then decided to split up; Julie wanted to take the trail down to the beach and ocean below, and I wanted to stay to explore the ruins some more and possibly find a secluded area where I could undertake a shamanic journey undisturbed. As Julie headed for the beach, I set off toward the south side of the ruins to visit a temple I'd been told was dedicated to Venus, a planet that had held extraordinary astronomical and ceremonial importance.

The ancient Maya carefully observed and recorded the individual astronomical cycles of the sun, moon, and Venus and also documented the complex interrelationships among the solar calendar, lunar calendar, and phases of Venus. They recognized and celebrated a repeating eight-year cycle, when the 24-hour sun cycle, the 29½-day moon cycle, and the 584-day Venus cycle all aligned and synchronized around Venus rising at dawn as the Morning Star. Taken together, the rhythmic movement and subtle interaction of the sun, moon, and Venus as they traveled through the heavens created a magnificent celestial tapestry recreated every eight years. In the mural art at Tulum, Venus was closely associated with the Moon Goddess, Ix-Chel.

The Venus astronomical phases were tracked meticulously by the ancient Maya and provided the basis for one of the Maya's most important calendar cycles. Venus was the Morning Star for almost one half of the calendar's 584-day cycle, and the Evening Star for nearly as long. As a manifestation of the great cosmic cycles of time, Venus was represented as a deity in stucco sculptures at Tulum.[7] Scholar Arthur G. Miller also believes the astronomical relationship between Venus and the sun reinforces the theme of rebirth at Tulum. Venus as the Morning Star can be seen dramatically rising in the east shortly before sunrise at dawn. Ancient Maya iconography suggests that Venus was seen as the "precursor and herald of the sun" and in this role could "pull up the sun each morning."[8]

I was alone in the temple; no one else was nearby in the ruins.[9] Sitting on the floor, I rested my back against the stone wall, which had been warmed by the sun, closed my eyes, and let myself sink into the experience. The air was balmy and I could hear the surf below the bluff. I didn't have anything particular in mind. I was just grateful to finally be at this remarkable site. As I had done at Balankanche, I lit some copal, smudged myself with the smoke, and prayed for the health and well-being of the ancestors of Tulum. I asked for their help and guidance in understanding more about this sacred site, hoping I would be able to journey deeper into their sacred mysteries.

Julie and I had spent the morning and early afternoon exploring the main ruins within the confines of the stone wall. I had thoroughly enjoyed every minute and relished the feeling of being at Tulum, but nothing out of the ordinary had occurred and I'd seen nothing I felt drawn to investigate further. As I sat in the temple, my intuition told me there might be something of interest and importance outside the city wall to the north. The more I thought about heading outside the main ceremonial area, the stronger the feeling became that this was the right thing to do and the more excited I became about exploring less accessible parts of the ruins. I said a brief prayer of thanks, stood up, left the temple, and headed back north through the ruins.

As I walked toward the vaulted stone passageway that passed through the north wall, nearest the ocean bluff, I had the distinct impression that unseen ancestor spirits were guiding me to this area of the ruins. I knew the buildings I passed were ceremonial structures and that thousands of sacred rituals and observances had occurred here over the centuries. I also knew that pilgrims had undoubtedly visited here and conducted ceremonies on their way to Cozumel to honor Ix-Chel. It dawned on me that I too was on a pilgrimage, and I vowed to stay open to my experience and be receptive to whatever might be revealed to me. Approaching the stone passageway, my mindset shifted from that of a tourist to that of a pilgrim.

When I arrived at the passageway I stopped for a moment before proceeding. The thick masonry wall was composed of rough-hewn stone and crude mortar. It lacked the refinement and sophistication of much of the other masonry architecture I had seen at other Maya sites, but the entire structure had a wonderfully protective, nurturing feel to it. The wall was quite thick and the passageway through it was deep, almost like a tunnel. I could see a dirt trail leading off into the forest on the other side. As I stood gazing through the tunnel, the energy seemed to intensify, as if a sacred portal were being created between the world inside the wall and the world outside. I wasn't sure if the portal had just now formed or if it had been there all the time and I was just now able to see it.

I walked slowly through the entrance, imagining myself as a pilgrim moving into sacred time and space. The energy in the tunnel had a distinctly different feel from the other parts of the ruins. It also felt much different from the cave at Balankanche. But as I had in the cave, I experienced myself moving into an altered dimension. With each step I became increasingly curious about what I would encounter on the other side. Once through the passageway I could see a trail headed north, following the coastline and meandering through dense semi-tropical foliage. It also passed a small compound of contemporary buildings that looked as if they might be housing or work areas for park personnel, bordered by a large "No Trespassing" sign.

I stopped, not sure what to do. Looking to my right I could still see the dazzling aquamarine waters of the Caribbean; I still savored the sunshine and warm breeze. Ahead of me, dark shady woods engulfed the path I wanted to follow. The rhythmic, repetitive sound of the waves breaking gently on the shore below the bluff triggered thoughts of the ancient Maya's veneration of the sacred rhythms of time and life, never-ending cycles of rebirth, regeneration, and renewal unfolding in a dynamic equilibrium. I desperately wanted to continue forward but didn't want to be disrespectful of the site or the ancestors.[10] Moving ahead on the path, I said a silent prayer asking for guidance and resolved to turn back if something didn't feel right.

I passed the compound. It seemed deserted. My body felt light and my movements effortless as I followed the rough path through the dense foliage. The air was cooler and the forest canopy provided a welcome change from the intense sun. It felt as if I were moving deeper into sacred time and space, somewhat reminiscent of the feeling I'd had as I journeyed deeper into the cave at Balankanche. My thoughts turned to the thousands or possibly tens of thousands of others who had followed this same path. I wondered what had brought them here; were they, like me, all seeking a better life, a better understanding of themselves, a clearer sense of purpose, and an expanded ability to express their true selves?

I began to feel a wonderful, energizing connection to the ebb and flow of the abundant life around me. The whole area seemed to be alive and pulsing with the flow of primordial universal energies. The movement of the ocean seemed to mirror other less visible movements deep within the earth, and both seemed to reflect the vast cosmic energies so important to the Maya. Their sophisticated astronomical observations and intricate calendar system documented and predicted the natural and supernatural rhythms of their world. Agriculture, politics, warfare, and individual well-being were all intimately related to these great cycles of planetary movement and time.

I sensed that Tulum might have played a role in restoring and maintaining balance and alignment among the great cosmic forces that govern our lives, not only in the physical universe but in the other planes of existence as well. This unique ceremonial setting provided a window to the vast cosmic cycles through the movement of tides influenced by the cycles of the Moon. Here along the shore of the Caribbean, the vast, largely unseen interplay of planetary energies and cosmic forces was visible in a very immediate and tangible way. I pondered whether the great cosmic cycles governing the moon and tides on the physical realm might mirror cycles existing in the supernatural realms as well as within personal consciousness.

The ocean setting and cenotes at Tulum provided a unique glimpse into the profound spiritual and ceremonial significance of water to the Maya. The Maya used waterways to transport goods and people. The journey over water was also a metaphor for their journey through life. We know from sacred texts and hieroglyphics that the Maya envisioned the earth as the back of a huge reptile swimming on a primordial sea, not unlike the American Indian concept of "Turtle Island." Rivers and other bodies of water served as entrances to the Lower World and water was associated with the transition between life and death, between this world and the next. Contemporary Maya ceremonial leaders still use water for blessing, healing, and purification.

After covering about a third of a mile, I saw a small, ancient, one-room shrine to the right of the trail. The shrine had a door facing west toward the trail, but away from the ocean, and a stone bench along its south side. The area surrounding the

shrine and bench had been cleared somewhat of the dense vegetation lining much of the path. I decided to pause here for a few
minutes and take some time to open fully to the experience of the
setting. Sitting on the bench, I closed my eyes. Almost immediately, I sensed an ancestor spirit beside me in the shrine—a powerful
sacred Grandmother spirit. It felt as if she had been here for centuries and would remain for centuries to come.

Sitting in the stillness of this setting, I unexpectedly began
thinking about my friend and mentor, Tom Mails. Tom had spent
many years with the revered Lakota Indian holy man and healer Frank Fools Crow and had written a marvelous book, Fools
Crow: Wisdom and Power, about the esteemed spiritual leader.
In his book, Tom recounted the distinction Fools Crow made between curing and healing. In his healing ceremonies, Fools Crow
referred to curing as "getting rid of symptoms," getting some-
body well. He referred to healing as "getting someone 'right' with
Wakan Tanka," right with Spirit, right with God. Fools Crow believed not everyone could be cured, but everyone could be healed.
It was becoming clearer to me that the spiritual journey I was on
was about healing. My vision quests, inipi ceremonies, and other
ritual experiences had been leading me deeper into the realm of the
sacred. Now, my awakening at Balankanche and my presence at
Tulum were getting me closer to, and "right with," the Divine.

At that moment, I realized that I was being led on a journey
to heal myself, a journey that would help me become whole and find
a greater sense of balance in my life. I was beginning to realize it was
possible to find a way of being in the world that would allow me to
express my highest potential and become a more fully realized human
being. I was beginning to appreciate it might be possible to grow,
evolve, and develop as a soul so that I might move closer to a sense
of oneness with the universal source of all that is. It certainly was becoming clearer to me that my life in Los Angeles was much more lim-

ited and confined than I had realized, and that the world was much more mysterious and miraculous than I had ever imagined.

Sitting on the stone bench beside the small shrine, I felt completely relaxed and at peace as I listened to the sound of the ocean behind me and watched the dancing sunlight filter through the foliage of the jungle canopy overhead. I wondered how this ceremonial structure had been used and how it related to the structures in the walled precinct I had just left. My experiences with American Indian elders had taught me that everything in a ceremonial setting has meaning as well as purpose. Every ceremony follows a particular progression. I tried to imagine what had occurred here and how it might have fit into a larger mosaic of ceremonial activities.

Closing my eyes, I had a vision of a pilgrim leaving the main ceremonial center at Tulum at night, heading north on the same path I was following. I could actually see her ceremonial journey to the ocean for purification, healing, and blessing as if it were happening right there in front of me. I marveled at her journey's unfolding, illuminated by the light of a full moon under a magnificent canopy of dazzling stars. Rays of light from distant planetary homes, spanning the infinite reaches of space, filled the heavens; the sound of ocean waves breaking gently on the shore provided a rhythm for the ceremony and a reminder of the perpetual cycle of birth, death, rebirth, regeneration, and renewal. It seemed to me her journey was occurring in both the physical realm and the non-physical realms at the same time. She was walking on the earth while moving through the other worlds, journeying through time and space.

In my vision, the pilgrim stopped in front of the shrine where I now sat. She knelt reverently in front of the doorway, facing into the small stone structure. Seated inside was the same ancestor spirit I had just seen. This Grandmother spirit was a warm, loving, yet stern presence, a being of light, a non-physical guardian, a silent witness, and a guide and counselor. Although obscured by the darkness, she was fully awake and fully present to her encounter with the pilgrim. The pilgrim said a prayer of thanksgiving as she addressed the spirit. She asked for help and guidance in finding and experiencing her true spiritual self. Beneath the heavens, beside the ocean, without judgment and with total honesty, the two of them conducted a life review.

The pilgrim asked for help leaving behind that which no longer served her, and for help releasing the barriers that prevented her from moving to a new level of well-being. She reflected on what she had accomplished with her life so far, what she had failed to accomplish, and what she wished she had done. In the presence of the ancestor spirit, she confronted the truth about how her choices and behaviors had shaped her life for better or worse. She was clear about what she needed to shed to transform her life and realize her spiritual rebirth and renewal. And she understood that her personal transformation would help all beings become a purer expression of the Divine.

The pilgrim knew that having looked back over her life, it was now time to consciously choose the direction she would take going forward. She prayed to be cleansed and purified by the holy waters at this sacred place. She asked for clarity and honesty leading to self-awareness and self-knowledge. She prayed for the spirits to watch over her and assist her in finding the path whenever she felt lost, asking them always to whisper in her ear, reach through time and space to tap her on the shoulder, or send her a sign when she needed assistance. She asked for blessings and guidance from family, friends, and helpers from the physical and non-physical realms. And then the pilgrim and Grandmother together sang a hymn to the Goddess Ix-Chel.

A rustle of leaves and a noise in the brush suddenly brought my awareness back to the present. I looked up and saw a large iguana scurrying off into the undergrowth. I felt the hard stone bench beneath me and became aware of the sounds of the ocean. Deciding it was time to continue on my way, I stood and turned to my right to face north and stepped back onto the path. As I passed the doorway that opened to the shrine, I glanced inside. It was empty and the spirit I had experienced was gone. I had a fleeting thought that the sacred Grandmother had departed with the iguana. When I looked around the interior of the shrine, however, I could still sense her essence, as if it had somehow been imprinted there.

As I continued on the path I had a most remarkable sensation. I experienced myself in present time, in Tulum, walking a path on a spiritual journey, but at the same time I felt I was the pilgrim in my vision, moving through sacred time and space. It seemed as if our two experiences were superimposed: two pilgrims simultaneously following a ceremonial path to wholeness and renewal. She had traveled at night while I was traveling during the day. We had both paused together at the shrine, both encountered the Grandmother spirit, and were both now continuing on our way. The distinction between past and present was gone. The distinction between the physical and non-physical realms had vanished. What remained was a sense of eternal holiness.

I continued to follow the path north, exhilarated by the sensation of moving through multiple spaces and realities simultaneously. Eventually, the path emerged from the tall overhead foliage and continued along the crest of the bluff. The path became very rough and was strewn with small boulders, but the view of the Caribbean was breathtaking and the sun seemed to have lost a little of its intensity. The path dropped down somewhat and in the distance I saw a magnificent small, one-room stone temple with a beautiful stone roof characteristic of Maya ceremonial architecture. The temple had been built facing the ocean and was situated in a deserted cove with a sandy beach. The path led directly to the temple.

The entire area around the temple felt infused with energy. The temple shimmered in the light of the sun and seemed almost alive, pulsing with vibrancy. Looking to my right across the sandy beach, I saw small Caribbean waves gently breaking on the shore. Although I felt grounded and solid in physical reality, I also felt I was the pilgrim in my vision, standing now at the edge of the ocean, gazing at the temple in front of me. Suddenly, this experience began to disorient me. If the environment hadn't felt so peaceful and serene, the fear I was beginning to feel might have turned into panic.

I took a few deep breaths to help me relax and realize I was completely safe. My fear subsided, my disorientation lifted, and my confusion vanished. Following my intuition, I stepped off the path, walked over to the edge of the temple, and without really thinking, took off my shoes, socks, and all of my clothes. I folded them neatly and placed them on the stone steps beside the structure. I turned to face the ocean and started walking to the water although I had no idea what I was going to do once I was at the ocean's edge. I felt self-conscious walking naked on the beach, but the area was completely deserted.

As I walked toward the ocean, I found myself thinking about inipi purification ceremonies I had participated in with North American Indian elders. This experience at Tulum brought a similar feeling of purification and renewal. When I left my clothes behind at the temple, I felt as if I were leaving other aspects of myself behind as well. My nakedness seemed a metaphor for my willingness to reveal myself completely so that I could know myself at a deeper and more complete level. I felt a renewed sense of purpose and direction, a certainty that I was open and ready to receive any blessings from the spirit realm. I found myself once again enjoying the sensation of moving simultaneously through multiple dimensions of reality.

The bright white coarse limestone sand was hot under my feet and I was relieved when I made it to the cooler sand at the edge of the ocean. I moved slowly into the water and soon felt smooth, slippery rocks underfoot. A little way farther, where the water was about two feet deep, I encountered a smooth rock shelf. As I moved along its ledge, I felt something with my feet and then looked down in disbelief—I was standing in a shallow basin that seemed so perfectly formed it appeared to have been carved by hand. As I sat down in the basin, my right and left hands found handholds, also perfectly formed and seemingly created for that purpose, in the exact position to stabilize me as I sat. I was absolutely astonished.

While I sat in the basin, gentle Caribbean waves washed over me at chest height. Above me, the sky was deep blue and cloudless; the beautiful, translucent aquamarine water around me was cool and soothing, and the stone beneath me was solid and reassuring. It was one of the most magnificent experiences I'd ever had. I felt a tremendous sense of liberation and aliveness and felt grounded and fully present in my body. As I sat, using the basin's handholds to keep my body from drifting with the waves, I found small depressions in the rock where I could place the heels of my feet. A sense of joy and euphoria filled me as I sat and allowed the gentle waves to move over me, cleansing my body and soul. I completely lost track of whether I was the seeker by day or the pilgrim by night.

As each wave washed over my body, I felt purified and renewed; for the first time in my life I felt a sense of release and surrender, a sense of giving up and letting go. Every wave brought a feeling of greater balance and alignment. Peace and tranquility filled me as they never had before—I was completely in harmony with everything around me. Sitting there, gently caressed by the sacred waters, I felt connected to the great cosmic cycles of time, blessed by the Goddess Ix-Chel, and guarded by the tender, loving presence of the Divine. My mind and heart were calm and I was filled with a profound inner peace. Something mysterious was happening, something holy, a state of grace full of compassion and unconditional love.

Suddenly, I began experiencing my time in the ocean from the perspective of the pilgrim. The bright daylight faded into night and the cove was illuminated by stars and the brilliant light from a full moon. I sensed the beating of her heart, and the flow of her breath, aligned with the rhythm of the waves, the movement of the moon in the heavens, and the orbits of the planets in the cosmos. I experienced an intricate dance of physical energies and natural rhythms, a symphony of ceaseless, effortless movement set within a great galactic mosaic of being. I sensed subtle, unseen currents and eddies of energy flowing through non-physical reality as well, movement that mirrors the physical universe yet is just outside our normal awareness. I was the pilgrim, reuniting with the universal cosmic energies and aligning with the complementary planetary energies so important to the Maya.

I was overwhelmed with the realization that this must be how the ancient Maya experienced their world. Their unbelievably sophisticated multi-layered calendars, which recorded cycles within cycles spanning thousands of years, bear witness to this reality. Their beautifully realized ceremonial practices utilized this knowledge that energy and matter seamlessly interpenetrate the physical and non-physical realities of worlds within worlds. They recognized that sacred, divine energy—with both masculine and feminine aspects—was present within everything, and that everything was a manifestation of the Divine. In short, I understood that their world was richer, more complex, and far more expansive than anything I had imagined.

The pilgrim in my vision had come to Tulum to encounter these great cosmic truths. And now I had the extraordinary good fortune of following in her footsteps. At that moment, I had no way of knowing whether I had been that pilgrim in some other life or whether somehow our destinies were mysteriously intertwined, but I was overwhelmed with gratitude for this remarkable revelation. I gave thanks for the Maya ancestors and their legacy of sacred architecture, devoted spiritual practices, and transformational wisdom teachings. I gave thanks for the profound insight of my connectedness with the great celestial cycles of time and change. I gave thanks for the euphoria of experiencing my unity with the great cosmic cycles of being. My heart was filled with joy and fulfillment.

As the night of my vision dissolved back into day, I sat in the stone basin for a while and savored the gentle water washing over my body. I felt the dampness of my hair from the waves' spray and tasted the salt from the ocean water on my lips. Everything around me seemed alive and pulsing with life and I felt again as though my spirit were being washed clean. I sensed myself releasing—and the ocean taking—limiting beliefs, character defects, and old ways of being that had been hampering me or were no longer needed. I felt freer to become the person I wanted to be, not trapped by a more limited perception of who I thought I was. I felt reborn, renewed, and, in the moment, alive to the realization that we are all an aspect of the Divine.

When I sensed that my experience was complete, I slowly raised my body from the stone basin and turned away from the ocean to face the temple. The structure shimmered in the sunlight, infused with an inner radiance that beckoned me away from the water. I walked slowly to the temple, feeling my body tingling and awake. Warm sand oozed up between my toes and a light crust of salt formed on my skin as the hot tropical air dried my body. At the doorway to the temple I knelt on one knee, placed both palms on the sand, bowed my head, and said a silent prayer of thanksgiving. I prayed both as seeker and pilgrim, in the day and at night, in the present and in the past.

Suddenly my earlier vision returned and I saw the pilgrim pause at the temple doorway. Inside a priest was visible, waiting to bestow a greeting and blessing. The priest extended his hand and placed a gift in the pilgrim's hand—a palm-sized packet wrapped in a portion of corn husk and tied with a braided band of corn silk. The gift had been prepared to offer her guidance and protection during the upcoming ceremonial cycle. I saw the pilgrim accept the packet and place it over her heart, holding it there with her open palm. Her heart opened and sacred energy moved from the packet though her heart and through her entire body, permeating her whole being. I saw the pilgrim look into the kind eyes of the priest. Feelings of gratitude and joy seemed to be washing over her like the ocean waves she had just experienced.

My vision of the pilgrim dissolved and I stood up from where I had been kneeling. I turned toward the path and walked over to the stones where I had left my clothes. The sun was moving down from its zenith and would be lost behind the tropical foliage in a few hours. It was still hot, but the air seemed softer and soothing. I dressed slowly, savoring the experience, feeling prepared to go back into the world with a renewed sense of awareness. I felt more alive—cleansed, balanced, and healed.

Without looking back, I stepped on the path and retraced my steps toward the walled ceremonial precinct of Tulum. I followed the path along the edge of the ocean, heading toward the shrine I had encountered earlier. The pilgrim might still have been traveling with me in the moonlight; at one place on the path I thought I heard women's voices softly singing sacred songs for her as she passed.

In most ways, things in my life were good. I was happily married and had an exciting, challenging job doing work I loved. I enjoyed living in Los Angeles and could see myself being there for a long time. I particularly liked the fact that I could have a successful professional life and at the same time pursue my interests in personal growth and spiritual development. In an urban center like L.A., I had wonderful access to American Indian elders, teachers from Eastern faith traditions, and healers skilled in almost every imaginable healing art. My biggest struggle was the conflict between the demands of my professional life and finding time for myself and my family. My career provided material benefits and my spiritual work nourished me at a very deep level.

I continued thinking about this conflict as I followed the path back to the ceremonial precinct. I thought about how I could bring the expansiveness and openness I had just experienced back to my life in Los Angeles. I considered new ways of seeing my life and new possibilities that could open up for me. I reflected about actions I could take to achieve a better balance between the world of work and the world of Spirit. I realized I needed to find ways to bring more of my spiritual self to my work and to let my work experiences be part of my daily spiritual practice.

Ahead on the path, I could see the dense foliage open up as I neared the passageway leading through the wall and back into the ceremonial center. I began hearing sounds from the crowds of tourists on the other side of the wall and feeling the hectic energy inside the ruins of the ceremonial precinct. My sense of peacefulness began to evaporate and I started to feel anxious. The transition back into the normal world from the sacred realms was always difficult for me and I wasn't quite ready to return this time, but I took a deep breath and remembered what I had just experienced, reminding myself that I had choices. I couldn't control the crowds or their behavior, but I could stay open to my feelings of peace and expansiveness.

As I entered the passageway, I continued to calm myself with the thought that I could keep my experience at the ocean alive within me and return mentally whenever I wanted or needed to. I felt better as I walked through the ceremonial buildings to the place where Julie and I had agreed to meet. The parking lot was filled with empty buses waiting to take groups of tourists back to hotels in Playa del Carmen or Cancun. The bus drivers had left their engines running as they waited and the air was heavy with a haze of diesel exhaust fumes—quite a shock after the beauty and serenity of the deserted temple, pristine beach, and glorious ocean—but I was able to just let things happen around me and maintain my own inner peace.

Chapter Notes

1. In 1994, access to the site was redesigned so cars could no longer park next to the ruins.
2. Milbrath 1999: 148
3. Ibid., 148
4. Tozzer 1941: 109
5. A cenote is a deep, natural sinkhole opening to under ground water sources. Cenotes are common on the Yucatan peninsula; one of the most famous is the ceremonial cenote at Chichen Itza.
6. Sharer and Traxler 2006: 760
7. Venus was considered a celestial deity and was the most important of all the planets to the ancient Maya. The astronomical phases of Venus played a major role in the complex cycles of the Maya calendar and influenced agricultural activities during the rainy season as well as warfare and martial activities during the dry season. The cycles of Venus have also been linked with the founders of some Maya lineages. Scholars have noted cases where the combined imagery of Venus and the moon reflect the theme of resurrection or rebirth. The cycles of Venus were also studied carefully by the ancient Maya due to their belief that Venus could bring misfortune; they often

referred to Venus as the "Wasp Star" because Venus, like the wasp, could harm humankind.

8. Miller 1982: 89

9. Unfortunately, the passage of twenty-five years has dramatically changed the experience of the city I visited back in 1985. At that time, there were few tourists wandering within the city precincts and I had whole buildings and plazas practically to myself. If I climbed to the top of a temple because I wanted to see whether I could connect with the ancestors and spirit beings who lived there still, I had only to wait a short time to find myself alone, free to open myself to the sacred energies that are still so powerfully present in these ancient Maya cities and to receive visions and messages from the other worlds that still exist parallel to modern Tulum. Now, however, the site is filled with tourists, up to a thousand a day, and is the third most visited ancient site in Mexico. People are no longer permitted to freely roam the architectural area, climb many of the temple pyramids, or approach the coast and the ruins of the smaller sacred outbuildings.

10. On an earlier trip to Chaco Canyon, while exploring the ruins I wandered into an area where I started having apprehensions about a presence I felt there. Rather than follow my intuition and turn back, I continued on until I was forcibly confronted by Anasazi ancestor spirits and ordered to leave. I was distressed by the encounter and disturbed that my lack of awareness had resulted in my intruding where I was not welcome. I resolved that, in the future, I would be more mindful of my presence in sacred areas and always follow my intuition if I felt I should leave, regardless of how much I wanted to continue.

THE GOOD ROAD CEREMONY

Las Pinturas Temple-Pyramid, Coba
Quintana Roo, Mexico – 1985

The weathered remnants of ancient stone pyramids, temples, ceremonial platforms, and roadways *(sacbeob)* seemed to be struggling to keep from being overcome by verdant tropical vegetation. Everywhere I looked, crumbling, poorly preserved structures were engulfed by lush vibrant green foliage covered with dewdrops glistening in the early morning sun. Orchids, lianas, and brilliant red and yellow flowers provided a stunning contrast to the muted grey and brown tones of ancient stone and mortar. Coba has a much higher annual rainfall than Chichen Itza and Tulum. As a result, the ancient city is surrounded by a rich tropical rain forest of sapodilla, cedar, mahogany, cocoyol palms, ceiba, and wild cacao. Walking along the main ceremonial causeway on this glorious morning, I was trying to absorb everything I could.

The night before, Julie and I had arrived at the Villas Arqueologicas, where we were staying while visiting Coba. Even though the drive from Tulum was short, we had arrived too late to visit the ruins before the park closed for the evening, so today I'd risen early to explore by myself. The farther I ventured into the ruins, the more excited I became. Coba was much less commercialized than any of the sites we had visited so far. It was more remote and had far less tourist traffic. Only a few of the ceremonial structures had been restored to the degree we found at Chichen Itza and Tulum, and much of the site looked as it probably had to early twentieth century archaeologists. Its wilder, less-manicured quality made the ancient sacred energies seem closer and more palpable.

Coba is translated as "water stirred by wind," an appropriate name for a city that contains five lakes. In addition to the lakes, another of Coba's defining characteristics is a massive system of sacbeob (singular *sacbe*), more extensive than any other system yet discovered. Sacbeob, often translated as "white roads," are straight raised roads or causeways that link temples and other architectural groupings. Each causeway is about fourteen feet wide and varies in height from two to eight feet. The sides of sacbeob are faced with rough-hewn stone; the top roadway surfaces are coated with a smooth, fine limestone plaster that originally gave them a brilliant white finish. The longest causeway runs sixty miles from Coba to the ancient Maya site of Yaxuna.

Coba was built during the Classic period, ca. 600 CE, and reached its apogee during the Late Classic and Terminal Classic periods between 730 and 1000 CE, when Coba was the dominant center of northeastern Yucatan. With the completion of the extraordinary system of sacbeob, Coba established itself as the master of a region that encompassed 1544 square miles, a sphere of influence twice the size of the famous lowland kingdom of Tikal when it was at the height of its power. Coba's sacred temple pyramids, palaces, outlying residential buildings, and road systems covered eighty square miles of the total area. Scholars believe its peak population exceeded fifty thousand people. As Coba grew and prospered, many perimeter communities also sprang up during this time of rapid expansion.

Coba fell around 1000 CE when Chichen Itza attacked and captured the site. Over the next two hundred years, the city dwindled until it was abandoned around 1200 CE. Coba continued, however, to be used as a pilgrimage site by neighboring dynasties, and portions of the site were reoccupied in the fourteenth and fifteenth centuries. Even today, the Maya still perform ceremonies at some of its temples. Unfortunately, most of the causeways, temple pyramids, and other architectural structures have deteriorated dramatically. Only a few temple complexes have been excavated and restored, most only partially, and they represent only a tiny fraction of the city at its peak.

I didn't have a particular destination in mind. I just wanted to be open to energies of the site and allow my intuition to guide me, so when I came to a side footpath off the main trail, I decided to follow it. The path led to a small complex of ceremonial structures known as the Las Pinturas group. The centerpiece of the cluster is a stepped pyramid with a small one-room temple on top containing remnants of stucco paintings that once covered the inside walls. The structures were named for the vague remains of these paintings *(pinturas)*, deteriorated yellow, blue, and red paint splotches visible in the top corner of the temple.

I was immediately drawn to the pyramid and temple; they seemed to have a vibrant, beckoning energy, and I knew I wanted to spend some time here while it was still early and the buildings were empty of tourists.[1] As I stood at the base of the pyramid, I marveled at the aliveness of the jungle around me. Tulum and some of the other sites we had visited lacked the lush tropical forests of Coba, and the areas immediately surrounding their restored ceremonial structures were clear of vegetation. Here, forests teaming with plant and animal life crowded the sacred architecture, imbuing the ancient masonry structures with energy and intensity beyond anything I had previously experienced. I sensed the myriad life forms I found here in such a dramatic display of shape, color, and sound, might be a metaphor for my expanding sense of self.

I paused, closed my eyes, and said a silent prayer for the ancestors of Coba. I expressed my gratitude for their sacrifices and for the extraordinary stone monuments they had left behind. I prayed for their health and well-being in the other worlds and asked to receive their blessing and guidance. Opening my eyes, I let my gaze travel up the steps of the pyramid to the top, set dramatically above me. The treads of the steps ascended gently, harmoniously, and beautifully. They seemed to lead up into higher, sacred realms of spirit.

North American Indian vision quests frequently take place on the tops of mountains or buttes and often the phrase "going up on the hill" or "going up on the mountain" is used instead of "vision quest." Standing at the base of the pyramid, I felt I was about to climb a sacred mountain that would bring me closer to Spirit. Many years later I learned that the Maya did conceive of temple pyramids as sacred mountains and of the temples on top as the abodes of ancestors and deities. Not surprisingly, I felt once again that I was embarking on a vision quest that would continue to lead me into the realm of higher consciousness, toward greater understanding and self-awareness.

I began a gradual ascent up the steps, purposefully and slowly, to make my way to the top of this sacred structure. I had heard that Maya priests ascended and descended their sacred mountain pyramids in a zigzag pattern, moving back and forth across each tier of the pyramid rather than climbing straight up. I repeated this pattern, mimicking the undulations of the serpent so revered by indigenous cultures. As I climbed, I continued to marvel at the beauty of the setting. Every so often, I saw flashes of brilliant color as tropical birds darted through the lush green foliage of the massive ceiba trees, coated with luxuriant Spanish moss. The rich musky smell of the rain forest infused the moist early morning air.

Moving up the face of the pyramid felt much like my experiences climbing mountains, buttes, and mesas to reach vision quest sites in California, Arizona, and Colorado. The energy patterns in my body seemed to become more aligned and balanced with each step. The distractions of my everyday physical world slipped away as I became more focused; I was moving into a refined state of being and an expanded level of awareness. Planting my feet firmly on the limestone steps as I gradually ascended the face of the pyramid, I felt unseen ancestor spirits guiding and welcoming me on this journey to higher consciousness.

Climbing higher and higher, I continued to observe the beautiful vegetation and abundant wildlife around the pyramid. Although I had spent a great deal of time outdoors, I was not used to the intensity of the animal life in this early morning jungle. The sounds of birds, howler monkeys, and small animals rustling through the brush were thrilling. I felt welcomed and embraced by all of creation. Looking up, I marveled at the richness of the blue expanse of sky overhead. I felt my consciousness expanding, and I began to experience myself as a sacred being with the ability to realize my highest potential and express my true soul nature.

As I reached the uppermost steps, I realized the top of the pyramid was a large rectangular platform formed of hand-hewn stone blocks, tightly fitted and mortared to form a flat surface. Toward the back of the platform was the small one-room Las Pinturas temple, no more than eight feet on each side at the base. The temple had two west-facing, side-by-side doorways separated by a thick cylindrical column supporting a lintel that spanned both doorways. As I had done at the other sites, I tried to imagine priests and priestesses performing ceremonies here for rain and abundant harvests, conducting rituals for the initiation of adolescents, and praying in honor of ancestors and supernatural deities. I tried to imagine initiates and pilgrims coming to the temple—some for enlightenment, some to heal or be healed, and some seeking guidance and wisdom.

I continued across the platform until I reached the base of three rough-hewn steps that led up to the twin entrances to the temple. I knelt while placing the palms of both hands flat on the ground. I said another silent prayer of gratitude for the opportunity to be here at this sacred site, a prayer of thanksgiving for the ancestors who had created, nurtured, and cared for this place, and a prayer for their blessing and guidance. Then I climbed straight up the three steps to the temple entrance and turned and sat with my back against the central pillar to face out across the platform. The sun continued to rise behind me, illuminating everything in front of me. As I sat quietly under the shade of a protective thatch covering over the top of the temple, I noticed my breath was becoming deeper and more expansive.

The magnificent spread of jungle canopy far below me filled my entire field of vision to the horizon, interrupted only by a series of beautiful small lakes and the tops of other ancient pyramids. Although the limestone block I was sitting on felt hard beneath me, it also possessed a warmth and vibrancy. Like so many of the ceremonial structures I had visited, the stone of this pyramid seemed to possess a quality of aliveness quite unlike the cold, inanimate attributes I typically associated with stone, and it had a healing effect on me. I was thousands of miles away from Los Angeles, in an environment unlike anything I had experienced in the States, and yet I felt safe, at peace, and quite at home.

As I continued to sit, I noticed the entire structure appeared to be pulsing with sacred energy. This energy flowed from the ground below, rose up along the four edges of the pyramid, and continued past the platform to meet at a point in the air above the center of the platform. Most Maya pyramids have a recognizable pyramidal shape but, rather than having four sides meet at a point at the top like the Egyptian pyramids, Maya pyramids are truncated; they end in platforms that stop well short of an intersecting apex. As I watched, the energy meridians from the sides of this pyramid converged, forming an energetic structure in the shape reminiscent of the pyramids of ancient Egypt.

I reflected on the sacred architecture of the Indian tribes of North America and wondered about its similarities to the Maya. For the Plains Indians, the four directions have specific powers and attributes. Here, sitting against the western edge of the temple, I felt certain that its doorways' orientation toward the west was not accidental. For the Maya, like other indigenous peoples, this direction would have had very a specific meaning and ceremonial implications. For the Plains Indians, the west is the place of introspection, the place of purification and renewal, the home of the Thunder Beings. *Inipi* or purification lodges (sweat lodges) were, and still are, often built in the western quadrants of ceremonial sites.

In thinking about the inipi purification ceremonies I'd participated in, I recalled a story Tom Mails had told me about Frank Fools Crow. In the darkness of the inipi ceremony, Fools Crow would often imagine himself sitting on the opposite side of the lodge, facing himself. In the fiery light from the heated, glowing stones in the fire pit, Fools Crow would ask Wakan Tanka, the Great Spirit, to help him take a hard look at himself and see what human weaknesses or faults he needed to correct. Fools Crow believed that sooner or later, we all have to face the truth about ourselves and confront our inadequacies, failings, and misdeeds.[2]

As I reflected on this, I noticed the energy in the central area of the platform was moving and shifting, miraculously set in motion by an unseen force. The energy continued to coalesce into a column that embodied a transcendent, spiritual quality and looked something like a desert mirage—fluid, undulating waves that shimmered in the hot tropical Sun. As I continued to gaze at the energy column, a form began to crystallize and take on a more substantive shape. I was startled to realize that I was seeing an image of myself in the center of the column, much as Fools Crow had described seeing himself sitting on the other side of the purification lodge. The image looked back at me and forced me to confront unrecognized truths about my life.

I began to see myself objectively as I was in the world—the self as seen by my friends, relatives, and coworkers. I watched as a rapid procession of images, thoughts, and emotions flashed by in a review of my life from childhood to the present. I saw aspects of myself shaped by my parents, my educational experiences, my friends, my beliefs, and my attitudes. I witnessed myself as a small child with a child's thoughts, beliefs, and feelings, then as an adolescent and a young adult. I remembered times when I was terrified by my father's alcoholic outbursts, when I was mean to my younger siblings, when I lied to teachers and cheated on homework, and when my friends and I stole our parents' cars for joy rides. As the images illuminated different aspects of myself at different times in my life, I saw mental and emotional patterns that had formed my personality and shaped my concept of my everyday self.

Sitting on the platform, I gazed at myself inside the column in a detached, almost dreamlike state. As I continued to watch my life unfold before me, the images shifted to the frenetic, pressured pace of my life in Los Angeles—sixty, seventy, and eighty-hour work weeks, constant business traveling, meetings, conference calls, presentations, and reports. I saw myself constantly on the go, chasing the American Dream of expensive cars, bigger and grander houses, exotic vacations, fancy restaurants, Indian art and rare book collections, and a bigger retirement portfolio. I saw Julie and me struggling to find time for ourselves, for each other, and for starting a family.

Suddenly, time itself seemed to slow down. The images of my life review dissipated and rather than witnessing a progression of events, I started to reflect on their meaning. As I began to question what was behind the frenetic, pressured pace of my current life, my thoughts turned to my childhood experiences with a hyper-critical father. As a young boy, my father found some fault with almost everything I did; humiliation and shame were constants in my life as I was growing up. I recalled incidents from my childhood that repeatedly reinforced the belief that I couldn't do anything right. I realized that these feelings had turned into adult fears of inadequacy and a belief that I wasn't good enough, all of which had pushed me to excel.

I began to see how my old beliefs and childhood feelings were behind my need to be perfect. The fear of failure I had experienced as a child was still lurking behind every project I undertook at work. I began to appreciate the enormous impact these self-doubts and limiting beliefs had on how I lived my life at that time. With this insight came the understanding that I'd never be able to fully experience my higher nature unless I let go of these self-imposed limitations. I realized that my spiritual journey required becoming aware of these aspects of my life and that the resulting self-knowledge and personal mastery would lead to wholeness and inner peace. I had the feeling this was the beginning of a long, very difficult, but ultimately rewarding process.

Taking a deep breath, I became aware that I was feeling drained; the old memories had brought up painful emotions, and these realizations and insights were all I could absorb for the time being. I was relieved to notice that the energy inside the column had subsided. To get some relief, I turned my head sharply to the left and looked out past the edge of the pyramid platform to the luxuriant jungle canopy that spread out to the horizon. It was still well before noon; the sun hadn't reached its searing zenith yet and this area of the ruins was still deserted. I wanted to stay a little longer and reflect on what I had just experienced. Taking another deep breath, I tried to shake off some of the more disturbing aspects of the images of my life and simply enjoy the beauty and peacefulness of my surroundings for a few more minutes.

Just as I was starting to relax, I saw a second energy column begin to form to the left of the first. The initial, mirage-like quality of the energy changed as the boundaries of the column became better defined and more sharply focused. The column was infused with intense, radiant, crystalline energy with a blue tinge. The energy continued to coalesce as a human-like form. I saw myself again, only this time I was in the Lower World. In this energy column I was in the realm of the shaman, similar to the experience I'd had at Balankanche earlier that week. This was the realm behind the portal that had opened for me at Chaco Canyon, the realm of ceremony, healing, rebirth, and renewal.

I witnessed myself moving through sacred shamanic time and space, through the world of ancient wisdom teachings and lost spiritual knowledge, watched over and guided by the energy of the Goddess. I saw myself exploring this vast, magnificent realm hidden from our ordinary state of consciousness, pursuing a journey of self-discovery leading to the sacred Tree of Life at the heart of the unseen realms. All indigenous spiritual traditions to which I'd been exposed recognized the power of the Lower World and the sacredness of this unseen realm. They knew this realm held the key to a deeper, richer understanding of self and the world around us. This was the world that had been calling to me ever since I was a young boy, the realm of underground kivas, sacred caves, mysterious altars, and ancient spiritual chants.

Now I began to realize there was much more to this shamanic realm than I had ever imagined—more than acquiring guardian spirits, discovering power animals, and retrieving lost parts of the soul. I understood there was still much I needed to learn about how to apply the insights and spiritual awareness from this realm to my personal healing and the healing of others. I also had much more to learn about balancing and integrating this aspect of myself. As a young child, I had longed to understand the great mysteries of life. My intuition now told me that somewhere in this world I would find the key that would help me understand those mysteries and, in the process, achieve a fully integrated life.

I took a deep breath and shifted my legs, trying to find a more comfortable position on the platform. Suddenly, I glimpsed something out of the corner of my eye. A third column of energy was forming, this time off to the right of the center column in front of me. This one was much like the other two except that it was infused with radiant, pure white, crystalline energy. Once again I saw myself forming out of a coalescing energy vortex in the center of the column.

This world was distinctly different from the ones I had seen in the other columns of energy and yet there was a profound symmetry and interrelatedness among all three worlds. From the vantage point of this world, I was able to view my life with a pristine clarity, as if from a much higher perspective. I comprehended that a higher and grander purpose was guiding my destiny and leading me toward unity and oneness with the Divine. I could recognize my spiritual roots in primal, infinite creation and experience the pure, unlimited aspects of Divine consciousness and the Universal Soul. My heart was open and touched by the vibrant energy and aliveness of the universal love and compassion for all beings that emanated from this sacred realm.

This was the world I had encountered but not fully entered at Balankanche while sitting at the base of Wakah-Kan, the World Tree, the portal to this higher realm. Now, in my vision, I was actually experiencing the tangible, physical manifestation of the highest levels of spiritual awareness—a realm where I was perfectly aligned with my own soul essence, in tune with my higher self and guided by the Divine. This was the path I had been seeking. And although, at the moment, I had no idea how to find my way back again, the images were so powerful that I was convinced this would not be my last experience of this world.

Unexpectedly, I found myself becoming anxious and agitated as these thoughts filled my consciousness. There was no doubt in my mind that the insights I was gaining were absolute and undeniable truth, and that recognition was extremely unsettling. I knew I was witnessing an actual aspect of myself, a future wholeness and integration that I could eventually manifest. But what did it mean for my life and my future? Although sometimes challenging, my personal and professional life in Los Angeles was familiar and comforting. Would this spiritual realization lead me to abandon this comfortable life and move in an entirely different, perhaps even more challenging direction? Even attempting to accept the implications of this experience felt uncomfortable to me. I wasn't sure I was ready for this insight that spiritually, and in every other way, I could be so much more.

While I was wrestling with these thoughts, the energy columns vanished, as if they had been pulled back down into the pyramid. I was left sitting alone on the platform, gazing into the area where they had been only moments before. The space seemed empty and somehow incomplete, as if the vortices were such an integral part of the pyramid that without them a critical dimension was missing. But I was also relieved that the experience had ended; I'd had enough for the time being. Unfortunately, my relief was quickly overtaken by doubt, confusion, and fear. The world I knew was crumbling—things were not at all the way I'd thought they were. Up until now, the idea that there were different aspects of myself linked to multiple worlds had been a benign, abstract concept. Now, I couldn't deny the reality of this phenomenon. I struggled to make sense of what I had just witnessed and to link it to something familiar and understandable.

I was familiar with the concept of three separate worlds and had had some experience of these realms through my shamanic studies and practices within the Lakota culture. The idea of three separate worlds is also a well-known aspect of Maya cosmology and had been repeatedly noted by Maya archeologists and scholars. This tripartite reality is also a common theme among other civilizations around the world. Egypt, Mesopotamia, Greece, China, India, and numerous other cultures have rich mythologies involving a Lower World, an ordinary world that we inhabit, and a Divine, heavenly realm. Even the Sunday school lessons I had studied as a child presented a worldview that included both Heaven and Hell. What I had just experienced was perfectly consistent with universal human experience of the different aspects of reality.

Ten years after my experience at the temple, I found a beautiful description of how the Maya perceived these three worlds or "layered domains." In their book, *A Forest of Kings*, Linda Schele and David Freidel describe the three worlds as "the starry arch of heavens, the stony Middleworld of earth made to flower and bear fruit by the sacrificial blood of kings, and the dark waters of the Underworld below." However, the Maya did not see these realms or regions as distinct from one another, but as interrelated and connected, flowing one to the other, "alive and imbued with sacred power."[3]

Throughout time, human beings have had relations with all three worlds but, of course, some individuals, depending upon their gifts, spent more time in one realm than others did. For example, the Lower World, which the Maya named Xibalba, was visited by shamans during rituals and by kings when they experienced ecstatic trance during public bloodletting ceremonies performed for the good of their people and for the maintenance of life and right relations with all things. Just like the world of human beings, the

Lower World as the Maya conceive it, has its own inhabitants, sacred beings, animals, and plants. The Maya believe that it rotates at night above their heads to become the starry sky. In other words, it is transformed into the heavenly realm.

For the Maya, the Lower World is connected to the human world by Wakah-Kan, the World Tree at the center of existence, creation, and the universe. As the archetypal *axis mundi*, the World Tree is the unifying element of the three worlds, its roots penetrating deep into the Lower World, its trunk running through the Middle World, and its branches soaring to the heavens and the Upper World. In ancient ceremonies, the king himself would be transformed into the embodiment of the Tree of Life during ecstatic vision, standing atop the sacred mountain pyramids. Wakah-Kan had no specific geographic location, but could materialize anywhere, through rituals.

The Middle World, the place where human beings lived, was considered no less sacred to the Maya than the other worlds. Like the North American Indian cultures and many others, they based the natural world on a grid made up of the four directions. Each of these directions had its own special tree, color, bird, god, and rituals associated with it. The horizontal axis of the Middle World was the sun, bisecting the physical realm as it passed from horizon to horizon every day. Each of the four directions was concentric, connected to the World Tree, the *axis mundi*, at the center. Even though everything in this world was considered sacred, human beings still had to work to be in right relation to nature and to one another. Life had to be lived mindfully, or disharmony and chaos entered in.

For this reason, daily life for the ancient Maya was supported within a framework of ceremony, remembrances, and spiritual practices to keep human beings on the path of balance and harmony. Although in the modern world we have all too often lost these tools and practices that help maintain health and harmony, many indigenous cultures, including the Maya, have managed to keep these practices alive. The admonitions I had been hearing from elders over the last few years—to "walk in balance and harmony," "follow a path with heart," and follow the "good red road"—were beginning to make much more sense to me. And now I was developing an appreciation for the extraordinary power and profound influence of other worlds that my own culture didn't even recognize.

For the Maya and other indigenous cultures, the Upper World, Middle World and Lower World were all unified aspects of a greater whole; a sacred trinity existing simultaneously and available here and now. After seeing myself from the perspective of these three different worlds, it struck me that my spiritual journey involved exploring the aspects of myself represented by and expressed through these realms. My physical, emotional, and psychological dimensions were only a small part of a much larger whole. The journey that had started for me at a weekend workshop at the Esalen Institute was now turning into the pursuit of a miraculous body of ancient spiritual wisdom.

I pressed my back against the column in the doorway to the temple to give myself more support. It was dawning on me that during my visit to ancient Maya ceremonial sites, I had crossed a threshold from which there would be no turning back. My journey into the realm of indigenous spirituality had become an essential and substantive element of my life—much more than a passing interest, hobby, or diversion. These ceremonial experiences provided a critical missing dimension to my everyday life, something I cherished and longed to pursue. I had no intention of abandoning my family or my professional obligations, but I knew my journey now was taking on a deeper, richer, more committed dimension.

The loud rustling of a large animal in the underbrush at the base of the pyramid startled me and brought my thoughts back to my present setting. I wondered if it might be a tapir or peccary, since both were common in this area. My back felt stiff, my legs were on the verge of cramping, and I'd had enough for now. I closed my eyes and said a silent prayer of thanks for the honor of being in this sacred space and for the insights I had received. Bracing myself against the central pillar, I pulled myself stiffly upward and leaned against the pillar until my legs felt steady enough to start the trip down the pyramid. It wasn't noon yet and the area was still deserted. I savored my last few moments alone on the top of the pyramid.

There was still much I hadn't seen in the ruins, but I needed a break, so I began following the path back to the main entrance. The jungle was quieter on the walk back than it had been earlier that morning. I could still hear an occasional howler monkey in the trees, and every once in a while a parrot or macaw, but the loud morning stirrings of wildlife had receded and the intensity of movement in the forest had died down. I passed dozens of large iguanas with subtle green banded shadings; they scurried away from the path toward the dense jungle undergrowth. The iguanas brought back long-forgotten childhood memories of chasing frogs, turtles, and salamanders near muddy Midwest ponds on hot and humid summer days, and hunting for snakes in the tall grasses. Being here felt a little like being in heaven.

Chapter Notes

1. Like Tulum, Coba is much different today than it was when I first visited in 1985. Although not as popular as Tulum and less accessible, the ruins are now crowded with tourists on foot and bicycle. In the early 1980s a new, paved road was opened to Coba and the site started becoming a bigger attraction for visitors on day trips from Chichen Itza and the Riviera Maya. It is not possible to climb Las Pinturas pyramid today, and access to other structures has been restricted as well. When I last visited, in 2009, I couldn't find any area

near the ceremonial structures with enough privacy to conduct a personal ceremony.

2. Mails recounts Fools Crow's practice in his biography, *Fools Crow: Wisdom and Power* (1991: 112).

3. Schele and Freidel 1990: 66

MANIFESTATION OF THE GODDESS

Ixmoja Temple-Pyramid, Coba
Quintana Roo, Mexico – 1985

I was awestruck as I stood at the base of the magnificent and formidable Ixmoja temple-pyramid, an inspiring presence looming twelve stories above the dense rainforest floor. Like many of the structures in the Nohoch Mul group at Coba, Ixmoja had only been partially restored. Except for the grand stairway leading up to the temple at the top, and the surrounding pyramid face, dense jungle vegetation engulfed the majority of the structure. The stairway and stonework were composed of rough-hewn limestone blocks and gritty mortar joints—a sharp contrast to the smooth finished surfaces, crisp lines, and fine architectural details characteristic of fully restored ceremonial buildings. But the coarseness of the masonry work, standing in sharp relief against the brilliant green jungle, gave the impression the ancient temple-pyramid had emerged from the distant past to serve as a portal to a lost world.

The sun was well past its zenith as I started the long, arduous climb up the massive grand stairway that rose majestically before me. It was still uncomfortably hot and the humidity was as close to 100 percent as it could get without raining. I was soaked with perspiration and had a hard time catching my breath in the dense air. Looking down as I climbed, I had a terrific view of the entire Nohoch Mul group, a cluster of ancient structures that included a colossal elevated ceremonial platform, temples, pyramids, and other unexcavated mounds. Off in the distance I could see a few small groups of tourists exploring other areas of the ruins. I had hoped that by waiting until late afternoon I would have Ixmoja to myself and it looked as if this were going to be the case.[1]

The view from the top of Ixmoja, sometimes called Nohoch Mul, was even more spectacular than I had imagined. Looking out across the jungle canopy, I tried to visualize the boundaries of the eighty square miles that comprised Coba at the height of its power and influence (about the same land area as Seattle or Baltimore). In the distance I could see hills everywhere, completely covered by lush tropical foliage, the remnants of unexcavated temple-pyramids, and other ceremonial and secular ruins. As I scanned the seemingly limitless expanse of jungle, I imagined the dense green vegetation receding and the ancient masonry architecture revealed in all its former glory, and I began reflecting on the spiritual worldview of this great civilization.

The ancient Maya did not differentiate between the secular and spiritual realm as we do today. As a result, their "urban" environments, like Coba, are often referred to by scholars as "ceremonial cities." All were organized around a central sacred precinct with temple-pyramids, ancestral shrines, and other structures for religious functions. Adjacent to the central precinct were other groups of buildings, often constructed on elevated masonry platforms, for political, administrative, commercial, social, and residential uses. Sacbeob traversed secular areas to reach the spiritual core of the city.

The spiritual realm pervaded the secular world of the ancient Maya through their constant contact and interaction with ancestor spirits, supernatural beings, and deities. By deciphering ancient hieroglyphics, scholars have learned that "this group of beings formed as much a part of society as any royals, nobles, farmers, artisans, or traders."[2] Kings summoned spirits for assistance, oracles were consulted for guidance, astronomers determined favorable dates for military campaigns, and ancestors were routinely petitioned for advice and blessings. Ixmoja, the tallest pyramid in the Yucatan, must have been at the heart of one of the truly remarkable ceremonial city centers of the ancient Maya, one that attracted many pilgrims to its rituals precisely because of Coba's enormous political, economic, and spiritual influence throughout the region.

From the top of the pyramid I could see Macanxoc Lake about three-quarters of a mile directly in front of me—a large trapezoid-shaped body of brackish water approximately two-and-a-half miles in circumference, with its shorter, truncated shore nearest the pyramid. To my right, near the park entrance and the Villas Arqueologicas, was Lake Coba, a large oval-shaped lake about the same circumference as Lake Macanxoc. Two smaller lakes, Xkanhá (about one-half the size of the larger lakes) and Sacakal (about two-thirds the size of Coba and Macanxoc Lakes), were to my left. Large groups of lakes were quite unique in the Maya realm, but it was the spatial relationship between Lake Macanxoc, Ixmoja, and the sacbeob that particularly fascinated me.

Before coming on this trip, I had found a copy of a 1932 publication by the Carnegie Institution of Washington titled: *A Preliminary Study of the Ruins of Cobá - Quintana Roo, Mexico*, authored by J. Eric Thompson, Harry E. D. Pollock, and Jean Charlot. The publication had excellent academic observations on Coba, but it was one particular illustration,[3] a fine line drawing on fragile tissue depicting the relationship among the Nohoch Mul ceremonial complex, Macanxoc Lake, and a series of sacbeob causeways, that particularly caught my attention. I became increasingly excited as I studied the illustration and reflected on the possible significance of the unique architectural layout.

As I studied the illustration, I first noticed that the Ixmoja pyramid had an unusual northeast/southwest alignment that oriented it directly toward the midline of Macanxoc Lake. Most ancient Maya ceremonial structures are oriented to the four cardinal directions and I was unaware of any other ceremonial structures oriented toward a lake, instead. The drawing also showed five separate sacbeob radiating out from, or converging on, the Nohoch Mul ceremonial center—another characteristic that does not appear at any other site. Two of the five sacbeob originated at the base of the pyramid and radiated out toward Lake Macanxoc, hugging the shoreline of the trapezoid-shaped lake on the sides that angled in toward the pyramid. Another sacbe, following the precise midline of the lake, emerged from the rear of the pyramid and extended three miles in the opposite direction to a small ceremonial complex known as Sac Mul. The fact that the temple-pyramid had been built to align perfectly with the midline of the lake, and that the sacbeob that originated at the pyramid precisely followed the lateral shorelines, suggested to me that the ceremonial relationship between the temple-pyramid and the lake represented something quite extraordinary.

As I sat on the edge of the platform at the top of the pyramid, I recalled the details of the illustration and noticed heavy jungle foliage had completely overgrown the ancient sacbeob lining Lake Macanxoc. Small wavelets, caused by the gentle breeze, were forming on the surface of the dark brackish waters. The shadow of the great pyramid, cast by the sun descending to the west behind the pyramid, was slowly moving across the lake. For the Maya, as in other indigenous cultures, water was an aspect of the Goddess, the Divine Feminine. As a result of my studies with North American Indian elders, I knew that lakes, natural springs, and sometimes rivers were often considered places of sacred power. Some of the most sacred shrines of the Hopi Indians were at natural springs. The Zuni Indians consider lakes to be portals to the realm of the ancestor spirits and supernatural beings. Many years after my first trip to Coba, Maya scholars determined that water, whether in springs, lakes, or cenotes, always had to be present where a city was founded because the element of water recalled the mythological moment of primordial creation. For the ancient Maya, like the Hopi and Zuni, some lakes were believed to be portals to the Lower World and as such, were considered particularly sacred.[4]

In order to take full advantage of the light and my solitude, I immediately turned to face the temple at the far end of the platform. I knelt, placed both palms on the platform, silently said a brief prayer of thanksgiving, and asked for blessings and guidance from the ancestors. Although Ixmoja was much larger than the Las Pinturas pyramid, it had the same truncated top and smooth platform with a temple built toward its back. The rectangular temple aligned perfectly with Macanxoc Lake. Its longer side was perpendicular to the midline of the lake and the six-foot wide center doorway was oriented to face the middle of the lake. The inside of the temple measured twenty feet by four feet, with a twelve-foot high vaulted ceiling. Except for an area six-feet wide and two and one-half feet deep at the temple entrance, a one-foot high stone platform used as a bench occupied the entire interior of the temple.

Walking slowly and mindfully across the platform toward the temple, I focused on my breath and brought my attention to my immediate surroundings, tuning into the energy of the lake, the pyramid, and the temple. As my mind quieted, I began to feel a vibrant, radiant aura emerging from the pyramid, almost as if the entire structure were a powerful beacon. I felt unbelievably grounded and anchored by the pyramid's sheer size and mass. At the same time, I could sense delicate, ethereal vibrations shimmering off the sides and platform of the pyramid. It struck me that this pyramid and lake were the archetypal sacred mountain and sacred waters; one reached for the heavens, the other led into the watery Lower World.

When I reached the opening to the temple, I said another brief prayer, asking the ancestor spirits for permission to enter. Once inside, I sat down on the center of the bench facing out through the doorway toward the lake, with my back resting against the rear wall of the temple. I noticed immediately that the air around me had an electrified quality and that my body seemed supercharged with energy. Every time my thoughts turned to the relationship between the pyramid and the lake—sacred mountain and sacred waters—I felt a jolt of adrenalin shoot through my body. I was overwhelmed by the intensity of what I was sensing, intuiting, and experiencing. For the first time, I had perceived myself simultaneously in all three of the worlds I had encountered at Las Pinturas the day before.

I was clearly in the everyday physical world but felt myself being pulled toward the heavens and drawn into the depths of the watery Lower World. I sensed that the lake and pyramid were mirror images of each other, ascending and descending into their respective spiritual realms. Each was a unique manifestation of the Divine, an essential element of creation. Like the classic Chinese yin-yang symbol, they were perfectly balanced energies coexisting in absolute harmony and exquisite alignment. I remembered the fear I had felt at Tulum when I struggled with the confusion of being in two worlds at once. Yet now my mind was clear and focused. I was able keep myself grounded even as the three worlds coalesced around me.

Suddenly, I took a deep involuntary breath. Realizing that this revelation had literally taken my breath away, I intentionally resumed the pattern of my deep, slow breathing and gradually became calm and centered again. I settled back against the wall of the temple, shifted my legs to get more comfortable, and closed my eyes, hoping to just sit for a while and absorb all I had just experienced. The moment I closed my eyes, however, I began to experience a vision of a ceremony that had occurred at Nohoch Mul possibly a thousand years earlier—a ceremony involving the healing nurturing power and presence of Ix-Chel, the Moon Goddess, the feminine aspect of the Divine and goddess of fertility and childbirth. I was enthralled by the vividness of the images unfolding before me.

In my vision it was evening; brilliant starlight pulsed in the dark tropical heavens in a rich three-dimensional celestial tapestry. A magnificent full moon was rising in the northeast; its proximity to the equator made it look enormous. Above the far end of Lake Macanxoc, it traced an arc aligning perfectly with Nohoch Mul and with the central doorway to the temple at the top of the pyramid. Moonlight flooded the ceremonial center and created dancing patterns of light on the breeze-ruffled lake surface; it illuminated the sacred mountain-pyramid and turned the sacbeob into ribbons of white light.

Thousands had gathered, lining the shores of the lake and congregating in the space between the lake and the base of the pyramid. Most were women. Some had come to pray and receive a blessing for children not yet conceived or already in their wombs. Some had come with their young children to pray for healing and well-being. And some had come in old age to pray and receive a blessing before they passed on to the realm of the ancestors. The mood was reverent yet joyful, filled with gratitude and hope. This was not the first time Ix-Chel had appeared at this sacred site and it would not be the last, but for many, as for other pilgrims throughout the ages, this would probably be a once-in-a-lifetime experience.

The evening was filled with the sounds of the gathering crowd as well as the chirping of birds, buzzing of insects, croaking of frogs, and screeching of howler monkeys. In the distance a jaguar growled in a hoarse, raspy cough. Young children splashed and laughed in the murky shallow water at the edge of the lake as they chased turtles scurrying to the safety of deeper waters. Occasionally, a large fish broke the surface and landed with a loud plop, disrupting the dancing pattern of moonlight on the water. Some of the women talked softly in small groups as they waited for Ix-Chel's arrival. Some stood or sat quietly, rocking to soothe the children in their arms or wombs. All were filled with excitement at the prospect of the arrival of the Goddess.

As the time for Ix-Chel's appearance drew near, the pace of preparation intensified. The interior of the temple and the platform around it gleamed from a fresh coat of plaster. Now eight priests and priestesses flooded the temple with the sweet, aromatic smoke of sacred copal incense. They took their positions in two groups of four, sitting cross-legged on the wide stone platform bench, each group in two rows of two, facing the center of the temple. Attendants lit torches placed at the four corners of the platform at the top of the pyramid and then swept its plaster surface. On each of the massive pyramid's seven terrace levels, torches flanking the grand stairway were lit and attended by a priestess and priest standing beside each torch, guarding the sacred spiritual fire emanating from each level.

More torches, lining the sacbeob that hugged the shore of the lake and elevated on poles high above the heads of the pilgrims, were lit and attended by priestesses, priests, and acolytes. Moonlight reflecting from the small, irregular portions of the freshly-plastered sacbeob that weren't crowded with pilgrims created the illusion of a pulsing ribbon of light supporting the gathering crowd. Light from the torches created graceful patterns on the rippled surface of the lake, guiding the flowing, circular light mandala the moon created moving slowly up the midline of the lake toward the pyramid. As I looked down from the sacred heavenly mountain, the torches appeared almost as runway markers, defining a path for the approaching Goddess.

Suddenly, the trumpeting of a chorus of conch shell horns erupted from the distance on each of the five sacbeob. In perfect unison, long sustained tones punctuated by short periods of silence reverberated through the warm, moist tropical air. Far from the ceremonial center, birds took flight, startled howler monkeys scrambled through the treetops, and animals in the brush rushed for cover. Each series of tones crescendoed and then abruptly stopped, giving the echoes time to fill the silence and die before a new series erupted. The tones from the conches washed over the pilgrims, sending chills up their spines; the waves of sound opened and balanced their energy fields, helping them enter sacred time and space. My heart was racing, and I was filled with awe as my body involuntarily opened to receive these tonal blessings at the threshold to the other worlds.

At the base of the sacred mountain, converging sound waves created a rapidly-growing energy vortex. Each pulse of tones added richness, depth, and intensity as the vortex swelled and gained momentum. Massive concentric circles of sound radiated out laterally and vertically for hundreds of yards, engulfing the priestesses, priests, acolytes, and pilgrims in an ocean of sound vibrations. Each tonally pulsed shock wave thinned the ethereal veil between the physical and non-physical realms, blending the realms effortlessly and seamlessly.

As abruptly as they started, the conch shell horns ceased and their last echoes faded into the night. For a moment the jungle was absolutely still, completely empty of sound or movement. Suddenly, amid the stillness and silence, a remarkable transformation began. The energy vortex at the base of the pyramid began to penetrate the stones of the sacred mountain, their resonances blending as the mountain came to life, filled with the presence of the Divine. The massive limestone blocks pulsed with the heart-beat of the cosmos. The entire structure seemed to shed its massive weight and float suspended in space and time, transformed into a great cosmic beacon of pure holiness.

At the same time, the energy vortex at the base of the pyra-mid began to merge with the waters of the sacred lake, their resonanc-es blending as the lake also came to life, also filled with the Divine. The dark, turgid waters cleared to allow light from the torches and the moon to penetrate the watery roof of the Lower World and illuminate the realm of the ancestors and sacred beings below. All assembled found themselves at the heart of the Great Mystery, fully present in the physical world and the realm of the senses, but at the same time able to experience sacred time and space—to witness the reality and the majesty of the non-physical realms above and below.

The moon continued her movement through the heavens above the awakened water and the temple-pyramid, piercing the depths of the sacred lake and flooding the contours of the sacred mountain with light. In this multidimensional state—where the physical and non-physical realms had merged, and the world of matter and the world of spirit had become one—the light stream-ing from the moon slowed in vibration and frequency, assuming an ethereal physicality. Within the matrix of light energy, a form began to coalesce, slowly and indistinctly at first, then quickly gaining fo-cus and definition. As the priestesses, priests, acolytes, and pilgrims looked on in awe, Ix-Chel, the Moon Goddess, patroness of fertility, pregnancy, and childbirth, fully emerged from the energy matrix en-cased in the moonlight that connected the heavenly realms with the earth and the Lower World below.

Slowing Her vibrational resonance, She assumed an increas-ingly solid and recognizable form as She descended into the physical world to bestow Her blessings, guidance, and healing grace. She was simultaneously present in all Her manifestations and aspects—

as a beautiful young woman, as an old crone, as a tender, nurturing mother, and as a strong, formidable protector. She was in this world but not of this world. She had come from the other worlds to serve those who had assembled at the sacred lake.

As She reached the surface of the lake, Her transmutation was complete and Her healing work began. Her feet glided effortlessly over the sacred waters. Every heart was open to Her, every secret was revealed, and every need was known. She saw all things in those present—personal shortcomings, weaknesses, faults, resentments, guilt, and shame—and in return She helped them see Her in themselves—the wholeness, perfection, and grace of the Divine Feminine. Seen through the eyes and felt through the heart of the Cosmic Mother, Her unconditional love and compassion touched all assembled at the deepest levels of their souls. She flowed through sacred time and space, looking here, pointing there, and raising Her hand to offer a blessing.

On the shore, in the warm, humid jungle night, a transformation occurred among those who had come to experience Her presence. Tears flowed and fell onto the liquid light surface of the white road; the soft gentle sounds of weeping drifted through the tropical air, sobs of grief released to find a home elsewhere. Faces were bathed in radiant ecstasy, eyes softened with gratitude, and smiles of joy abounded. During Ix-Chel's journey across the lake, the pilgrims let go of physical, emotional, and mental aspects of their being that no longer served them. Many were cured of illnesses and physical limitations. All were healed through experiencing their connection with the Divine and finding the Divine within.

Completing Her journey between the lakeshore and the pyramid, Ix-Chel reached the steps that led up the sacred mountain to the temple and began Her ascent. She moved slowly and gracefully up each of the seven levels, passing priestesses and priests with bowed heads and open hearts. Her form was solid enough to leave the impression of faint footprints on each step, yet remained fluid, oscillating between Her many aspects and manifestations. Hearts opened to feel Her grace and souls unmasked to receive Her blessings. Back at the lake shore, some turned their eyes to follow Her progress; others embraced their children or fellow pilgrims. All continued to bask in the glory of Her presence.

Ix-Chel stepped onto the platform and made Her way across the smooth plastered surface to the temple. Her presence was a dazzling display of light-energy from the Moon, radiating and pulsing in physical form, moving through sacred time and space, sending ripples through the ethers. Once She crossed the threshold of the temple, She turned and sat on the center of the stone bench facing the doorway, with the two groups of four priests and priestesses facing Her from each side of the temple, and the lake clearly visible beyond the far edge of the platform. Her energy was so exquisite, so refined, and so intense that several of those seated to either side of Her were nearly overwhelmed by Her presence. All experienced the Goddess's gift—a magnificent state of grace and personal healing.

Before She departed, Ix-Chel telepathically imparted Her wisdom to those with Her in the temple, providing guidance and direction for the upcoming cycles. Some heard Her voice inwardly. Some experienced a healing touch. Others simply sat in Her presence, allowing sacred energies to pour over them and wash their spirits clean. This was a night none would forget, an opening that would never close. All assembled were in the presence of the Divine, all experienced a state of grace, all recognized their interrelatedness, and all were one.

As the moon arced over the roof of the temple and began to descend behind the sacred mountain, Ix-Chel's physical form began a transmutation. Her eyes were closed; Her breath was slow and even. The backs of Her hands were resting on Her lap, Her palms open to the heavens. Her physical body trembled and began to lose its substance as Her vibrational rate increased, creating an energy vortex that shifted between the physical and non-physical realms. Her form became less solid and more ethereal as the cells in Her body dissolved into particles of light swirling in energy plasma that reached toward the heavens. The vortex filled the temple and drew Her back firmly into the holy realm beyond the material world. Her physical presence had departed but She was, and always would be, present and available in the realm of the Divine.

Slowly, gently, everything began returning to its natural state. The plaster-covered stone masonry of the pyramid regained its solid, weighty dimension. The dark, brackish appearance of the lake water returned. Stars in the heavens immediately above the pyramid and lake filled in the void the moon had left. A sense of deep and abiding peace pervaded the ceremonial site and surrounding area. Pilgrims relaxed into the deep, rich darkness of the night, inwardly reliving the highlights of the coming of Ix-Chel.

Inside the temple, priestesses and priests felt the sacred energies recede and began to bring their attention back to the everyday world. They moved out to the center of the platform to prepare the prayers, chants, and offerings that were the evening's final tribute to Ix-Chel. Those who had guarded and attended the torches on the pyramid steps and sacbeob near the lake joined those already assembled on the platform.

Pilgrims completed their own ceremonies alone or in small groups that formed spontaneously. Some spent the night at the lake or near the base of the pyramid, keeping vigil until the sun rose. Some left offerings as well as prayers of thanksgiving. Others returned to family or friends carrying carvings of Ix-Chel they had brought to the lake to be bathed in Her radiant energy. And some from distant locations spent the night in group shelters constructed for them.

Ix-Chel continued Her journey through the realms of sacred time and space, threading Her way through the non-physical worlds, keeping the portal open for anyone who desired to experience Her presence and grace. This was Her gift to humankind, a legacy for Her daughters and sons. She was always available through prayer, meditation, and journeying—in times of good fortune or times of distress—offering Herself for the health, safety and well-being of all. Standing beside Her children, she was always ready to bring new life into the world, always ready to bestow Her healing powers and spiritual graces. She was at the center of the great cosmic cycles and tides that govern everyday lives. And all were in Her heart, enfolded in compassion and unconditional love.

Taking a long, slow, deep breath I allowed my attention to return to the present before I opened my eyes. The temple bench I was sitting on felt hard and uncomfortable and my back and legs were stiff. The physical world I had reentered had a rigid, sharp quality that had been absent from the world of my vision. I was sorry to have to leave the luminous, ethereal realms behind. But it was getting late and I wanted to have time for a leisurely hike back to the park entrance. I said a few last prayers—for the ancestors, for the Maya people of today, and for the caretakers of this sacred site. I also offered prayers of thanksgiving for the honor of witnessing the manifestation of Ix-Chel.

As I descended the stone steps of the pyramid, passing each of the seven terraced levels on my way to the ground, I pondered the new insights I had received from my vision. It was becoming clear to me that these other realms coexist with us as integrated rather than independent realities. Each realm seemed to have unique qualities and attributes, yet could be experienced in the here and now. I reflected on some reading I had done about Australian Aborigines and their concept of the Dreamtime. Although the

Dreamtime had connotations that were unique to the indigenous Aborigines, their experience of Dreamtime as a state of being and a way of perceiving the world seemed an accurate description of the Lower World experienced by the ancient Maya. At the same time, it seemed to me that the higher spiritual realm I was experiencing at Maya ceremonial sites was also a way of being and perceiving the whole of creation in the here and now rather than as a distant reality that we would hopefully encounter after death.

The next day, Julie and I were to have a long day of travel to reach Palenque, our final destination before returning to Los Angeles. I was still confused, still searching for answers, still unsure where my spiritual journey would lead, but I was more at peace with my uncertainty and doubt. Although I was excited about heading deeper and deeper into the sacred realms of indigenous spirituality, I was feeling emotionally drained by the intensity of my experiences. I hoped that our time at Palenque would be uneventful and restorative. I was comforted by the prospect of returning to my normal life in L.A., and excited about bringing these new spiritual insights back home to help me live a fuller, better life.

Chapter Notes

1. The afternoon I visited the Nohoch Mul ceremonial complex, I saw only seven or eight other visitors on my way to and from the pyramid. There was only one person on the pyramid when I arrived. I waited for her come down before I climbed up; no one else was at Ixmoja when I was there. When I visited the pyramid again in 2009, I was shocked to find it was overrun with visitors. At any given time there were at least thirty people climbing or resting on the pyramid, with at least a dozen resting or taking pictures at the top and five or six inside the temple. Most visitors approached their Ixmoja experience as they might a

trip to an amusement park, with seemingly no respect for the sacredness of the site. As with the other sites I revisited, it would be impossible for me to have the experience today that I had in 1985.

2. Houston and Inomata 2009: 193
3. Thompson, Pollock and Charlot 1932: Plate 13
4. Grube 2006: 298–299

JOURNEY WITH THE CELESTIAL BIRD

Of all the Maya ceremonial centers I studied before our trip, Palenque, often referred to as one of the most awe-inspiring Mayan ruins, was the one I was most excited about visiting. This Late Classic site (600-900 CE) is like something out of a dream, a shimmering white gem of a city resting on the limestone shelf of the first level of the Tumbala Mountains in the modern state of Chiapas in southern Mexico. It rises above the brilliant green of a mist-shrouded forest that stretches from the Chiapas Mountains to the beaches of the Gulf of Mexico. Bubbling springs and streams rising from the limestone strata help create the magical beauty of the city and surrounding lands. As Linda Schele wrote in *A Forest of Kings,* this calcium-rich water flowing up from the earth

> ...fashions a fantasy world of crystal lacework by encasing the decaying leaves and branches of the forest in what will become the fossil-laden strata of floriferous limestone a million years hence. The

163

pearly deposits shroud temple and tree alike, creating a mirror to the Otherworld, like a cave turned inside out.[1]

In fact, an ancient name for Palenque, derived from the many springs within the site, was Lakam Ha, which means "Wide Water."

Palenque was built by people who shared common ancestry with those at other sites up the Usumacinta River, such as Piedras Negras, Yaxhilan, and Bonampak. Between 300 and 600 CE, Palenque served as a small regional center with trade connections to the Petén region, the Chiapas highlands, and the Grijalva valley. At the height of its glory, Palenque's influence and control stretched up the Usumacinta River and across the wide plain of what is now known as Tabasco. But like many Maya kingdoms, it was torn by power struggles between dynasties who fought to legitimatize their power. Ironically, many of the city's most magnificent structures, greatest works of art, and longest hieroglyphic texts, were created to consolidate that power. These include the four great "king lists"[2] placed by Janaab Pakal I ('Radiant Sun Shield'), also known as Pakal the Great, in the corridors of his funerary building, The Temple of Inscriptions. The obsession with history, royal lineage, and religious iconography left behind by Palenque's rulers has been endlessly fascinating to scholars who have struggled to decode the political and mythological stories of the city.

When I was there in 1985, epigraphers and archaeologists were just starting to assemble the puzzle pieces of the language and the temple-pyramid complexes into a cohesive story. Most of their work in translating the inscriptions within the Maya ruins had not yet been widely published, at least nowhere a "civilian" like me could read about it. So these inscriptions and the purpose of the temple-pyramids were as mysterious to me as they were to the great adventurers of the eighteenth and nineteenth centuries, such as John Stephens and Frederick Catherwood, who captured the imagination of the European world with their drawings and speculations about this clearly advanced, yet "abandoned," civilization.

Palenque was the last stop on our trip before traveling to Mexico City and returning to Los Angeles. We had scheduled four days to explore the ruins, visit the waterfalls and pools of Agua Azul and Mishol-Ha, and relax at a beautiful resort village outside of Palenque. In planning our trip, we had hoped that our visit to Palenque would be a perfect combination of relaxing in the midst of a spectacular, lush tropical setting and having one last chance to spend time among some of the greatest archaeological treasures in the world. Our brief late-afternoon incursion into the otherworldly beauty and magic of Palenque on the day we arrived convinced me we had made the right decision.

The next day, Julie and I left early for the ruins and spent most of the day with a guide exploring the archeological site. The ruins were as stunning in reality as in the photographs. The entire site was open to the public and there were no restrictions on access to architectural monuments and ceremonial buildings.[3] The highlight of the day was a climb to the top of the sixty-six-foot-high Temple of Inscriptions, the famous burial pyramid built by Palenque's best known ruler, Pakal I, and a descent down the narrow, claustrophobic interior stairway to his burial chamber and sarcophagus, located deep within the pyramid at ground level. The Temple of Inscriptions is one of the best preserved, most widely recognized Maya temple-pyramids, and Pakal's tomb is one of the most magnificent of ancient Mesoamerica. The discovery of his funerary crypt was the first confirmation that Maya pyramids were often both funerary structures and temple platforms.

This burial chamber had been discovered by the Mexican archaeologist Alberto Ruz Lhuillier in 1952. While doing restoration work in the inner sanctum of this temple, he noticed there were twelve symmetrical stone-plugged holes in the room's floor, which he correctly assumed had been used to position a stone seal into place. When he and his team lifted this massive stone slab, they discovered a stairwell tightly packed with rubble beneath the floor. It took them four seasons to remove the debris from the stairway. At a depth of eighty feet, he discovered a short corridor leading to a sealed door. In June of 1952, after nearly fourteen hundred years, that door was reopened and one of the most remarkable discoveries of the Mesoamerican world was revealed.

Climbing down the dark, narrow, claustrophobic passageway that led to Pakal's burial chamber was one of the most intense experiences of my life. The space was barely large enough for me to pass through. The massive stone walls and corbeled arch ceiling of the stairwell pressed in on me from all sides. The air had a stale, musty smell, and without much ventilation it was difficult to breathe. About half way down to the chamber, the stairs abruptly changed from their initial east-to-west orientation and doubled back. It was almost impossible to comprehend how this small tunnel passageway could exist within this massive mountain of stone without being crushed by the weight of surrounding masonry. My heart was racing in anticipation as I neared the small burial chamber.

Even though the lighting in the tomb was still quite poor, the view of the exquisite carving on the lid of Pakal's sarcophagus was breathtaking. I had seen some of the world's most famous art and sculpture in museums in Asia, Europe, and the Americas, but I had never seen anything quite like this—the fantastic mystical imagery, extraordinary detail, and remarkable state of preservation made this thirteen hundred-year-old work of art truly exceptional. Standing on the small platform overlooking the thirty by thirteen foot chamber, deep within the magnificent pyramid, I was filled with a sense of awe and reverence. Even though the humidity was oppressive (I was drenched in sweat), the heat intense, and the stale air stifling, seeing this stunning tribute to Palenque's revered ruler in this sacred setting was unbelievably expansive and uplifting.

Our entire first day at the archaeological site was filled with memorable experiences, with visits to the Temple of the Sun, Temple of the Cross, the Palace complex, and the Ball Court. But for some reason I had been uncomfortable while exploring the ruins ever since we'd arrived that morning. As beautiful as the city was, and as much as I loved being there, I was feeling quite anxious. I decided, however, that my discomfort had little to do with Palenque itself and was probably the result of the accumulated stress of my intense spiritual experiences during the earlier part of the trip. While those visionary experiences were sublime, insightful, and often transformative, I often felt confused, disoriented, and sometimes frightened. My anxiety continued to build throughout the day.

As I was trying to fall asleep that night, I was haunted by the memory of an experience at Coba that I thought I had left behind in the ruins. As I followed the path back to the park entrance after my vision of Ix-Chel at Ixmoja, I was excited and confused, struggling to somehow reconcile the world that had been described to me in school and in church with the world I was experiencing at these sacred sites. I was lost in thought and only partially aware of my surroundings when, out of the corner of my eye, I spotted a narrow side trail almost completely overgrown with tropical underbrush. It led off toward what appeared to be a crumbling, unrestored ruin of a temple with a large carved stone stela nearby.

I was intrigued by the thought that this out-of-the way structure might hold some secrets that would move me further along in my understanding of the ancient spiritual mysteries of the Maya. so I followed the path to the small clearing in front of the temple and stopped and faced the stela. It was similar to many found throughout the Maya world; this one appeared to depict a warrior or priest engaged in some sort of ritual or ceremony. Standing there, I did something that turned out to be incredibly stupid and very, very dangerous. Closing my eyes, I took long, deep, relaxing breaths and used the techniques I had been taught to enter a shamanic state of consciousness that would enable me to connect with the energy of the image carved into the stela.

A wave of pure terror rocked my body as I realized something terribly wrong was happening. All of the warmth from the hot humid tropical air was being sucked out from the space around me and I was surrounded by an icy chill. A powerful, overwhelming, menacing presence was emerging from the stela and I saw a dense cloud of heavy yellow fog rapidly move forward to engulf me. I could feel the fog trying to penetrate my consciousness. I instinctively knew that something horrible would happen if the fog engulfed me and overtook my mind. I started involuntarily backing up toward the main trail. I felt like an irresponsible and inept psychic tomb raider who had stumbled, completely unprepared, into a place I had no business being and was now suffering the consequences.

Hundreds of thoughts flashed though my head so quickly they seemed simultaneous. Since my earliest shamanic experiences I had been warned to be prepared, always protect myself psychically, stay alert, and never let down my guard when working in the shamanic realms. The elders I studied with always wore a headband at sacred sites, asked the spirits for permission before entering a sacred area, and prayed for guidance. I had done none of these things this time and now I was confronting something dark, sinister, and incredibly dangerous. I was alone without any protection or guidance and completely outmatched by the presence I was confronting. Nothing I had encountered before had been this menacing or evil.

I had discovered during my early childhood experiences at the Field Museum and during my shamanic journeys and trips to sacred Indian sites that I was particularly sensitive psychically. In many ways this sensitivity was a great gift, but it had been a source of challenges as well. Now, I'd been lulled into a false sense of security by the marvelous visionary experiences on this trip, and I was paying a price for my negligence.

I recalled that during one of my earliest shamanic journeys I had unintentionally encountered dark, negative energy and needed help protecting myself. Another time I had refused to obey a telepathic request from ancestor spirits to leave an abandoned ceremonial kiva after I had finished performing a prayer ceremony. The spirits had come to use the kiva and wanted me to leave immediately, but I lingered. That night at camp I experienced the most extreme headaches, stomach cramps, fever, and diarrhea of my life. By the next morning I was fine, and although it occurred to me that getting sick might just have been a coincidence, it seemed more like a powerful warning.

Now, at Coba, I forced myself to imagine my physical body and consciousness flooded with protective white light, and I tried to create an impenetrable light-energy barrier against the encroaching fog. The adrenalin coursing through my body helped intensify the barrier, increasing its strength. I kept backing up toward the main trail, focusing all my energy and will on solidifying my white light barrier and fighting off the sinister yellow fog. I started singing a North American Indian prayer song that petitioned the spirit Grandfathers for help and healing. I sang as if my life depended on it; at that moment, I was sure it did.

By the time I reached the main trail I felt more protected and somewhat relieved. It seemed that I had left the immediate danger behind. While trying to compose myself as I headed back to the park entrance, I realized I was still very shaken up. I had been given a hard, brutal reminder that these sacred sites contained portals to non-physical realms that need to be approached with a great deal of preparation, care, caution, and respect. Through these portals, its possible to encounter both light and dark forces. I was extremely grateful for the lesson and vowed that I would never do anything as foolish as this again.

As I lay in bed that night at Palenque, the Coba experience returned like a nightmare. For some reason I couldn't shake it and the more I thought about it, the more real and present it seemed. And, as if that wasn't enough to deal with, another equally troubling phenomenon was occurring outside our room. My attention kept being drawn to what seemed like movement outside our casita. At first I thought the movement might be other hotel guests, but I heard no footsteps or rustling, and realized that ghosts—ancestor spirits—were rushing around in an intensely agitated state, creating a chaotic, disturbed energy. I had never encountered anything like this before during any of my vision quest experiences. I tried every conceivable thing I could think of to calm myself, but nothing worked.

I felt overwhelmed, vulnerable, and afraid. The disturbance was so troubling and was becoming so intense that I even considered checking out and finding a hotel somewhere in town, farther away from the ruins. As I tried to think of options other than leaving, I finally decided to go out by the pool in the garden to burn some copal, offer prayers for the spirits of this place, and softly sing some sacred songs. The combination of copal, prayer songs, and prayers had always had a marvelously calming and uplifting effect on me, so I was hopeful this would get me through this night. Without telling her specifically what I was experiencing because I didn't want to frighten her, I talked to Julie about what a hard time I was having and how anxious I felt and let her know I was going out to the garden for a little while.

It was a moonless night and the path was lit by only a few ground-level lights as it meandered through the dense, dark foliage of the rain forest. I kept my gaze downward as I followed the path through the garden to the pool. As I focused my concentration on the ceremony I was about to perform, I was able to let my unpleasant thoughts about Coba and the energy around the casita subside. Near the pool, I finally looked up and instantly froze as I found myself facing two spirit beings a short distance ahead of me on the path. Each was surrounded by an ellipsoidal field of radiant light energy. My fear returned. Adrenalin rushed through my body and it took all the self-control I could muster to keep from yelling, turning around, and running back to the casita.

The spirit beings remained motionless; the only discernible movement was the oscillation of the energy fields around them. My heart was pounding, my palms were sweating, and I was having trouble breathing as I stood and faced them. As the moments passed, the initial shock of the encounter began to lessen. I was still terrified, but as I calmed down, I didn't sense anything hostile or threatening about these beings. Their energy fields were bright and pure and seemed to be of a very high vibration level. I didn't sense any of the dark, cloudy, negative energy I had encountered on earlier vision quests when in the presence of threatening spirit beings. As my fear started to subside, I actually found myself feeling somewhat comforted.

Gradually, I experienced them communicating with me telepathically. They told me it was not necessary to make an offering that evening and assured me they would help clear the ancestor spirit energy that was making me so anxious and uncomfortable. They explained that many ancestors from Palenque had been unable to cross over to the other side at death and were still tied to the ruins by their grief, sorrow, and emotional encumbrances. They also said I had important work to do at the ruins the next day and that they would make sure I was guided and well protected. They instructed me to get up early the next morning so that I could be ready to enter the park exactly when it opened. By the time they finished speaking, I felt much calmer.

The light energy faded as the beings departed and I was alone in the garden. I turned and followed the path back to our casita. When I arrived, the disturbing energy I had experienced earlier in the evening had lessened dramatically. I was still feeling anxious but I knew I'd get through the night. I thought briefly about not returning to the ruins at all, but my intuition told me I should obey the instructions of the light beings. I had a good feeling about those spirits and felt I could trust their guidance. I wondered if some great tragedy had befallen Palenque and had resulted in an enormous loss of life. Perhaps the spirits I'd sensed outside the casita had been victims of warfare or plague.[4]

The next morning, inside the rental car while on our way to the ruins, I sensed once again the presence of the two spirits. Their energy was not as intense, but I could tell they were definitely with me. Again, I didn't sense anything dangerous or threatening. They instructed me to go directly to the temple-pyramid known as the Temple of the Foliated Cross[5] as soon as the park opened, to climb to the top of the pyramid, and to sit in front of it with my back to the main door, facing the Temple of the Sun to the east.

Continuing with the instructions, they told me that once I was sitting in front of the temple, I was to burn several small pieces of copal incense, one piece at a time—three pieces for the Palenque Triad, as the three pyramids in the complex were known,[6] four pieces for the four directions, nine pieces for the sacred nine count and the Nine Lords of the Underworld,[7] and one piece for Hunab-Ku. Each time I burned a piece of copal, I was to recite a brief prayer: "May the souls of these children, travelers, and pilgrims[8] descend to the heavens; may they free themselves from their grief and sorrow and seek a better life." I was to immediately leave the temple when I was finished, leave the park, and not return until the next day. I was not to go inside the temple or stay to explore the ruins.

As I was listening to the instructions, part of me questioned what I heard. I was moved by the simplicity and beauty of the prayer but the phrase "descend to the heavens" didn't make sense to me at all. I wrestled with the apparent contradiction. At one point I even considered reciting the prayers but changing the wording. As I struggled to find the right action, it finally dawned on me that in Maya cosmology, departing souls descended first into the Lower World to pass through a series of trials and tests, and then ascended to the heavens. When I realized that in light of Maya cosmology the prayer made perfect sense, I started to get annoyed at myself for questioning the guidance I had received.

I arrived at the park early, was the first in line to enter the ruins, and went immediately to the Temple of the Foliated Cross. The temple is part of the Cross Group that includes two adjacent sister temples, the Temple of the Sun and the Temple of the Cross. These three shrines were built by Pakal's oldest son and successor to the throne, Kan Balam II. The Temple of the Foliated Cross was never restored and is surrounded by lush rainforest foliage; the pyramid itself is covered in a thick blanket of brilliant green vegetation that hides the entire masonry substructure except for a narrow set of irregular steps leading to the top. The temple has lost its entire front wall and the front surface of its mansard roof, but the side of the roof still has some fragmented stucco relief remains. A carved panel depicting sacred rituals is also still in place in what is left of the once-elaborate roof comb. Like the other shrines, the Temple of the Foliated Cross has three doorways, and the central entry leads to a main sanctuary and two side rooms at the rear of the temple. With the front of the structure missing and the interior exposed, the temple has an eerie, otherworldly air.

I followed the narrow stairway to the top of the pyramid, walked a short distance toward the entrance to the temple, turned, and sat cross-legged on the pyramid platform with my back to the shrine. Closing my eyes, I said a few silent prayers asking for guidance and protection and then began following the instructions I had been given. I was completely alone on top of the pyramid in front of the temple. I felt neither the presence of the two ancestor spirits who had accompanied me to the ruins, nor any of the spirits who had been wandering restlessly outside the casita the night before. Although I was anxious about being interrupted as I started the series of prayers to release the souls bound to the physical plane at Palenque, I was committed to faithfully carrying out the request that had been made of me.

As I lit my first piece of copal, my eyes followed the smoke rising toward the heavens. I watched incredulously as an elliptical energy vortex with fluid, undulating waves radiating out in all directions began forming around the smoke above me. The vortex shimmered in the early morning sun as the energy intensified around its core, creating rhythmic, concentric ring formations. Slowly, a large circular opening materialized, surrounded by pulsing, vibrating energy, and a portal to the Lower World appeared. The disturbed chaotic energy I had experienced since coming to Palenque was subsiding and I felt completely calm and uplifted. I wasn't aware of the presence of any ancestor spirits and didn't have any visions of souls progressing on their journey to the Lower World, but I definitely experienced the energy around me transforming. I knew something important, magical, maybe even miraculous was occurring.

My intuition told me not to look into the vortex above me but rather to focus my gaze on the burning copal, which I did. I sat in a state of awe and humility as I sensed the souls of many ancestors being drawn toward the portal. As they passed through the vortex, the energy field was cleansing and purifying their souls. Their grief and sorrow—described in the prayer I had been given—evaporated, along with other negative emotions that had trapped them on the earth plane. Once they reached the portal, they were easily able to pass through and enter the Otherworld to continue their long-delayed journey. The sense of intimacy, holiness, and reverence surrounding this transmigration of souls was profound almost beyond belief, and I was filled with gratitude for the privilege and honor of assisting in this sacred rite of passage.

As my prayers continued, I glanced out and saw a group of tourists approaching the pyramid from below. I became concerned about having the ceremony disrupted, but I was still alone as I finished burning the last piece of copal and said the last prayer. As the final wisps of smoke drifted up toward the heavens and vanished, the energy vortex dissipated and the portal closed. The entire temple area seemed immersed in a state of profound and deep, abiding peace. I said a brief, silent prayer of thanks, stood up, and began descending the pyramid stairs. I wanted to stay longer so I could explore the temple and process all I had experienced, but I knew it would be disrespectful and foolish to disregard the instructions I had been given.

I passed the group of tourists on the steps—the ancestor spirits had cut it close—and then walked directly toward the park entrance without looking back, got into the rental car, and drove back to the resort. Since I was still in a little bit of a daze from the ceremony, I was glad that Julie and I had already decided to spend the rest of the day away from Palenque, exploring the gorgeous waterfalls and translucent blue water pools at Agua Azul. Our afternoon was spectacular. After hiking around the falls and swimming in the pools, I felt completely rejuvenated. Although I was still anxious about spending another night at the resort, by the time we got back to our casita late in the afternoon, the disturbing energy I had struggled with the night before had completely cleared.

Later that evening I sat by myself in the resort garden and spent some time reflecting on the events at the Temple of the Foliated Cross. It was a warm, peaceful evening and I was completely alone. I didn't have another encounter with the two spirits from the night before, but I did have a strong sense that I should return again to the ruins first thing in the morning for another ceremony. I was beginning to trust my intuition more and was completely willing to let it guide me to areas within the site that might hold important encounters for me. My plan for the morning was to go immediately to the area of the ceremonial center known as the Palace because it was a good distance away from the park entrance. That way I could avoid the tourists who usually started their visit at the structures near the gate.

The next day I left early by myself; Julie had decided to spend the morning at the resort. Almost no one else was at the park entrance when I arrived. I followed the path that led east through the Central Plaza, past the Temple of Inscriptions (Pakal's tomb), and headed for the group of structures known as the Palace. This group of adjacent buildings and interior courtyards is one of the most intriguing and complicated in Mesoamerica. The Palace includes vaulted galleries and rooms that scholars believe were royal residences; these surround two courtyards, East and West. The centerpiece of the complex is a beautiful square four-story structure built just before the city's collapse. Known as the Tower, it's a signature element of Palenque's exquisite, graceful architecture. All of the buildings sit on an artificial, thirty foot high platform three hundred feet long and two hundred forty feet wide.

I climbed the stairs to the top of the platform and slowly wound my way through the labyrinth of ancient structures. Their corbeled vaults (Maya arches) and sloping mansard roofs are supported by pillars with spectacular bas-relief images carved in stone or modeled in stucco. Palenque artists were among the most highly skilled in the world of the ancient Maya. Their carvings here depict lifelike scenes of royal life with elaborately dressed rulers and lords, ceremonial regalia, scepters, and objects connoting political authority. There are also depictions of fantastic supernatural deities and scenes from the other worlds.

When I reached the Tower I saw the sunken West Court-yard at its base. It was the smaller of two courtyards on the north side of the Palace complex. Something about this long, rectangular, four-sided area was magnetically inviting, as if I were being guided to enter. When I did, I lit copal and smudged myself and then moved around the edge of the courtyard, smudging its perimeter with the thick fragrant smoke. I ended at the southeast corner, at the top of four stone steps leading down to the grassy field in the center of the courtyard. As I descended the steps, I was enthralled by the beauty of the early morning and the courtyard's magical quality.

The sun was still low on the horizon. A light mist rose from the grass and wafted gently in the morning breeze. As I looked around me, I noticed a recessed, throne-like stone seat built into the wall near the steps. I sat down in it, facing west, resting my back against the wall and letting myself relax into the rich, soothing energy that filled the space. After saying my normal prayers, I took a few deep breaths and opened myself to the beauty of my surroundings and the warmth of the sun as it travelled farther along its arc across the brilliant blue sky. Everything seemed alive and filled with vibrant, nurturing, healing, transforming energy. It felt as if I were in the presence of K'inich Ajaw, the Sun God.

As I studied the courtyard, I noticed that the stone and masonry wall along the perimeter had broad stone piers protruding a short distance into the courtyard at irregular intervals. The piers were faced with panels of stone on which I could see the weathered remains of intricate bas-relief stone and stucco sculptures. The energy within the open area of the courtyard seemed dramatically different from the energy on the main level of the Palace group above me. The courtyard seemed alive with sacredness, the stone and stucco sculptures pulsing with radiance. It felt almost as if I were submerged in a pool of pure, crystalline energy.

At the time, I knew nothing about the content or meaning of the sculptures in the courtyard. Decades later I learned they were images of little stone casitas (houses) covered with stucco, representing *waybilob* (places of sleep or "god houses"). Each *waybil* contained figures of ancestors, gods, animals, and what scholars believed to be other supernatural beings.[9] Waybil shrines were constructed as resting places of ancestors or deities that were contacted, "woken up," and summoned during rituals and ceremonies.[10] The sculptures in the courtyard also included a representation of K'awiil, the Maya god of transformation and visions.[11] I now know that as I sat in the courtyard I was surrounded by the resting places of Palenque ancestors and deities and watched over by the divine manifestation of transformations and visions.

Sitting in the niche in the courtyard wall, I felt myself moving into sacred time and space. The faint aroma of the copal still lingered in the air. As I looked out around the upper edge of the courtyard, the energy seemed to be shimmering as if the copal smoke had created a vertical, broad, curtain-like vortex around the perimeter. To my left, on the opposite side of the courtyard, at the top of the wall I began to see a procession materializing within the vortex created by the copal smoke. The procession was led by a priest, resplendently dressed in full ceremonial regalia—a lavish quetzal feather headdress, elaborately embroidered tunic, jade necklace and pendant, and ceremonial rings—similar to depictions in one thousand-year-old paintings and on ceramics I had seen. In his extended hands, he solemnly held an object that I couldn't clearly make out but could see was bathed in radiant white light.

The stately procession of twelve men and women made its way along the opposite wall of the courtyard along the same path I had used earlier when I was smudging the upper perimeter. Everyone was dressed in what seemed to be ceremonial attire, similar to the lead priest's but not as dramatic—richly embroidered tunics for the men, *huipils* for the women, with both men and women wearing necklaces, pendants, rings, and immaculate ornamented sandals. As my eyes adjusted to the vision, I noticed that the object in the priest's hands seemed alive. A few moments later I realized the object wasn't bathed in radiant, white light, but rather it was radiant white light, and was in fact a holy being—a sacred bird from the spirit realm.[12] My heart raced at the thought of being in the presence of this holy and magical being.

I watched, transfixed, as the procession moved through the center of the broad, curtain-like energy vortex created by the copal I had smudged the courtyard with. Turning the corner at the opposite wall, they continued along the perimeter, moving purposefully and majestically. Soon they reached the upper portion of the courtyard wall where I was sitting and began to pass behind me. Thinking I should not turn and watch as they moved behind me, I kept looking ahead toward the east and eventually closed my eyes. Their passage sent shivers up my spine. When they reached the four broad, stone steps just to the left of where I was sitting, the priest led the procession down into the courtyard itself. He then walked in front of where I was sitting and approached me while the others followed, moving to stand behind him, facing me on the grass.

As the priest approached me, my heart pounded and my palms were sweaty. It was hard to breathe. A thousand random thoughts flooded my consciousness. I wasn't frightened by his presence or the procession waiting in front of me, but I was terrified that I would be invited to participate in a ceremony that I didn't understand or wasn't prepared for. I had no idea what to do except just be there in the moment. The priest's hands, bathed in pulsing, radiant, white light, extended toward me, offering me the Celestial Bird, the Bird of Heaven, the same way I'd seen North American Indian elders offer a sacred *chanupa*, a ceremonial pipe. I could clearly see the bird within the light and recognized it as a sacred being that embodied the everlasting holy consciousness that pervades all life. The gift from the priest to me was a gift of peace, a gift of celestial light. I sat in the presence of the group, my eyes riveted on the bird, and I was awestruck and unable to move, overwhelmed by what was happening.

The energy that surrounded the Celestial Bird began to shift and vibrate as the bird rested in the priest's outstretched hands. The bird itself began oscillating and morphing into alternative forms that seemed to reveal subtle nuances of its true nature, each embodying elements of holiness. I saw the bird as a dove symbolizing the Holy Spirit—everlasting peace, the consciousness of the avatars and masters. I saw it as the Phoenix rising from the ashes, symbolizing rebirth, renewal, regeneration. I saw it also as the Quetzal—symbol of the great feathered serpent, spiritual wisdom, and divine knowing.

Without thinking, I extended my open hands. The priest placed the Celestial Bird gently into my cupped palms. I could feel its feathers against my fingers and its chest moving with its heartbeat. It was both solid and ephemeral, substance and spirit, in this world but not of this world, a powerful divine, celestial energy. This was truly a gift from Hunab-Ku. Somehow I knew this sacred creature would allow me to journey outside of time, into a sacred space from which I could live my life in an expanded state of knowing and awareness.

As I sat holding the Bird of Heaven, my thoughts turned spontaneously toward the images of my own "spiritual self" that I'd seen earlier at Coba, and of my higher spiritual nature that is different from my limited physical body. My awareness began expanding and the physical boundaries that usually defined my sense of self began to evaporate. I automatically focused on my breathing, aware of the air flowing in and out through my nostrils, mindful of the rhythmic, gentle cycle of inhalation and exhalation. The energy around me began to thin. The others in the courtyard seemed to recede into the background and my own awareness began to expand. With each breath the air seemed more alive and vibrant. As I felt the Celestial Bird stirring in my palms, my spirit essence began to disengage from my physical body and effortlessly leave my body through my breath. I felt the bird take flight, pulling my spirit out of my body as it rose toward the heavens.

This was a phenomenon I had never experienced before. I had read about out-of-body travel, but even with all the shamanic journeying I had done I had never actually done any spirit traveling. I felt remarkably calm as I rose upward, even though I probably should have been terrified. I was so focused on the immediacy of the experience that everything else left my awareness. The ancient city of Palenque disappeared far below as I followed the bird into the heavens, journeying through sacred time and space, gliding and climbing with ease. Eventually, we stopped our ascent and began orbiting the planet, following the Maya's conception of the progression of life from birth (east) to death (west) to rebirth (east).

Our speed increased as we continued our circular orbit around the earth. As we accelerated, I experienced the childhood beliefs and old emotional patterns I had witnessed earlier in the trip at the Las Pinturas Temple in Coba sloughing off my spirit body and being cast aside—thoughts of abandonment and rejection and of not being good enough, self-doubt, fear, self-pity, even hopelessness and despair. Limiting beliefs, negative emotions, and self-defeating behavior patterns were released to evaporate into the ethers as we hurtled along our cosmic orbit. As we traveled faster and faster I felt myself being pulled to a new level of awareness and knowledge, moving beyond self-imposed limitations and free from old karmic ties.

After several revolutions, our speed caused us to escape our trajectory and soar away from orbit. Eventually, my momentum slowed as I floated with the Celestial Bird until we stopped at what seemed to be our intended destination. The energy seemed vaguely familiar and in a moment I realized I was once again in the presence of the World Tree I had encountered at Balankanche. Only now I was experiencing a dimension far different from the dense, earthy Lower World manifestation in the cave. Here, at its crown, Wakah-Kan displayed glorious, divine, cosmic energy that both transcended and integrated the three worlds of the Maya. Its core—the axis running through all of existence—connected the heavenly realm I was travelling in with the Middle World and the Lower World.

As I struggled to take this all in, I telepathically heard the Celestial Bird describe our destination:

This is the Center of Spiritual Creation.

This is the place where you are free
to become what you want.

This is the place where you are free
to create what you want.

This is the temple of the spirit,
the temple of the Jaguar Priest,
a way station on the path
through the cycle of birth, and death,
and rebirth.

This is the place of all knowingness,
of calmness and serenity, of clarity,
insight and wisdom.

This is the place of the fulfillment of the spirit
and freedom from that which you are not.

This is the place of perspective,
of non-judgmental discernment,
and true understanding.

This is the place to pause and be renewed
and regenerated, the place to heal oneself,
and the place from which to heal others.

This is the place to shed your illusions and
from which you can confront the great mysteries.

This is the place of Samadhi.

This is the place that is nowhere and everywhere,
nothing and everything, lightness and darkness,
sound and silence, being and nonbeing,
having and not having, doing and not doing.

This is the center of the crossroads,
the core of the sacred Tree of Life,
the breath of the everything,
the heartbeat of the universal soul,
and the womb of the Creator.

This is where life begins and ends,
where the circle starts and finishes,
where the cycles come and go.

This is the source and the destination.

This is the beginning and end of time,
the beginning and end of life,
the place of heavenly peace.

I was astonished to realize that this must be the home of the Celestial Bird, messenger of Hunab-Ku, here at the crown of the World Tree, the central axis, high in the heavenly realm of the Upper World.[13] I sensed that I would be able to return in the future, but that to reach this place I would once again have to leave behind everything that was unworthy of my true nature and held me back; I would have to empty and purify myself. But once I was here, I knew I would be able to transform myself.

Suddenly my euphoria began to turn to fear, bordering on panic. I felt completely overwhelmed, deep in an alien world, far from the comfort and familiarity of my "ordinary" life, and afraid I might get lost and be unable to find my way back. I looked over and saw the Celestial Bird beside me, a reassuring presence and lifeline back to the Middle World. I'd had enough and was anxious to return. I gently placed my open palms under the bird and raised them until I could feel its weight. Cradling its sacred energy, I closed my eyes and prayed for help and guidance in returning to Palenque. With a soft upward thrust I released the Celestial Bird and willed myself to follow it. With the bird leading the way, I effortlessly followed it back to our previous orbit in the heavens, but this time we circled in the opposite direction, eventually slowing as we approached Palenque. When the courtyard came into view below, we headed directly for the bench where the journey had started.

Slowly, I felt myself coming back into my body and felt the hard limestone beneath me and against my back. The sun had risen higher and the heat was more intense. I became aware of the humming sounds of insects and the chirping of birds. It was hard to judge how long my journey had lasted but I guessed it had been no more than an hour. Taking a deep breath, I noticed the pungent, musky order of the lush tropical vegetation. The priest and the members of the procession were still with me although they had moved off to either side of the courtyard and left a large space open in the center.

They seemed even clearer and more present than when my journey began. Although I could hear human voices faintly in the distance, for the moment no visitors were in the immediate area.

The energy began to shift at both the north and south ends of the courtyard as nine other spirit beings began to materialize. I couldn't tell whether they had returned with me from the journey or whether they were spirits from the waybilob in the courtyard and had been awakened. They moved to the center of the courtyard and sat in a council circle, facing each other, with the Celestial Bird in the center. They seemed to be having a discussion and I had the impression that this was what it was like in ancient times when priests and rulers summoned ancestors and supernatural beings for prophecy and council on politics and wars, civic and spiritual affairs, and agricultural plantings and harvests.

As their discussion progressed, I remembered the prayer I had been asked to say at the Temple of the Foliated Cross and the nine pieces of copal I had burned there for the Nine Lords of the Underworld. I wondered if these nine spirit beings were in fact those lords. I closed my eyes and silently asked for their help and guidance on my journey so that I would be able to fully understand and appreciate my experience with the Celestial Bird. I thanked them for the spiritual wisdom that had been shared with me, and then I asked permission to call on them in the future. Feelings of peace and joy washed over me and I was filled with gratitude for the remarkable spiritual gifts, love, nurturing, and help I'd received from the Maya ancestors during my last two weeks in their ancient realm. The world would never look the same to me again. Sitting in the courtyard, I realized I had found my way to my spiritual home, a path out of the darkness into the light, a way to make myself whole, and a way to express my True Self.

Chapter Notes

1. Schele and Freidel 1990: 216
2. Kings lists are royal genealogies, typically carved in stone, documenting succession and family relationships for a specific Maya site. Although they have been discovered at ceremonial sites throughout the Maya realm, the king's lists at Palenque are by far the most comprehensive and best understood.
3. When I returned to Palenque in 2007, I found the Temple of Inscriptions, as well as many other buildings, had been closed to visitors, and it was no longer possible to climb the pyramid or view Pakal's tomb. Archaeologists' and preservationists' concerns that a dramatic rise in tourism and increased visitor traffic would lead to further deterioration of ceremonial structures resulted in the Mexican government drastically restricting access to at-risk structures.
4. Earlier in the day, our guide at the ruins told us that when Palenque was being excavated and studied by contemporary archaeologists, the ancient remains of hundreds of bodies were discovered. The skeletal remains did not bear any markings of mutilations and damage characteristic of victims of warfare. Our guide informed us it was believed these deaths were probably the result of a mass epidemic of some sort. This may have occurred during the mysterious collapse and abandonment of the city in the ninth century, or during the sixteenth century when indigenous Maya may have revisited the site during the smallpox epidemic at the time of the Spanish Conquest. I have not yet been able to corroborate our guide's story through my personal research.
5. For years I was curious about why I had been asked to perform the ceremony at the Temple of the Foliated Cross instead of some other location. During my return trip to Palenque in 2007, I learned the Temple of the Foliated Cross contains a magnificent

carved panel with a cross-shaped image of Wakah-Kan, the World Tree. The center of the cross is the place in Maya cosmology where the heavens and the Lower World meet the land of the living—much like my experience in the cave at Balankanche. Decades after I had performed the ceremony, it excited me to learn that I had been directed to the sacred structure that symbolized the perfect setting for the transmigration of souls—the journey from the physical realm to the Lower World, and from there up to the heavens.

6. The Palenque Triad is the term used for three mythical Maya divinities. They were particularly revered in Palenque and accorded honor as guardian deities of the city. Today, scholars refer to the three gods as GI, the Maize God aspect of Chaak; GII, the god of royal dynasties; and GIII, the Sun God (Grube 2006: 435).

7. The Maya conceived of the Lower World as consisting of nine levels. Each level had a corresponding supernatural being associated with it. The ancient Maya referred to those beings as the Nine Lords of the Underworld.

8. When I was given the prayer, I was told there was a word in the ancient Mayan language to describe approaching death as a spiritual pilgrimage from a state of child-like innocence, a single word that included the concepts of child, traveler, and pilgrim.

9. In her magnificent 1985 publication on the sculpture of Palenque, Merle Green Robertson identified the bas relief stone and stucco structures on the panels as houses or "casitas" (74-75). Later research determined that a common element of Maya spiritual belief included the concept of shrines, known as waybilob (waybil, singular) or "god houses," depicted in small three-dimensional stone structures, bas-relief sculptures, or paintings. I believe that the casitas documented by Robertson in the West Courtyard are actually waybilob dedicated to deities, supernaturals, and ancestors associated with Palenque.

10. Grube 2006: 270

11. Ibid., 96

12. At the time of my experience in the West Courtyard in 1985, I had no knowledge of the Maya concept of the Celestial Bird (also referred to as the Bird of Heaven). None of the publications available to the general public at the time referenced this entity. I was first introduced to the concept of the Celestial Bird through *The Blood of Kings* exhibition at The Cleveland Museum of Art in 1986, and the book that accompanied the exhibition, by Linda Schele and Mary Ellen Miller. In my field notes from Palenque, I used the term "Spirit Bird" when describing my experience, but the moment I saw Schele and Miller's reference to the Celestial Bird, I recognized it as the Spirit Bird I'd seen.

13. As research progressed in the late 1980s and early 1990s, scholars' understanding of Maya iconography and symbolism increased dramatically. In Schele and Freidel's book, *A Forest of Kings*, they expand on the concept of the Celestial Bird and its relationship to the World Tree. When I wrote a draft of this chapter fifteen years after my experience at Palenque, I reviewed Schele and Freidel's writings and I now believe my personal experience revealed a deeper spiritual aspect of the Celestial Bird and the World Tree phenomenon. I also believe that Wakah-Kan is the portal, the magical passageway, that allowed journeys between the Middle World and the other worlds—a multidimensional energy field that connected ancestors and other supernaturals to the realm of the living. And I believe that this is the site of "the door or hole to heaven" referenced in *Maya Cosmos*, Freidel, Schele and Parker (1993: 414): "At the center, the realm of humans and that of deities are joined at *kumuk' lu 'um*, 'the center of the sky' where the [shaman] believes *u hol gloriyah*, 'the door or hole of heaven' to exist."

RIVER OF RUINS

Julie and I could hardly contain our excitement as we listened to Mary Dell Lucas in the dining room of our hotel in Belize City describe our upcoming trip. We had joined Mary Dell, the Founding Director of Far Horizons, and a small group of fellow travelers for the "River of Ruins" archaeological tour. Julie and I had avoided traveling with a group before, but the Far Horizon tour itinerary was so exceptional that we couldn't pass up the opportunity. For the next ten days we would visit ancient Maya ceremonial centers in Guatemala and Mexico. Our trip would take us to exotic, deserted ruins located in the midst of some of the most spectacular, unspoiled jungle rainforest in the world.

The past two years had been hectic and professionally challenging for both of us. We were routinely putting in sixty- to seventy-hour work weeks, Julie as an associate in the litigation department of a large law firm, and I as a partner in a rapidly expanding management consulting firm on *Inc. Magazine's* list of the "500 Fastest Growing Companies" in the country.

Since our last trip to Mexico, I had continued my studies with Bear Heart, including a trip to Wild Horse Mesa in New Mexico for a vision quest; I had also participated in several inipi ceremonies at friends' lodges in the Los Angeles area. Since returning from Mexico, I had also made a commitment to use my business and management skills to assist social service organizations on a pro bono basis and had recently led the board of a local youth shelter through a strategic planning process. The spiritual insights from my last trip were helping me live a fuller, better life, but I was still running at a breakneck pace and looking for more balance in my life.

A major breakthrough had occurred for me six months before this trip, in November 1986, when I visited the Cleveland Museum of Art to view an extraordinary exhibit of Maya art and iconography, titled "The Blood of Kings: A New Interpretation of Maya Art." The exhibition was curated by two of the most highly regarded Maya scholars, Linda Schele of the University of Texas and Mary Miller of Yale University. In addition to displaying a never-before-assembled collection of Maya art, the museum also chose to forego the customary exhibit catalogue and instead published a magnificent book with the same title as the exhibition—a landmark independent study of the Maya based on the latest scholarly research.

I'd had the good fortune of being able to visit the world's leading museums in this country, in Europe, and in parts of Asia, but nothing I'd seen before was as dramatic or thrilling to me. The exhibit contained a dazzling array of breathtakingly beautiful pottery; exquisite ceramic, stone, jade, flint, and stucco sculpture; photo murals of brilliantly colorful frescos; and intricately carved stone and stucco bas relief sculptures. The masterfully painted and flawlessly executed works of art depicted scenes of kingship, rites of accession, courtly life, ceremonial bloodletting, warfare and captive sacrifice, ball games, and the Maya cosmos. Revolutionary breakthroughs in deciphering hieroglyphics, epigraphy, and iconography had finally enabled scholars to understand the meaning of the written narratives and artistic representations on art objects and ceremonial sculptures. The lost world of the ancient Maya had come to life as never before and to a degree that would have been unimaginable even a decade earlier. And, for the first time, all the latest academic research findings were on full display for a general audience.

As I toured the exhibit I was stunned to see images executed by ancient Maya artists of the World Tree, the Moon Goddess, and the Celestial Bird. I'd found only brief, superficial references to the World Tree and Moon Goddess in my earlier reading and no references whatsoever to the Celestial Bird. After returning from my last trip I'd spoken at length with Bear Heart about my visions, and he had provided helpful insights. But he was not familiar with specific ceremonial practices of the ancient Maya or their spiritual worldview, and at the time I didn't know any Maya spiritual leaders to consult. As vivid, powerful, and inspiring as my experiences had been, for the last year-and-a-half I had desperately longed for some assurance of the authenticity of my visions. Here, for the first time, was independent scholarly confirmation of the veracity and validity of my spiritual journeys with the ancient Maya.

My doubts about my visions vanished and I felt exhilarated. Memories of my ceremonies at Balankanche with the World Tree, at Coba with Ix-Chel, and at Palenque with the Celestial Bird came flooding back with pristine clarity and an almost overwhelming emotional intensity. The theme of ritual as a bridge between the supernatural and the mundane worlds was woven throughout the displays, and they provided independent support that the shamanic and ceremonial world I experienced with indigenous elders paralleled the spiritual world of the ancient Maya. I read the latest research findings confirming the shamanic perspective—specifically that the ancient Maya believed the universe was

> a three-level structure, consisting of the Overworld, the Middleworld, and the Underworld. The Underworld world was entered either through a cave or through bodies of standing water, such as an ocean or lake. The Middleworld, the world of human-kind, was oriented to the four cardinal directions, each associated with a tree, bird and color ... The Overworld, also called the Upperworld, best described as the heavens, was marked by the passage of the sun across the sky.[1]

Although the extraordinary artistic creations were truly stunning, the insight I was gaining into the spiritual realm of the ancient Maya made the biggest impression on me. Scholars now understood that the ancient Maya believed the World Tree, the *axis mundi,* rose "from the center of the cave," was "at the center of the universe," and was regarded as "a sacred being."[2] Further, there was a consensus that "the souls of the dead and the supernaturals of the Maya cosmos traveled among the [Underworld, Middleworld and Upperworld] via this tree."[3] Research had also revealed that the supernatural Celestial Bird, "chief" among the many birds of the Maya cosmos, resided "at the top of the *axis mundi,* the World Tree of Maya cosmology;" and the Moon Goddess, patroness of fertility, pregnancy, and childbirth was represented as "a young woman who sits in the crescent of the Moon."[4] The exhibit also contained meticulous drawings, detailed descriptions, and stunning interpretations of the images on the sarcophagus lid in Pakal's tomb that I'd marveled at but hadn't understood—Pakal, at the instant of his death falling into the

Lower World in the presence of the World Tree and the Celestial Bird.

With the insights I had gained from the exhibition and book, my expectations for this trip were even higher than those for the first. In addition to the well-known and accessible site of Tikal, our itinerary included remote, difficult-to-reach ancient ceremonial centers that were usually visited and studied only by archaeologists. Much like the ancient Maya, we would travel by the Pasión and Usumacinta rivers to reach many of our destinations. Some sites could only be reached by boat. For others, river travel was the most direct route. Several sites we would visit had been discovered within the last thirty years, and had been explored by archeologists to only a limited extent. In short, these were definitely not tourist destinations. By traveling and camping in the same rustic fashion as the archaeologists who studied these sites, we would have the jungles, rivers, and sites completely to ourselves most of the time. This was as close to an Indiana Jones experience as a non-archaeologist like me was ever going to have.

Aside from hotels in Belize and Tikal and a stay at a rustic fishing camp on the Petexbatún Lagoon, the majority of our lodgings on this trip would be campsites along the river or in the jungle near the ruins we planned to visit. Traveling pristine rivers by *lanchas*—large, flat-bottomed, canopied river boats, hiking through jungles teaming with wildlife, and camping at isolated ruins in Guatemala and Mexico was like a dream come true for me. This was not Julie's idea of the perfect vacation but she was willing to share the experience. As Mary Dell began our pre-trip orientation at the hotel, Julie and I became increasingly excited about our adventure. As the evening progressed, however, our excitement was tempered by factors we hadn't yet considered.

The jungle where we would be spending most of the next ten days was among the most exotic and pristine in the world. The Pasión River in the western lowlands region of northern Guatemala cuts through dense tropical rainforest. The river basin is designated an "archaeological zone" and contains the three ancient Maya ceremonial centers we were going to visit: Aguateca, Dos Pilas, and Altar de Sacrificios. The Usumacinta River, a natural border between Guatemala and Mexico, runs through the heart of the spectacular Lacandon jungle, one of the most biodiverse rainforests in the world and the setting for two ancient Maya sites we would visit, Yaxchilan and Bonampok. While there, botflies, poisonous spiders, and venomous snakes would be a real and ever-present danger.

Botflies—so densely haired that they resemble bumblebees—belong to a large group of fly species whose larvae are internal parasites. They are ubiquitous in the jungle and their bites can cause real problems. They deposit their eggs under the skin during a bite; eggs later develop into larvae which, in turn, eat their way back out through the skin—an extremely unpleasant and painful process. To prevent bites, we were told to keep as much of our skin covered as possible, all while hiking through the jungle in 100 degree temperatures with near 100 percent humidity.

Then there was the matter of the snakes. An encounter with a fer-de-lance—a deadly, poisonous type of pit viper—could be life threatening. They were a menace because they were so aggressive and deadly; cases had been reported of individuals severing the snake's head to prevent a lethal bite only to find themselves being attacked by the severed head. The precaution here was to make sure we avoided any such encounters.

Despite these concerns, my longing for the type of spiritual experiences I'd had on our first trip to the Maya ruins two years earlier far outweighed the potential risks of this trip. I was sure I would have similar or even more profound experiences at these more remote settings. With the exception of Tikal, our tour group was likely to be the only visitors at each destination, and I knew we would have unstructured free time during the trip. Following the pattern of Julie's and my previous trip to Mexico, I planned to spend time alone on a spiritual quest in each of the ruins, praying for the well-being of the ancestors and asking for their guidance in exploring the realm of Spirit and the other worlds. I would remain open to any insights or revelations I might receive.

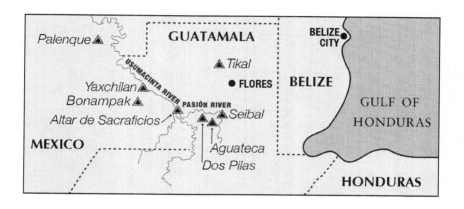

TIKAL, GUATAMALA

The next morning, we took a quick tour of Belize City, visited a small local zoo where we saw our first live jaguars, and then headed to Tikal. By the time we reached it later that day, we were completely enthralled by our surroundings. Tikal, sometimes translated as "place of spirits" or "place of spirit voices," is forty miles from the city of Flores. It has the remote, isolated feel of Coba, but the surrounding Guatemalan jungle is even more verdant and the native wildlife more exotic and abundant. The sheer size of the site, the massiveness of the ceremonial structures, and the remarkable restoration were all breathtaking.

I had been fascinated by Tikal ever since I saw the images of the ruins depicted as the rebel base in George Lucas's first *Star Wars* movie in 1977. In reality, the ruins were even more magnificent than I could ever have imagined. Our lodgings were right in the park, only a short walk from the ruins, in casitas with open thatched roofs. Our concerns about botflies, fer-de-lances, and other dangers of the jungle had almost vanished until we asked about the mosquito netting draped under the thatch and were told it was there to keep the tarantulas that lived in the thatch from dropping down into the rooms. Nevertheless, it wasn't worry about tarantulas that made it hard to sleep that night, but the excitement of the trip and the sounds of the jungle—droning insects, exotic nocturnal bird calls, and screeching howler monkeys.

The next day we began a systematic tour of the ruins, spending time exploring the sacred architecture and several of the many groupings of buildings and ceremonial structures around the extensive site. We climbed temple-pyramids and studied sacred carved stone altars. We followed miles of ancient causeways that connected building complexes through verdant rainforest teeming with tropical birds, howler monkeys, and other wildlife. Along the way we were tutored on the latest research findings and discoveries of archaeologists and scholars. There were a few other visitors besides our group, but compared to Chichen Itza the ruins were practically deserted.

During our two full days at Tikal, we had a chance to explore the Temple of Inscriptions, the Lost World Complex, and the Bat Palace. Julie and I climbed to the top of the colossal pyramid-base of Temple IV, the Temple of the Double-headed Serpent; at two hundred twelve feet high it is the largest at Tikal and one of the tallest in Mesoamerica. From its top, we had a breathtaking view of the other massive pyramid structures, their temple roof combs towering over the rainforest treetops. The afternoon of our last day at Tikal, I returned to Temple I, the Temple of the Great Jaguar, located in the Great Plaza. The temple-pyramid was the most glorious I had ever seen. The Grand Plaza and other nearby ceremonial structures were breathtakingly beautiful and were imbued with palpable sacred energy. It was here that I hoped to have an encounter with spirit beings or to journey once again to the supernatural realm.

I climbed the impossibly steep steps and sat in the temple doorway[5] atop the mortuary pyramid of the ancient ruler of Tikal, Jasaw Chan K'awiil I ('K'awiil that Clears the Sky'), who had ruled Tikal for fifty-two years.[6] His victory over Calakmul thirteen years into his reign established Tikal as the dominant military presence in the area and sparked a political and social revitalization. Tikal remained stable and prosperous through the remainder of his reign.

I was overwhelmed by the spectacular view. Possibly the most iconic of all Maya structures, the one hundred fifty-four foot high temple-pyramid is the centerpiece of one of the most extraordinary complexes of ceremonial architecture in the world. Looking straight ahead from the temple toward the western border of the Great Plaza, I could see the shorter but equally impressive Temple II which scholars believed was built for Jasaw K'awiil's principal queen Lady Lachan Unen Mo' ('12 Baby Macaws')[7]. Farther in the distance, Temple IV majestically soared two hundred thirty feet above the dense, verdant jungle floor. Together, the three temple-pyramids defined one of the Maya's most stunning sacred ceremonial centers.

To my right on the northern boundary of the Great Plaza were the remains of a once-magnificent grouping of twelve temple-pyramids, known as the North Acropolis. Although some of the earliest construction dates back to 300 BCE, the majority of the structures were built between 1 and 500 CE as sacred burial monuments for Tikal's rulers. Many of the earliest structures had been built over and encapsulated by larger structures that came later. At the time of Tikal's heyday, the acropolis also contained thirty altars and forty-three stelae. During the 1950s and 1960s, archaeologists dismantled the more recent layers of buildings to reveal the older, underlying temple-pyramid structures. Looking at the ruins of the remains of the acropolis, I couldn't help thinking that the archeologists had desecrated this sacred setting.

To my left, the southern border of the spacious Great Plaza contained portions of the Central Acropolis, a massive complex of structures covering almost four acres. The complex includes forty-five buildings and six courtyards with an intricate arrangement of stairways, halls, and doorways that connect the buildings and plazas. Scholars believe several of the structures in the acropolis were used as residences for the ruling family and that others may have been governmental and administrative offices. To be sitting in the temple, high above the jungle in this extraordinary setting, was a rare privilege.

I was alone on top of the pyramid; the rest of the group was exploring the areas off the Grand Plaza. Before the trip, I had participated in an inipi purification ceremony, a traditional Plains Indian pipe ceremony, and an overnight vision quest, all with the intent of readying myself for this journey into sacred Maya time and space. Now, moving to the center of the temple, I sat down and opened a small bag and removed the ceremonial objects I had with me: a ceramic bowl and charcoal tablets for burning copal; a small, wrapped bundle with four hundred and five multi-colored prayer ties; and a small wrapped bundle with six prayer flags. The prayer flags represented the four cardinal directions, plus the earth and sky.

I lit a charcoal tablet and placed it on the bottom of the bowl, and then placed a large piece of copal on top of it. As plumes of pungent, fragrant copal smoke spiraled upward, I passed the prayer ties and flags through the smoke to cleanse them and to reaffirm the prayers and intentions I had focused on when I prepared them back in Los Angeles—prayers for the well-being of the ancient and contemporary Maya, prayers that I would always conduct myself in a respectful and reverent manner at these sacred sites, and prayers that I would remain open to receiving spiritual wisdom during my ceremonies. I set the ties and flags next to the bowl and used my cupped hands to draw the copal smoke over my head and around my body to clear my energy field. Closing my eyes, I began to sing the sacred Plains Indian prayer songs I had learned over the years: a song to the spirits in the six directions, a song for filling the sacred *chanupa* (prayer pipe), and a prayer song to the Great Spirit. The temple acoustics were fantastic. The hard stucco surfaces on the walls and ceiling caused the tones from the songs to reverberate through the entire structure, even though I was singing quietly.

As the last sounds from the last song faded, I opened my eyes and placed more copal on the charcoal. The burning copal cast dancing shadows on the walls of the temple, which were just beginning to capture the startlingly beautiful hues reflected from the imminent sunset. I concentrated on relaxing my body and letting my breath soften and deepen. I continued to sit, anticipating that something would happen, perhaps a spontaneous journey to the Otherworld or a spirit encounter. But I didn't experience any of the phenomena I had encountered two years earlier. After a while, I realized that nothing out of the ordinary was going to happen and that I needed to rejoin the group.

I carefully placed the bundles of prayer ties and flags back into my bag, grasped the bowl—still hot on the bottom from the charcoal—and stood and walked to the temple doorway near the pyramid steps. My Far Horizons group mates had all assembled below in the Great Plaza and were admiring the brilliant jungle sunset. The pyramid steps looked impossibly steep as I prepared to descend; I was glad to have the heavy chain handhold that had been added to the structure. On the way down, I thought about the group in the plaza and wished I could have been with them so I could have looked up and seen the smoke from the burning copal and the shadows on the temple walls. I also realized that I was feeling disappointed and a little sad. I knew better than to try and force an experience in a ceremonial setting, but it felt as though I had missed something.

About halfway down the steps I was still struggling with the fact that I hadn't had an encounter with the spirit realms, and wondering if I had done something wrong. Suddenly, I sensed an energetic presence behind me and slightly to my right and, in my mind, I heard a strong, clear male voice say "You can come here as a tourist or you can come here as a priest, but you can't do both." As I heard his words, chills ran up my back. I knew he was right. I had never thought of myself as a priest or even wanted to be a priest. I just thought of myself as someone who loved the ceremonies, the sacred songs, and being in the sacred energies. Now I immediately realized I needed to approach this trip differently. My intent should not be to just "collect" otherworldly experiences or chase after supernatural phenomena. I needed to approach these ancient ceremonial centers as Bear Heart or the other elders I studied with would, as an intermediary between the human and spirit realm, not as an inexperienced initiate.

Julie and the group had gathered on the steps that led to the North Acropolis at the far end of the plaza and it took me a while to reach them. Several in the group said they had been watching me in the temple at the top of the pyramid and had enjoyed the prayer songs. I was stunned to hear this. I had been at the opposite end of the plaza, inside the temple, one hundred fifty feet in the air, singing in a relatively soft voice, but the group had heard me as loudly and clearly as if I'd been sitting at their feet. I realized that these ceremonial structures had been engineered for acoustical perfection. It was clear to me that a Maya priest in the temple could have addressed a crowd of hundreds with the same ease as a Catholic priest saying mass in a modest cathedral.

Daylight was beginning to fade as we started back across the plaza toward the series of trails that would take us out of the ruins. I was glad to see Julie again and being with the group helped me feel more grounded, but as we passed the base of the pyramid of Temple I, I realized I was still feeling unsettled. I wasn't exactly sure what to make of my encounter descending from the temple and I felt caught between two worlds, the familiarity and safety I felt with Julie and the group, and the excitement and solitariness I felt in the sacred time and space of the ancient Maya. At the moment I was feeling a little removed from each reality and grounded in neither. This wasn't a completely new feeling—I'd felt the same after our trip in 1985 and, to a lesser extent, every time I completed a vision quest or other intense ceremonial experience. But it was a fresh and vivid reminder of how I had struggled to find balance while living with one foot in the everyday physical world and the other foot in the world of ceremony and spirit.

At dawn the next morning we boarded *combis* at the hotel for a thirty-mile trip to Flores followed by another forty miles to the town of Sayaxché on the banks of the Pasión River. There we met the boatmen who would be with us for the remainder of the trip. We boarded lanchas and headed upriver to the Petexbatún River, a tributary of the Pasión River, and followed it to the magnificent Petexbatún Lagoon, a small rainforest lake surrounded by the lush, rainforest jungle. The lagoon and its environs were teeming with the most diverse, colorful, and exotic wildlife I had ever seen in one place. The lagoon was filled with dozens of species of fish, water turtles, frogs, and an occasional crocodile or caiman. We saw herons, snowy egrets, storks, and spoonbills in the surrounding marshlands and, in the jungle, brilliantly colored hummingbirds, macaws, parrots, parakeets, and trogons. Our base for the next several days was a rustic fishing camp on the lagoon—a well-worn structure of exposed weathered wood and timbers that seemed to blend perfectly into the dense jungle foliage.

AGUATECA, GUATEMALA

The next day we visited the ruins of Aguateca perched on top of a three hundred-foot-high limestone bluff near the southern shore of the Petexbatún Lagoon. The ancient city is surrounded by a system of defensive walls over three miles long. Although Aguateca lacks the monumental temple-pyramid structures of other sites, it does have a modest Main Plaza with well-preserved terraced platforms, altars, and stelae, as well as a nearby Palace Group.

That day I was able to go off by myself and perform a prayer ceremony on one of the altar platforms, much like the one I had done at Temple I in Tikal. I was hoping that here, at a remote site in the heart of the jungle, I would have an encounter with the spirit realm, but it was not to be. I finished my ceremony, expressed my gratitude for the privilege of being at Aguateca and, somewhat disheartened, rejoined the group. When I first thought about this trip, I had been certain that by spending time in these remote sacred sites I would be able to easily access the Otherworld and ancestor spirits. I tried to push my disappointment aside and focus my attention on the breathtakingly beautiful jungle surroundings.

Toward the end of the afternoon, we re-boarded our lanchas and returned to the camp for the night. On the river we enjoyed the constant presence of brightly colored tropical fish, fresh water turtles, and crocodiles. Occasionally our lanchas flushed an egret or heron from the dense vegitation; the rainforest foliage we glided past was constantly exploding with flashes of brilliant color from the feathers of toucans, macaws, and parrots. Empty of all human habitation, the jungle was absolutely pristine. Even though I was still disappointed that I hadn't had a supernatural experience, I was excited about how the trip was unfolding and looked forward to what was ahead.

Dos Pilas, Guatemala

At daybreak, we traveled again by lancha to a trailhead leading to the remote ruins of Dos Pilas on the eastern shore of the lagoon. It was a grueling ten-mile hike through dense jungle on an old, narrow, partially cleared dirt trail. Because of the potential threat of botflies, most of us wore wide-brimmed hats with mosquito netting around our faces, long pants, and long sleeved shirts; only our hands were exposed. Breathing the dense tropical air was a struggle due to the sweltering heat and oppressive humidity. Fortunately, our camping gear and supplies for the two nights we were to spend at the ruins were being transported by burros. Arriving safely at the ruins that afternoon was a tremendous relief.

Like Aguateca, Dos Pilas is rather modest in size. The ruins were first reported in the early 1950s, and the first archaeological expedition occurred in 1960. When we visited, the site had still been only partially cleared and not yet excavated or restored. In fact, since 1960, archaeologists had visited the site only infrequently and had taken photographs of monuments and done rubbings of some of the intricately carved stelae and a glyph-carved limestone stairway, known as the Hieroglyphic Stairway I. Although parts of Stela 16 had deteriorated, the main image on the carved limestone monument depicted an imposing male figure, possibly a ruler, in sharp detail and high relief. He was realistically portrayed in richly detailed ceremonial regalia that included an elaborately embroidered tunic, necklace, wrist cuffs, and shield-shaped chest pectoral as well as a dramatic headdress. The remnants of Stairway I that had been cleared of jungle overgrowth, although also poorly preserved, had limestone risers faced with beautifully detailed, crisp hieroglyphic images carved in high relief. Although scholars speculated the site might be much larger, relatively little was known about Dos Pilas and few of the hieroglyphics had been deciphered.[8] The leading guide to Mesoamerican ruins at the time gave Dos Pilas a rating of "one star" due to the fact that it was the most difficult site to reach of all one hundred forty sites discussed in the guidebook.[9]

Despite its small size, meager structures, and difficult accessibility, I loved every minute of our stay. I relished the steamy jungle setting, mysterious hieroglyphics, and meticulous stone carvings of magnificently attired individuals who appeared to be rulers or priests. Twice I was able to get away from the group and perform ceremonies like the one I did at Tikal. Sitting on the jungle floor, surrounded by monumental carved stelae and piles of weathered stone blocks from decomposed, ancient structures, I said prayers and sang sacred songs for the ancient and living Maya. By this time I was beginning to doubt that I would have any supernatural experiences on this trip and, sure enough, I didn't have one here. But I was finding something profoundly moving in the simple act of being prayerful.

ALTAR DE SACRIFICIOS, GUATEMALA

The hike out of Dos Pilas seemed easier than the trip in. We were better prepared mentally and had learned that drinking lots of water to stay hydrated made a world of difference. We took the lanchas back to the fishing camp to spend the night, and were back on the water early the next morning. We left the lagoon and headed up the Petexbatún River to the Pasión River and then motored upstream toward where the Pasión and Salinas rivers converge to form the Usumacinta River. Our destination was the ancient Maya site called the Altar de Sacrificios (Altar of Sacrifice), located on a small island along the southern bank of the Pasión River. Also a modest site, Altar de Sacrificios was first discovered in the 1890s and investigated by archaeologists from the Peabody Museum of Archaeology and Ethnology from 1958 to 1963.[10] The site was first inhabited between 800 and 600 BCE. Altar de Sacrificios grew to dominate the river trade route and reached its peak in the seventh century CE. Its fortunes waxed and waned over the next two hundred years and archaeologists believe the site was abandoned by 950 CE. Three small main building complexes and two plazas cover an area approximately 1300 by 1300 feet.

It didn't take long to study the ceremonial structures and the twenty-nine inscribed monuments (most badly eroded and unreadable) on the small site, including a small temple-pyramid, ball court, burial tombs, stelae, and carved altar stones. Again, I was able to leave the group and find a somewhat secluded spot near Altar 3 to perform a ceremony.[11] I burned copal, laid my prayer flags and ties on the altar, sat cross-legged on the ground, sang sacred songs, and prayed for the Maya. This time I had absolutely no thoughts about the other worlds and just let myself be immersed in the experience of prayer and song. As I finished, I had a startling realization. Several years earlier I had asked Bear Heart what the purpose of a vision quest was and he had replied with one word: worship. I finally understood what he meant; there was no other "purpose"—just the experience of the sacred.

BONAMPAK, MEXICO

When we had finished our exploration, we boarded the lanchas and continued upstream. We were traveling in a northwesterly direction on the Usumacinta River, the natural boundary between Guatemala to the northeast and Mexico to the southwest. Our immediate destination was Frontera Corozal, a small border town on the Mexico side of the river. This community was founded in 1976 by families from indigenous Ch'ol, Lacandon, and Tzeltal Maya groups. We learned from our guides that the Maya at the Frontera community were living descendants of the ancient Maya who, contrary to popular belief, had never "disappeared." Although some ancient Maya cities were abandoned by the time of the Spanish Conquest in the 1500s, Maya groups in Mexico, Guatemala, and Honduras were still thriving.

Our lanchas put in at Frontera Corozal, where we left the river and piled into the back of a vintage 1930s logging truck for a rough two-hour trip over old, rutted, dirt roads to a trailhead leading to the ruins of the ancient Maya city of Bonampak. After a two-hour hike through the Lacandon jungle, we finally arrived at a small, unimposing site containing one of the most spectacular treasures we would see on the trip. Bonampak was first seen by a group of Americans in 1946 when they were taken to visit the ruins by local Lacandon Maya who still performed spiritual ceremonies in the ruins. The site was given the name Bonampak ("painted walls" in modern Mayan) by the noted archaeologist Sylvanus Morley, in recognition of the spectacular frescos that archaeologists discovered in Structure I, Temple of the Murals.

These ancient fresco murals are Bonampak's treasures. They were painted on the interior walls of a long, narrow temple structure built atop a relatively low, stepped pyramid base. The temple had three mural-covered rooms, each with a unique series of scenes and images. The murals date from 790 CE; artists used natural pigments to paint images onto moist freshly-applied plaster on the temple walls and vaulted ceilings. Although it had been a long, arduous, uncomfortable trip to reach this place, my fatigue evaporated almost immediately as I stood in front of these brilliant, exquisitely detailed works of art. They were as stunning and breathtaking as any artistic masterworks in the world; Bonampak's reputation as the "The Sistine Chapel of the Americas" is well deserved.

The walls and vaulted ceilings of each of the three rooms were entirely covered with magnificent lifelike scenes from the Maya world of thirteen hundred years ago, and each had a built-in, rough-hewn stone bench positioned to allow a seated visitor a magnificent 360 degree view of the dramatic images. Featuring human figures about two-thirds life size, scenes included a royal family and attending nobles, war scenes and captive prisoners, ritual blood-sacrifice, musicians, singers, dancers, and actors. All were amazingly realistic and were rendered in stunning red, blue, green, and yellow hues that, although faded, were remarkably intense and well preserved. As I stepped into each room, I was surrounded and immersed in ceremony and ritual so alive that the painted participants seemed to be moving and the drama unfolding before my eyes. The gorgeous murals brought the ancient Maya civilization to life for me, and suddenly their long-abandoned and deserted cities seemed reborn.

While I was in the temple, others in the group joined me and then left to explore other parts of the city, but I didn't want to leave. I could have spent days in those three rooms and still not have had enough time to absorb all I was witnessing. At some point, however, I realized it was impossible to take it all in, so I decided to see a little more of the ruins before we had to leave. When I walked around the site, the bleached, weathered stone structures took on new meaning for me as I superimposed scenes from the murals onto the architecture around me. Bonampak seemed infused with the fullness and richness of the mural images, and for the first time I experienced the humanity of the ancient Maya and their civilization. Their joys and sorrows, triumphs and tragedies, and hopes and fears all seemed as real to me as my own.

It was mid-afternoon when we started our hike back to the trailhead. Just before we boarded the truck, we were approached by some Lacandon Maya who lived in the area. I spoke very little

Spanish but enough to let one of the young men know I would like to purchase some copal. He ran off through the jungle and returned a few minutes later with a sticky, fist-size ball of fresh copal resin. I had never seen fresh copal resin before, only dried, brittle chunks. This was copal in the form that contemporary shamans, and presumably ancient priests, used for their ceremonies. As I held the copal in my hand I had a startling shift in perception—back in L.A. the copal would have very little monetary value, but at this moment, for me, it was a small, precious treasure. Even without burning, the fresh copal had a pungent, sweet aroma that faintly resembled fresh pine sap. The smell of the sticky resin had a wonderfully calming effect on me, and I knew it would help make the long truck ride back more bearable.

YAXCHILAN, MEXICO

The sun was just starting to dip below the horizon when we arrived back at Frontera Corozal. I felt incredibly relieved to be off the truck and back by the water. The setting couldn't have been more magical. An enormous full moon was just beginning to rise; near the equator, the moon looks almost three times as large as it does in the States. The warm moisture-laden air was filled with the rich musky odors of the jungle, mingled with the crisp clean scent of the river. We sat on the bank of the Usumacinta waiting for two *cayucos*, small local fishing boats, that were to take us further upriver to the ancient Maya city of Yaxchilan. It had been a long tiring day of travel. Four hours in the truck and four hours hiking had been strenuous, but the trip to Bonampak had been worth the effort and waiting by the river seemed to rejuvenate us all.

Yaxchilan, like Palenque, which lies one hundred eighteen miles to the northwest, is situated within the spectacular, luxuriant Lacandon rainforest, the largest in North American continent. The

Lacandon is one of the most biodiverse areas in the world, with a stunning array of wildlife that includes scarlet macaws, eagles, tapirs, spider monkeys, howler monkeys, and swamp crocodiles—all increasingly rare or already endangered species. It is also one of the last jungles in North America to support jaguars, animals highly revered by ancient Maya rulers, who often chose jaguars to be their animal spirit doubles because they were the most powerful and dangerous animals known to them. The jungle rainforest was just starting to come alive with the sound of nocturnal fauna.

It was dark when the two weathered cayucos, with their small, battered outboard motors, finally arrived to pick us up. I could tell immediately by their dilapidated appearance and poor state of repair that the boats were used for everyday life on the river by the impoverished Maya who lived nearby, and weren't designed for tourist traffic. We made our way slowly, cautiously downriver, using moonlight and the boatmen's hand-held flashlights to keep an eye out for floating debris. Shallows and occasional rapids were a constant source of concern on the river, but we finally reached Yaxchilan without a mishap. As we stepped onto the riverbank we could see the dark shadowy silhouettes of the monumental ruins on the hills above us. I found myself as relieved to be off the river as I had been earlier to be off the trucks.

Using our flashlights, we unloaded our gear from the cayucos and headed toward our campsite at the entrance to the ancient ceremonial center. The trees and vegetation were too thick to allow a view of the ruins that night and it was late enough that everyone just wanted to get some rest. The jungle around us was alive with the sounds of wildlife and it was hard for me to sleep. But I felt as though I were in a paradise a million miles and thousands of years away from home.

Early the next morning, after breakfast, we followed the main trail a short distance to the entrance to the ancient city. The only way to enter the ceremonial precinct was through a massive building known as the Labyrinth. Constructed sometime between 400 and 800 CE to represent the Maya Lower World, this three-level structure consists of nine vaulted chambers, connected by sixteen long passageways. Once we stepped inside, this architectural arrangement plunged us into absolute darkness. Using flashlights, we followed the primary route through the Labyrinth and emerged abruptly onto the Main Plaza, a broad, elongated terrace platform elevated thirty feet above the level of the river. The brilliant sunlight was quite a shock after the darkness of the Labyrinth.

Once my eyes adjusted to the daylight, I was stunned by the beauty and majesty of the site. At the time I knew very little about Yaxchilan, and the only colored photographs I'd seen of the site had been in an October 1985 *National Geographic* article.[12] As I took my time walking through the Main Plaza, I was overwhelmed by the incredible setting. We were surrounded by towering ceiba, mahogany, cedar, and gum trees covered with long, hanging, ropy vines and jungle flowers. Enough low brush and jungle overgrowth had been cleared to reveal the exquisite architecture and sculpture of the city, but dense jungle nonetheless pressed in on all sides. Trails and ancient stone staircases led up the steep hillsides to temples, stelae, and massive stone ceremonial altars.

Looking out from the Main Plaza, I could see the graceful bend of the Usumacinta River that cradled the ancient city. Starting in the mountains of Guatemala, the river flows six hundred miles northwest to the Gulf of Mexico. Yaxchilan had been built on the Mexico side of the river at a point where the land protrudes into a great horseshoe-shaped bend. From the riverbank, the land rises dramatically in a series of naturally terraced hills. Unlike other Maya sites, where temples were constructed on stone pyramids that represented sacred mountains, here temples and other ceremonial structures, some as high as six hundred feet above the river, were built high on the natural hillside terraces. Stone steps up to these structures were built into the terraces.

We spent two amazing days here in the most beautiful setting imaginable, studying magnificent sacred architecture, faded murals, and extraordinary stone carvings. Yaxchilan lacks the colossal monumental structures and grand temple-pyramids of Tikal, but it has many of the finest stone bas reliefs of the ancient Maya kingdoms. In addition to hieroglyphic stairways and carved stone altars and stelae, Yaxchilan is known for its exquisitely carved stone lintels. Many of the ancient stone carvings are remarkably well-preserved and, as a result, have enabled scholars to make dramatic advances in deciphering texts and understanding the political and spiritual life of the ancient Maya.

Our guides pointed out altars, stelae, and lintels adorned with strikingly detailed portrayals of rulers ascending to the throne, ritual blood sacrifices, symbolic ball games, royal lineage histories, and key calendar dates. Hour by hour, the splendor of the ancient Maya civilization seemed to come alive through the dramatic artworks surrounding us. I spent most of my time at Yaxchilan with our group, learning of the latest academic findings. But I had planned to spend a portion of our last afternoon at the site doing a ceremony on my own at Temple 33 situated on the hill above the plaza. The temple had captured my imagination because if its imposing size (by far the tallest structure at the site) and its magnificent location overlooking the Usumacinta River. I waited until I knew the group would be visiting a different part of the ruins and then walked to the northeastern edge of the plaza where a magnificent structure, the Grand Staircase, leads up the hill to the temple.

Temple 33 was dedicated to Yaxun Balam IV ('Bird Jaguar IV,' the name preferred by scholars), ruler of Yaxchilan from 752 to 768 CE.[13] During his reign, which began when he was forty-three years old, Bird Jaguar distinguished himself as one of the most energetic rulers of the Classic period. Although he led several minor military incursions, he is best known for his ambitious building campaign and architectural transformation of Yaxchilan. He was responsible for the new construction or major modification of a dozen structures, including Temple 33. This imposing temple-pyramid, also sometimes referred to as the Palace, is a masterpiece of Maya architecture and Yaxchilan's most famous ceremonial edifice.

With the river at my back, I slowly climbed the massive stone steps that ascended the hillside until I reached a small, level plaza. The temple was situated at the far side of the plaza atop a tiered stone platform. In the middle of the plaza, an extremely large stalactite shaft—somewhat like a stone tree trunk—had been set into a shallow pit approximately fifteen feet in front of the temple. The extraordinary temple and the carved stela-like stalactite shaft[14] were absolutely breathtaking.

I paused at the stalactite to spend a few minutes studying the temple. The wide structure has three doorways that open into a long, narrow corridor with four alcoves along the back wall. The alcove behind the central doorway contains a larger-than-life-sized seated figure some scholars believe represents Bird Jaguar. The figure, though originally intact, was decapitated at some point; its head now rests on the temple floor. Above the doorways and main body of the temple is a taller, magnificently carved stone frieze capped by a spectacular, double-sided roof comb—composed of a tall lattice of stonework ornately decorated with high-relief stucco representations scholars believe may be of deities, supernatural beings, or important rulers. A niche in the center of the roof comb contains the remains of a life-sized, modeled stucco sculpture seated on a throne.

Continuing on, I climbed a series of intricately carved stone steps and risers to reach the temple itself.[15] I then sat cross-legged on the platform in front of the center doorway, facing northeast toward the Usumacinta River with my back to the seated sculpture thought to be of Bird Jaguar. Because of the position of the temple at the back edge of the terrace, the river wasn't visible from where I was seated, but I did have a fabulous view of the luxuriant Lacandon jungle stretching to the horizon on the Guatemala side of the river. As was the case during most of our time at Yaxchilan, there were no other visitors or groups at the site, so I was completely alone at the temple. Taking in the expansiveness of the view and the extraordinary beauty of the setting, I felt wonderfully removed from the cares and preoccupations of everyday life.

I had come prepared to conduct one last ceremony before the trip ended. This time I had no preconceived expectations. I was here to give thanks for the privilege of experiencing these sacred surroundings and to offer prayers for the ancient Maya ancestors and their descendants. I carefully took my prayer ties and flags out of my bag and placed them on the steps beside me. I set my bowl in front of me, lit a piece of charcoal, and placed it on a layer of earth on the bottom of the bowl. I then placed a large chunk of the Bonampak copal on the glowing charcoal and watched as a dense cloud of smoke snaked up into the sky. The sweet, pungent aroma of copal filled the air. Taking a deep, centering breath, I used my cupped hands to draw the smoke over my body. This was always a magical time for me as the ceremonial energies started to shift.

After unwrapping my ceremonial bundle, I first laid the prayer flags across my lap, passed them through the copal smoke several times to cleanse and purify them, and then placed them on the steps. Again I picked up the flags and passed them through the copal smoke. Something about the stalactite stela in front of the temple had captivated me the moment I saw it, and I instinctively decided to attach my prayer flags to it. In the North American Plains Indian tradition, prayer flags are often tied around the circumference of a tree trunk. Each flag is positioned on the trunk in the direction its unique color represents. I decided to honor this tradition and place the flags on the stalactite the way I had during ceremonies back in the States.

I walked to the stela and began to carefully tie the prayer flags on the stalactite, reaching up to fasten them above my head. Each flag was about eighteen inches long and seven inches wide with a round one-inch ball of tobacco tied in the cloth at the top. The string I used to tie the tobacco ball was intentionally left long so it could be used to fasten the flags to a tree limb or trunk. I tied four colored flags around the stela in the cardinal direction that each color represents in the Lakota Indian tradition (black for the west, red for the north, yellow for the east and white for the south). I was not aware then the traditional Maya color combinations were slightly different. I positioned the blue flag (representing the sky) and green flag (representing the earth) above and below the other flags.

After returning to the place where I had been sitting in front of the center of the temple, I placed another chunk of copal on the charcoal in front of me and watched another dense plume of scented smoke rise toward the heavens. As I gazed at the stalactite in front of me, it seemed to have let go of its earthly moorings and become suspended in time and space. It was surrounded by a vibrant, pulsating energy field radiating from its central core. Behind me, I sensed the temple radiating a complementary field of vibrant, pulsating energy. In some strange way I didn't understand, it seemed as if the stalactite were becoming "activated" and functioning as a cosmic lightning rod or homing beacon opening a portal to the other worlds. This was not at all what I had expected and I started to feel anxious. I had no idea what might happen now or what I should do.

I watched, incredulous, as the stalactite seemed to break free from the constraints of physical reality. The hard stone stela that had been so solid and secure only moments before was transforming into an ethereal spectral presence from another dimension. The solid form of the stalactite appeared to have receded into the background as its energetic aspect moved to the foreground. The stalactite seemed to be connected to an energy vortex located deep within the other worlds, tethered by some sort of cosmic umbilical cord. Its pulsing and vibrating synchronized with a distant rhythm emanating from within the unseen realms. Energy pulsed from the vortex through the cord and into the stalactite, making it vibrate like a tuning fork.

Rhythmic concentric rings of energy pulsed out from the stela like ripples moving across the surface of a still lake. These pulses pushed through the air, engulfing the temple and surrounding areas. In the process, the boundary between physical and non-physical reality seemed to shift, replicating the energetic shift the stela had undergone just minutes before. Across the entire platform the otherworldly non-physical aspect of the stela, temple, and ceremonial site moved to the foreground—completely present, fully realized, and perfectly manifested. It appeared as if a veil that usually separates physical and non-physical reality had been lifted and a barrier between the two had opened completely. I decided to continue my ceremony, hoping I would be protected from anything that might come through from the other side.

I picked up my prayer ties and held them in my hand as I started to sing the same series of sacred songs I had sung at Tikal. The fragrance of the copal and the feeling of the prayer ties were comforting; the melody and tones of the songs helped me stay centered and grounded. My anxiety slowly subsided and I let myself open to an expanded sense of aliveness and inner peace. As I came to the end of my last song, I found myself wishing I could keep singing, but every song had a prescribed format and I didn't want to violate the tradition I'd been taught to follow. I took a deep breath as the last tones from the last song faded into the distance.

The energy around the stalactite and the temple had subsided; the entire setting was pervaded with calmness and peacefulness.

I sat looking out past the stalactite toward the vast Lacandon jungle on the other side of the Usumacinta River. I'd finally gotten to the point where I simply appreciated the time spent in ceremony without any expectations about a specific outcome. My thoughts had even started to drift to other ceremonies I'd done at other ruins earlier in the trip when I suddenly felt a large, strong hand on my shoulder. A wave of pure terror shot through my body and a hundred panicked thoughts instantly raced through my mind. I was frozen to the spot with my heart racing and my palms sweaty.

I was sure I was completely alone up here. The Grand Staircase was the only access to the temple. The entire temple-pyramid structure was surrounded by dense, seemingly impenetrable jungle; only the stairway and small area immediately around the temple had been cleared. If anyone had come up the stairs I would have seen them. A picture flashed into my mind of a photo in the October 1985 *National Geographic* article of masked, heavily-armed, Guatemalan guerrillas who frequently crossed the river into this area. The guerrillas' incursions were the result of the Guatemala Civil War (1960-1996), fought mostly between the government of Guatemala and the indigenous Maya peoples. The government forces were later condemned for widespread human rights violations and for committing genocide against the Maya population. I wondered if somehow they had entered the temple area through the jungle and now were confronting me. I took a deep breath, expecting something bad to happen any moment, but nothing did.

I took another breath and started to regain my composure. I realized there was nothing aggressive or threatening about the hand on my shoulder. I thought to myself that if I were going to be attacked, it would have happened by now; I also realized that no words had been spoken. Shifting my weight, I turned to face whoever was behind me. No one was there; I was completely alone. For a second I thought I might be imagining things but I could still feel the warm imprint and pressure from the hand on my shoulder. The experience seemed so real and so vivid that I was sure I wasn't making it up. The only explanation that seemed plausible was that someone had reached out and physically contacted me from the other worlds.

I felt disoriented, weak, and shaken. While I was relieved there didn't seem to be any imminent danger, I was also perplexed as I tried to find a rational explanation. My thoughts turned to the portal that had opened through the energetic action of the stalactite. Whatever had happened, I knew it was time for me to complete the ceremony. I finished my prayers, walked to the stalactite to retrieve my prayer flags, returned to rewrap my flags and ties in a bundle, and repacked my bag. The bottom of my bowl was still hot from the charcoal so I carried it by the rim as I left the temple area without looking back. I carefully began to descend the Grand Staircase. Before reaching the bottom, I spotted my group at the far end of the Main Plaza. I took a few deep breaths as I walked over to them and tried to push my experience at the temple out of my mind.

That evening, our last at Yaxchilan, was as pleasant as any on the trip. I thought I might have a harrowing night like the one I'd had at Palenque two years earlier, but nothing out of the ordinary happened. I didn't mention the spirit contact to anyone, including Julie, and hoped that either the memory would fade or I would find an explanation later on.

We knew that being back in Los Angeles would require quite a readjustment, but we were ready to get back to work. It had been great to be so disconnected from our professional responsibilities for a little while, but work projects and commitments awaited us. As usual, getting caught up was so demanding and stressful that some of the memories of the trip faded quickly. Yet my experience at the temple that last afternoon still troubled me. Shortly after returning home, I had the opportunity to meet with Bear Heart and attend an inipi ceremony at a friend's house in Burbank. I took my prayer flags and ties from the trip into the sweat lodge that night, and during the prayer round I asked for help and guidance in understanding and integrating the experiences I'd had on the trip.

Later, after the ceremony, I spoke with Bear Heart about the trip and my encounter at the temple. By that time, I was certain that someone had reached out to me from the other worlds. Bear Heart agreed and told me that this was a powerful, protective spirit who was offering to help me on my spiritual journey. He told me that even though I had never experienced anything quite like this before on my vision quests with him, this type of contact with a tutelary or guardian spirit was a fairly common occurrence during indigenous spiritual rites. Bear Heart offered his guidance on working with this spirit and told me this could become a lifelong relationship if that was my wish. He then instructed me to burn my prayer flags and prayer ties from the trip in the inipi fire.

I watched with some sadness as the smoke from my flags and ties rose and disappeared above me, releasing all the accumulated energy from the sacred sites I had visited. The words of the ancestor spirit I had encountered on the steps of Temple I at Tikal suddenly came back to me with clarity and force, as if he were once again just behind me: "You can come here as a tourist or you can come here as a priest, but you can't do both." I realized that this trip had been a turning point for me. While my first trip had been a series of initiatory experiences and rites of passage, with this trip I had moved deeper into the spirit realm of the ancient Maya. My new role would be that of intermediary and intercessor: working with the ancestors and supernatural beings to bring forth their wisdom and healing energies.

I knew the spiritual challenge for me now was to integrate the insights I'd gained into my everyday world for my own healing and for the benefit of others. I had no idea how long it would be before

I would once again visit the sacred ceremonial centers, but I knew I would return. In the meantime, I vowed to stay connected to the spirit realm and honor my visions.

Chapter Notes

1. Schele and Miller 1986: 42
2. Ibid., 284
3. Ibid., 42
4. Ibid., 55
5. During our visit in 1987, all the structures in Tikal were open to visitors. When I returned to Tikal in 2007, Temples I and II, as well as other structures, were closed to visitors and it was not possible to climb the pyramids.
6. Martin and Grube 2008: 44
7. Ibid., 46
8. Major excavations at Dos Pilas started in 1989 and continued through 1994. As a result of building restoration and hieroglyphic decipherment during those years, the history of Dos Pilas has been reconstructed with an exceptional level of detail that is generally unmatched at other ancient Maya cities.
9. Kelly 1982: 459
10. Sharer and Traxler 2006: 407
11. The term "altar" is used by archaeologists to describe large carved stone sculptures associated with temples and other ceremonial buildings. The altars I've seen are typically squat, circular, drum-shaped sculptures that range in height from several inches to two-feet with a diameter of one to two feet. They are carved from single blocks of stone and often weigh between six hundred pounds and a ton or more. The altars are richly decorated with intricate hieroglyphic carvings scholars speculate are depictions of important ceremonial rituals or political events.

12. Wilkerson, Jeffery K. and David Hiser (photography). "The Usumacinta River: Troubles on a wild Frontier." *National Geographic* Oct. 1985: 514–543.
13. Martin and Grube 2008: 128
14. The stalactite stela, referred to by archaeologists as "Stela 31," has since been removed from the site and I have been unable to learn its current location. Pictures of Temple 33 that show Stela 31 in the foreground are included in Kelly 1982: 207 and Tate 1992: "Author Photos."
15. Although I was unaware of this at the time, the stairs and risers comprised Yaxchilan's famed Hieroglyphic Stairway. The sculptured stones depict, among other things, a ceremonial ball game, key political events of Bird Jaguar's life, and female members of the royal family (Martin and Grube 2008: 130).

REVELATION

PAKAL'S JOURNEY
TO THE WORLD TREE

PALENQUE
CHIAPAS, MEXICO — 2007

A light mist was rising from the dew-moistened grass as I headed toward the northern boundary of the Main Plaza at Palenque, looking for a place to sit and tune into the energy of the sacred site. Just beyond the main tourist path through the ruins, a towering, stately tree was growing in a semi-secluded area of the plaza. It seemed like the perfect spot to spend a little time before exploring the ruins. I found a place to sit on the ground at the base of the tree, between gnarled roots that protruded from the lower trunk and descended into the earth. Sitting cross-legged, I leaned back against the trunk, shaded by the tree's dense foliage high above. From my position I had a perfect view of the Temple of Inscriptions in front of me to the south, the Cross Group to the southeast, and the Palace to the east.

Palenque, known in antiquity as 'Lakamha', meaning "Great Water", was the first ceremonial center site I was visiting during a three-week solo pilgrimage to ancient Maya sites in Mexico, Guatemala, and

Honduras. I planned to stop at several ruins I had visited many years earlier and one I hadn't—the ceremonial center called Copan in Honduras, site of the stela that had first captivated me as a young boy. I had started in Mexico City earlier in the week and from there had flown to Villahermosa and then traveled by bus to Palenque, finally arriving the night before. Being back at Palenque was a homecoming of sorts for me and it seemed as if a new adventure was finally underway.

Seeing the Temple of Inscriptions, the Temple of the Foliated Cross, and the Palace in the distance brought back vivid memories of my visit more than twenty years earlier. Although the ancient ceremonial structures were exactly as they had been before, many other things had changed. The archaeological park at Palenque had a beautiful new museum and archaeologists had made exciting new discoveries since I'd been there last. Recent excavations at Temples XIX and XXI, previously identified but never before cleared and studied, had yielded a wealth of momentous hieroglyphic inscriptions and extraordinary bas relief sculptures. A magnificent tomb had been discovered within Temple XIII, next to Pakal's temple-pyramid, and was believed to contain the sarcophagus of Pakal's wife. Other lesser tombs had been discovered and new ceremonial structures had been excavated. Tourism had increased dramatically, so I knew it would be impossible to have the privacy I'd had before. The Palace Tower, Temple of Inscriptions, and Pakal's tomb were off-limits this time due to the influx of visitors. The nearby town of Palenque, where I was staying, had grown substantially over the years and was much more congested now.

Sitting in the plaza once again it was hard for me to believe it had taken me twenty years to return to the sacred sites of the ancient Maya. Other activities in my life had taken precedence. The small, start-up consulting firm I joined in 1982 had grown dramatically in the late 1980s and through the 1990s. In December 1987, the same year as our River of Ruins trip, Inc. Magazine had included the firm in "The Inc. 500" list of fastest growing companies in the country. The growth had been exciting, but it also required constant travel during the week and sometimes on the weekends. Outside of work, I'd also been doing pro bono consulting for a variety of service organizations. And finally, Julie and I had started a family. In 1990 our first son, Nick, was born, followed six years later by our second son, Chris. Those twenty years had been an extremely busy, challenging time.

The challenges of international travel in the mid-'80s and early '90s were compounded by the fact that there were no cell phones, PDAs, truly portable laptops, or internet cafes, so staying in touch—a necessity now in my private and professional life—had been a real problem. Because of my commitments at work, responsibilities raising a young family, and Julie starting a new career, I'd long felt that another long trip to Mexico or Guatemala wasn't possible.

Throughout those years, however, I'd continued to study with Michael Harner and Bear Heart, and I'd participated regularly in sweat lodges and annual vision quests with indigenous elders and friends. In the summer of 1990, I completed a traditional Plains Indian style Sun Dance at Pilot Rock, near Ashland, Oregon. Beginning in 1993, I spent two weeks of each of the next five summers on the Pine Ridge Indian Reservation in South Dakota, studying with indigenous Oglala Lakota spiritual leaders and participating in inipi, yuwipi, and vision quest ceremonies. On a shorter trip to the reservation during an overnight hanblechya in 2000, I had my direct encounter with the Divine, which I recounted in the Prologue. During those twenty years, although my spiritual work continued primarily with American Indian elders in the western United States, I also participated in two, ten-day Centering Prayer retreats at St. Benedict's Monastery in Snowmass Colorado, and several personal three-day silent retreats at Pendle Hill, the Quaker retreat center near Philadelphia.

In November 1989, I had the good fortune to be introduced to Maya Elder Hunbatz Men when he was visiting Los Angeles. His book, *Secrets of Mayan Science/Religion*, had just been published and a mutual friend made arrangements for us to meet. Maestro Hunbatz, who passed away in 2016, was born in Wenkal, Yucatan, and was an authentic Mayan Daykeeper and authority on the history, chronology, calendars, and cosmic knowledge of the Maya civilization. He is also a highly respected ceremonial leader and founder of the Mayan Itza Council. I found him charismatic, engaging, and enormously generous with his time and knowledge. During our several conversations we discussed the topics in his new book and he led me to a greater understanding of ancient Maya history, calendars, metaphysics, and cosmic knowledge.

I told Maestro Hunbatz about my visions at the ancient ceremonial centers and asked him why they had been so incredibly intense, much more so than any I had ever experienced on my quests in North America. He explained that the sacred sites vibrate at a "higher dimensional frequency," and as a result can raise a person's consciousness to "receive cosmic wisdom" and "information from higher dimensions of existence." Part of the genius of the ancient Maya, he observed, was their ability to design ceremonial structures to "store" sacred knowledge and facilitate access to "higher levels of consciousness." Maestro Hunbatz also stated that the sacred sites are still active and "alive" today and that performing ceremonies creates an "affinity that allows even more information to be revealed."

I was particularly grateful for the time he spent with me discussing and interpreting specific visions I had received. Sitting in the dimly lit underground kiva I had built behind our house in Hancock Park,[1] we talked about the Otherworld of the Maya; about Hunab-Ku the Absolute Being and our relationship to the Divine; about the ancient Maya concept of the three aspects of self—physical, soul and spirit; about the World Tree, Wakah-Kan, and its role in awakening consciousness within us; and about the Celestial Bird and the Moon Goddess, Ix-Chel. As I relived my visionary experiences with Maestro Hunbatz, the memories returned with stunning clarity and seemed to imbed themselves deeper and more profoundly in my consciousness, becoming part of my spiritual DNA. His encouragement and support were incredible gifts.[2]

Earlier in 1989, I met and began studying with Thomas Mails, a former Lutheran Minister who was a prolific author, artist, student of Native American spirituality, and gifted teacher. Tom's intimate knowledge of the esoteric aspects of Plains and Pueblo Indian spirituality provided a foundation for my understanding of the spiritual wisdom of these indigenous peoples. Those insights unexpectedly helped me penetrate the deep universal spiritual truths behind many of the sacred rituals and ceremonial practices of the ancient Maya decades after I first met Tom.

Although I had years of experience with Plains Indian ceremonial practices, I was still fascinated with the Pueblo Indian ceremonies I had first encountered at the Field Museum, as a boy. As much as I'd longed for the opportunity, I'd never been able to participate in a contemporary Pueblo Indian ceremony. I had carefully studied dozens of detailed ethnographic accounts written in the late 1800s and early 1900s, but none of them revealed an inner psychology of the sacred ceremonies. As a result of his work with Pueblo elders, Tom was able to reveal the inner meaning of these practices through his writings and workshops. With Tom's help, I finally understood the meaning of the sacred altars and kiva rituals that had captivated me as a child, and I comprehended the inner essence of the fascinating ceremonies I'd read about in ethnographic manuscripts. It was my sincerest hope that the knowledge I had gained of the esoteric spiritual wisdom teachings of the Plains and Pueblo Indians might provide me with insights into the lost wisdom teachings of the ancient Maya.

By 2006, the obstacles to continuing my spiritual travels had lifted. My sons were more independent, I had started my own consulting firm which allowed more control over my schedule, and technological advances enabled me to stay in touch; cell phone access was possible even at the most remote sites. With those conditions met, I started planning this trip to revisit ancient Maya ceremonial sites in Mexico, Guatemala, and Honduras. I was excited about experiencing the sacred spiritual centers using the new insights I had gained from Hunbatz Men, Tom Mails, and Plains Indian ceremonial rituals.

I would also be carrying new knowledge on this trip thanks to the continuing advances in deciphering hieroglyphic texts and understanding ancient Maya artistic imagery. Scholars had decoded texts that detailed royal lineages, kingship successions, military campaigns, political strife, and regime changes spanning hundreds of years at key sites. A much clearer picture of ancient Maya metaphysics had also emerged that confirmed the shamanic foundation of their core spiritual beliefs and documented the actual presence of deities, supernaturals, and ancestor spirits during ancient ceremonial rituals. Scholars now knew that "[deities, supernaturals and ancestor spirits] formed as much a part of society as any royals, nobles, farmers, artisans or traders."[3] Recent research had also confirmed the ancient Maya belief that all things in the universe were inhabited with an invisible, sacred quality, k'uh, the Divine principal I'd experienced on my vision quest.

I had started this trip by spending two days in Mexico City visiting the National Museum of Anthropology in Chapultepec Park instead of immediately going back to any Maya ceremonial sites. Julie and I had visited the museum briefly during our previous trip, but this time I had planned to spend much more time there visiting the numerous exhibits on all the indigenous cultures throughout Mexico, particularly those dedicated to the Maya. I was particularly eager to see an exhibit featuring a complete reproduction of Pakal's sarcophagus.

When I stood inside Pakal's actual tomb at the Temple of Inscriptions back in 1989, the cramped quarters made it extremely difficult, and at times impossible, to see the intricately detailed and beautifully executed images carved on the vertical surfaces of the limestone sarcophagus, and the life-size, modeled stucco bas relief figures on the walls of the tomb. But at the museum all these years later, I clearly saw the gorgeous sarcophagus images, ten figures representing Pakal's parents and royal predecessors, all historically identified and spectacularly depicted "emerging as trees sprouting from the earth."[4] It was an incredible and humbling experience to be able to view and understand the significance of imagery in Pakal's tomb and on his sarcophagus.

After I had finished studying and taking notes on the sarcophagus exhibit, I walked over to a large vertical display containing reproductions of his skeleton and the breathtakingly beautiful funerary objects discovered in his tomb: a full-face mask made of hundreds of exquisitely crafted pieces of green jade fashioned into a stunningly lifelike mosaic symbolizing rebirth and new life, a magnificent jade belt incorporating images of three masks, a jade sphere symbolizing the sky and the heavens, and a jade cube symbolizing the earth and the Lower World. The amazingly lifelike mask was beautifully modeled to match the contours of his face with white and black inlays for the whites and pupils of his eyes. The effect was stunning; Pakal's piercing gaze had reached deep inside me, his slightly parted lips opened as if to reveal a secret. The ancient ruler of a magnificent city seemed almost to come to life before my eyes.

There had been several times in my life when I had thought about pursuing a career as an archaeologist or anthropologist. I had also had times when I had wondered what would have happened if I'd started this spiritual journey with the Maya when I was younger, before starting a career or a family. Those thoughts returned as I stood there, captivated by Pakal's death mask. What would my life have been like if I'd gone to live with a Maya shaman in Mexico or Guatemala in my twenties instead of leaving for Los Angeles to start a career in business? I knew I had made the right decisions about my marriage, my family, and my career; to have missed those experiences would have been a mistake. But I also realized that having one foot in the world of commerce and the other in the world of spirit all these years had been a continual challenge for me. I was reaching a time in my life when I needed to honor my deepest longings and respond more directly to the inner call to the sacred that had been with me all these years. There at the museum, the pilgrimage I was about to undertake seemed to be my destiny.

The screech of a howler monkey jolted me out of my reverie, but as I continued to sit under the grand tree in the Main Plaza of Palenque, my thoughts kept returning to Pakal. I recalled my journey twenty years ago, deep into the heart of the temple-pyramid that stood across from where I was now, at the burial place of this ancient city's most iconic ruler. I mentally superimposed the dramatic images from the museum exhibit onto the tomb and sarcophagus surfaces I hadn't been able to see clearly at the time. I would not be able to revisit the tomb itself, since it had been closed to the public, but at least I could visit the ceremonial complex of temple-pyramids. However, before I ventured farther into the complex, I wanted to honor the memory of Pakal. Reaching into my small day pack, I removed the prayer ties and flags I had prepared specifically for my pilgrimage, a packet of copal, and a small bowl. I hoped I could perform a short ceremony without attracting attention from any of the park's other visitors.

Although it was still early morning, I was far from alone. Several tour groups and other, unguided visitors were already exploring the ruins. Local Maya artisans were setting up displays of sculpture, pottery, jewelry, and textiles on blankets near tourist paths between ancient ceremonial structures. Fortunately for me, almost everyone who entered the ruins focused on the major temple-pyramids farther into the site, so the southern border of the plaza was relatively deserted. I set my bowl in front of me, in line with Pakal's tomb at the other side of the plaza, lit a piece of charcoal, and placed it on a layer of earth on the bottom of the bowl. I placed a large chunk of copal on the glowing charcoal and watched it release a dense incense cloud with a sweet, pungent aroma.

I used my cupped hands to draw the smoke over my body, cleansing and purifying myself with the smoke, and then passed both the prayer ties and prayer flags through the copal smoke several times to cleanse and purify them as well. After setting them on the ground beside me, I leaned back against the tree trunk, took a deep breath, and gazed out at the Temple of Inscriptions on the far side of the plaza. The smoke rising from the copal created a thin, wispy veil in front of me but it didn't seem to be attracting any attention, so I added more copal, closed my eyes, and silently prayed for the spirits of Palenque, Pakal, and the indigenous Maya who were all around me. As I opened my eyes, I noticed that a subtle shift had occurred in my surroundings.

The activity and sounds in the plaza seemed to have receded into the background while the Palace and Temple of Inscriptions had moved to the foreground in dramatic clarity. My attention was drawn to the Palace on my left, and as I looked over I suddenly found myself watching events unfolding inside one of the Palace rooms. The scene was hazy at first but gradually came into sharp focus. With a shock of recognition, I realized that even though I still was fully aware of myself as firmly rooted in the present under the tree in the plaza, in my vision I was in the royal chambers witnessing the passing of the Great Lord Pakal.

I watched as soft flickering lights cast dancing shadows on the smooth stucco walls of Pakal's chambers. The aroma of copal incense filled the room where he was lying on richly embroidered pads that covered a wide limestone bench with an intricately carved edge. His back and head were slightly elevated to enable him to more easily converse with family, friends, courtiers, and priests making short visits to his bedside. Pakal's breathing was somewhat shallow and much of his former physical strength was gone from his eighty-year-old body—yet he was quite lucid, his eyes bright and his energy strong.

In the room near him were two younger men of regal bearing, who I presumed were his eldest son and immediate successor, Kan Balam II ('Radiant Snake Jaguar'), and his second son, K'an Joy Chitam II ('Precious Yellow Tied Peccary'). A chief priest and three assistants were by his side, attending to him. Summoned from the Otherworld, waiting patiently in the corner of the chamber for his transition to begin, were two spirit presences my intuition told me were his mother, Lady Sak K'uk' ('Resplendent Quetzal'); and his father, K'an Mo' Hx ('Precious Macaw Jaguar').[5] The ancestor spirits were there as silent witnesses from the sacred realms, inhabiting the space between the worlds, visitors from the heavens—not fully present on the physical plane yet unmistakable and comforting presences nonetheless.

Pakal knew his time in a physical body was drawing to a close and that shortly he would begin the transition that preceded his journey through the Lower World. His sons and attendants gazed attentively at the ailing lord, looking for the telltale signs signaling the end of his life as beloved ruler of Palenque. Pakal's breathing became increasingly shallow and labored, his physical body increasingly weak and fatigued. And yet I somehow knew that he could feel his spirit, strong and forceful. Very soon now he would abandon his physical body and journey though the Lower

World to join his ancestors. Stillness and peacefulness filled the royal chambers as Pakal felt himself moving closer to the other realms; he was at ease and filled with gratitude for the many blessings in his life.

I sensed that preparations for Pakal's death and journey had been meticulously planned, and now the plans were being carried out flawlessly. Pakal had journeyed to the Lower World during initiations and ceremonies many times since he had assumed the throne. Now Palenque's revered king would travel in much the same manner as he had during his physical life. But this time, the journey would have a different purpose and focus; it marked a monumental transition for Pakal as well as for his successor and the city he loved. He was on the threshold of beginning a new life, never again to return to his people in a physical body. In the future, Pakal's soul essence would materialize from the spirit realm when summoned for ceremonies or supernatural guidance. He would return then not as the Lord of Palenque, but as the Maize God representing the presence of the divine spirit in maize.[6]

In an anteroom outside Pakal's chambers, priests and attendants were readying the litter to be used to transport Pakal's body across the Main Plaza to the Temple of Inscriptions, for interment. Sacred jade objects that would adorn his body and accompany him on this journey were being blessed and sanctified. In death, a full-face jade mask and a magnificent jade belt he had worn for ceremonial occasions would be placed on his body. A jade sphere symbolizing the sky and the heavens would rest in one hand, and in the other there would be a jade cube symbolizing the earth and the Lower World. By the time Pakal returned once again to Palenque in spirit form, he would have traversed the Lower World and ascended to the Heavens. The jade cube and sphere symbolized his soon-to-be-achieved mastery of the other worlds.

Throughout the Palace, the pace of activity continued to increase as final preparations were completed for this solemn occasion.

Since Pakal had ruled for sixty-nine years, few in Palenque had experienced the passing of a king. Servants were busy preparing food and attending to accommodations for visiting dignitaries who had been arriving steadily during the last week, all wishing to say farewell to the beloved ruler and pray for his safety in the other worlds so that he could continue to work on behalf of the people. Plans for the official ceremonies, funeral procession, and interment were being reviewed and checked for any needed changes. Activities of state required for the transmission of power and the coronation of the future king were underway.

Outside the Palace at the Temple of Inscriptions, priests were in the final stages of completing preparations for Pakal's burial and journey to the Lower World. The surface of the Main Plaza, the steps leading up to the sanctuary at the top of the temple, the steps leading down into the burial chamber, and the chamber itself had all been ritually washed and covered with a fresh coat of brilliant white stucco. The entire route that Pakal's body would follow, from the Palace chambers to the sarcophagus in the temple burial chamber, had been smudged with copal and prayed over ritually. The path Pakal would follow out of this world and into the next had been cleansed, purified, blessed, and sanctified.

Deep within the heart of the temple-pyramid, four priests holding conch shell horns to their lips stood in each of four recesses in the walls of the burial chamber. Suddenly, the chamber was flooded with the rich, sonorous tones of the horns, punctuated with brief moments of silence, calling to the unseen realms in perfect unison. The toning of the horns was followed by deep, resonant chants of sacred songs, reverberating off the stone walls, opening the portal to the Lower World and summoning ancestors from the other side. As the veil between the worlds thinned and opened, prayers and meditations of the ancestors on the other side helped set the energies in motion, creating an energy vortex and portal between the two worlds.

As the chanting of the priests continued and intensified, a vertical, ellipsoidal energy field formed in the space occupied by the massive stone sarcophagus in the burial chamber. A sphere of energy within the center of the field pulsed with an ethereal heartbeat, expanding and rhythmically contracting in the space between the two worlds. As the energy in the vortex gathered momentum, a point of stillness was created in the center of the pulsing energy mass. The energy in the vortex drew away from this center, enlarging the still point until a crystal clear portal opened between the worlds and expanded to enfold Pakal's sarcophagus.

As the opening between the worlds expanded, the energy around the life-sized figures of Pakal's ancestors, molded in stucco in high relief on the walls of the chamber, began to transform. The once-lifeless plaster bodies appeared to come alive, animated by the spirit beings who had journeyed through sacred time and space to join Pakal at this historic moment. Using the stucco sculptures as a homing beacon, the etheric bodies of past rulers and ancestral lords and ladies of Palenque including K'uk' Balam I ('Quetzal Jaguar'), the founder of Palenque's Classic dynasty; Ankal Mo' Nahb ('Turtle Macaw Lake'); Butz'aj Sak Chiik ('Smoking White Resplendant Coati'); and Lady Yohl Ik'nal ('Lady Heart of the Wind Place'), the first female ruler of Palenque[7], emerged from the sculptures into the burial chamber after passing through the portal. Once the ancestral spirits had fully materialized, the chanting of the priests was replaced by silent prayers.

High above the burial chamber, in the temple at the top of the pyramid, priests and assistants had opened a second portal between the worlds to allow other ancestors and spirit beings to pass into the realm of the living. Within the innermost sanctuary of the temple, a few spirits of priests, holy men, healers, and guardians from the other worlds had arrived through the portal to guide Pakal at the start of his journey. They were a powerful, radiant presence—and they were clearly visible to the priests in the sanctuary as their spirit bodies became increasingly grounded in the physical plane. When their materialization was complete, they took their places around the opening to the stairs leading down to the burial crypt and intoned incantations from the Holy Books to ease Pakal's journey.

The spell of the vision was broken momentarily when I found myself taking a deep involuntary breath. I noticed my palms were sweaty and my heart was beating quite fast. The scenes I was witnessing in the royal chamber and in Pakal's temple-pyramid were much more intense than I was accustomed to, and I realized I had become so engrossed in this revelation that I had completely forgotten I was actually sitting under the tree in the plaza. I remembered looking at Pakal's death mask at the museum and wondered if this experience was the "secret" I'd imagined him imparting to me. If that were the case, it was much grander and more profound than I ever could have imagined.

My awareness was once again drawn inside the royal residence and in my vision I could not only see clearly everything occurring but somehow could also sense what Pakal was thinking and feeling. Those at his bedside began to see the signs they had been watching for and knew the time for his transition had arrived: Pakal's eyes closed and his shallow breathing slowed until it was almost imperceptible. His awareness of his physical body and immediate surroundings gently receded into the background and his attention turned instead to his sak nik nahal ("white flowery breath"), his *k'ulel* ("soul essence").[8] From a place that was simultaneously inside and outside his physical body, simultaneously in the realm of matter and spirit, Pakal felt and watched his k'ulel begin to separate and detach from his physical body.

For a moment, a feeling of pure terror flooded his physical body, an instinctual response engendered by his awareness of his imminent demise. But Pakal maintained his mental focus and continued to watch the process unfold. The terror subsided as his attention shifted to the dance of energies engulfing both his physical body and his k'ulel. Pakal had left his body to experience the non-physical other worlds many times before, journeying through the Lower World in his way or spirit companion form, journeying to the upper realms in his k'ulel. But during these journeys, he had always maintained his connection with his physical essence in the material world. This time, the separation was final and eternal.

From somewhere that seemed quite distant yet somehow quite close, Pakal felt the sound vibrations of sacred chants from the priests in his chamber opening an energy vortex, a brilliant sphere of sapphire-blue light tinged with radiant white light that infused his entire being. Although he had experienced this sensation before, he was surprised by the purity and intensity of the energy this time. The energy vortex magnified the transformational process, increasing the vibrational rate of the energy meridians in his physical body and easing the separation of his k'ulel body. Swirling energy eddies enveloped his k'ulel, creating a boundary between his physical body and his "white flowery breath," or soul body. Suddenly, the last remaining aspects of his k'ulel were drawn into the sphere of light.

Although free from its ties to his physical body, Pakal's k'ulel remained within its confines. In my vision I observed Pakal's k'ulel body rotating 180 degrees inside his inert physical body so that it faced down toward the bench on which his physical body was lying. He arched the neck and back of his k'ulel body so that the upper part of his head was positioned against the space created by the nostrils of his physical body. He drew up the arms and legs of his k'ulel from within the space of his physical body, placed both hands of his k'ulel against the inside of his physical body's upper back and the soles of his k'ulel's feet against his lower back.

Then, taking a full, deep breath, he pushed his k'ulel out through the nostrils of his physical body, freeing his k'ulel.

As in the process of giving birth, Pakal's k'ulel, his white flowery breath body, emerged transformed, suspended in the air over his physical body in the royal chamber. He had taken his last physical breath on earth and was now ready to leave his physical body behind for the last time. Within the sphere of brilliant, sapphire-blue and radiant white light, his k'ulel slowly began to take on a more physical-looking form, his soul essence becoming a more solid and recognizable presence. Pakal looked down upon his discarded body and acknowledged that now he was an ancestor. With that came the full realization of his Divine soul essence. Surrounded by his family, priests, attendants, and the spirits from the higher realms, Pakal shifted his attention to the Soul Keeping ceremony that was about to begin.

Pakal's chief priest had been designated as his "Guardian of the Soul," and he now approached his lord with two acolytes. Incensarios were lit and the small balls of copal placed on the smoldering charcoal immediately flooded the royal chamber with the aroma of the incense. The guardian and his helpers would remain with Pakal throughout the three-day soul-keeping vigil, fasting and praying in the manner prescribed by ancient manuals to purify their departed lord's soul and prepare him for his journey. From time to time they were joined by others—priests, priestesses, and family members—who came to honor Pakal and offer their prayers for his well-being. This was a sacred time and a holy event, a critical period in the soul's transition that would set the tone for the next steps in Pakal's journey.

Ancient purification rites, as prescribed by the Holy Books, were performed by the guardian and his assistants for three nocturnal cycles; Pakal's body was ritually bathed, smudged with copal, coated with cinnabar, and prayed over. When the purification rites were completed, Pakal's physical body was prepared for the procession from the Palace to the burial chamber within the temple. Adorned with his jade mask and other funerary objects, the body was shrouded in white linen and placed reverently on the royal litter. His two sons, along with his priests and their attendants, took their places as the procession formed in the Palace. Pakal's k'ulel accompanied the procession. The intensity of his energetic presence was a surprise to most in the procession; those closest to his k'ulel experienced the otherworldly life force emanating from his white flowery breath body.

The procession moved in a slow, stately manner down the stairs from the Palace and across the Main Plaza to the stairs leading up the pyramid to the temple. The route was lined with Palenque's elite, visiting dignitaries, and other well-wishers, all here to honor and pay tribute to the Great Lord, all offering prayers for his continued safety and well-being. Accompanied by his sons, the future rulers of Palenque, as well as priests and attendants, Pakal's physical body was carried up the stairs of the temple-pyramid and into the sanctuary at the top. There, in the inner sanctum, his k'ulel was rejoined by the spirits of his mother, father, and grandmother. Together they waited as his physical body was taken down the steps into the burial chamber.

Pakal's k'ulel, followed by the spirits of his ancestors, moved back out of the sanctuary and covered the short distance to the edge of the pyramid platform. Positioned slightly in front of the others, he gazed down at the crowd assembled in the Plaza and surrounding areas. Many in the crowd were awestruck at the vision appearing before them—the dazzling, radiant, spiritual presence of Pakal's k'ulel on his way to serve his people from the higher realms. Those who could not see his k'ulel could still sense the holiness surrounding his passing. With tears of joy and gratitude flowing from their eyes and prayers for health and well-being on their lips, they bade farewell to their beloved and revered ruler and petitioned for his safe rebirth and eventual return as the Maize God.

Pakal's k'ulel and his ancestors' spirits receded back into the inner sanctuary of the temple as the final preparations were completed inside the burial chamber deep within the pyramid. The lid of the massive stone sarcophagus had been rolled back to allow the body to be placed in the hollowed-out cavity inside. Pakal's body was laid to rest with his head toward the north end and his feet toward the south. The lid of the sarcophagus, with its magnificently carved images of Pakal's rebirth and resurrection[9] was moved back into place and Pakal's ceremonial jade belt was placed on top of it. Pakal's body was now symbolically embraced by the earlier generations of Palenque's rulers, his parents, and his wife through their representation in the carvings on the sides of the sarcophagus.

With the interment of Pakal's body now complete, the priests and their attendants climbed reverently back up the stairs through the small, narrow corridor illuminated by soft, flickering, torchlight. As they reached the top of the stairs, they emerged into the chamber at the top of the temple-pyramid and took their predetermined places along the side walls of the inner sanctum. It was now time for Pakal's k'ulel and the spirits of his ancestors to descend to the tomb chamber below and depart from the world of the living through the portal to the Otherworld. With the Guardian of the Soul leading the way, Pakal's k'ulel and the spirits of his ancestors, accompanied by Pakal's sons, and other priests and attendants, began their steep descent down to the burial chamber.

From the niches recessed into the chamber walls and the steps leading to the chamber, priests sang and chanted ancient incantations to assist the spectral party in departing from the physical realm. The sacred tones reverberating off the limestone walls of the crypt mingled with the energy surrounding the portal to the Lower World that had been opened earlier. Slowly, the vibrational rate of the energy of the portal shifted to synchronize with that of Pakal's k'ulel and the ancestor spirits until the separate fields were perfectly attuned, balanced, and aligned.

Pakal's k'ulel and the spirits of his ancestors moved to the edge of the portal and began to blend with its energy. The blended energies increased in intensity, pulsing rhythmically as if governed by a sacred heartbeat from deep within the other worlds, and filling the crypt with holy, radiant, ethereal light. The Keeper of the Soul, the other priests, and Pakal's sons began to feel the energy in the crypt being pulled toward the portal, drawn toward an energy vortex emanating from the Lower World in the non-physical realms. Pakal's sons watched spellbound as, one by one, Pakal's k'ulel and the ancestor spirits moved into the energy currents of the portal, into the open maw of the White-Boned Snake and, with a burst of energy and a flash of light, disappeared into the Lower World. Pakal had "entered the road"[10] on his journey to his next life.

With the passage of the last ancestor spirit into the Lower World, the intensity of the energy around the portal began to diminish and the opening to the non-physical realm began to disappear. The portal closed and Sak Bak Nakan, the White-Boned Snake, returned to Source. The incantations, chants and prayers continued until the priests were certain all were in the other realm. The final sounds of the last sacred tones faded from the chamber and seemed to drift into the ethers of the Lower World. The small, cramped, burial chamber was filled with a deep and abiding peacefulness that extended beyond the physical boundary of the chamber. Pakal's sons, priests, and attendants sat for a while in silence within the peacefulness and spaciousness of the moment.

Breaking the silence, the Guardian of the Soul rose and turned to begin the climb back up to the top of the pyramid, leading Pakal's sons, priests, and attendants to the inner sanctuary at the top of the temple. The four priests who had opened the portal in the burial chamber stayed behind in the chamber to keep a vigil during the early stages of Pakal's journey; the Guardian of the Soul and the other priests maintained a vigil in the sanctuary above. In the courtyard, at the foot of the temple-pyramid, many guests joined the vigil, some for a few hours, some for several days. Throughout this time, the Main Plaza was filled with the fragrant aroma of copal as prayers were said and flowers offered for Pakal during his journey through the Lower World.

Arriving in the Lower World, Pakal knew the ceremonies that marked his departure from the physical world would continue in his absence, but his attention was focused on the journey ahead. He was watched over and guided by the ancestors and other protective spirits, but this was a solitary venture, a trip he must make by himself. During Pakal's earlier journeys through the Otherworld, the non-physical realms had seemed to have a dreamlike quality; now, it felt as if he had awakened from the dream of a physical existence into a world of spirit that possessed a clarity, richness, and intensity he had never experienced before. Pakal was prepared for this moment and his resolve was strong.

His destination was Wakah-Kan, the sacred World Tree, the *axis mundi* at the center of the Lower World. Wakah-Kan represented the portal through which he would be transported to the Upper World, much as Sak Bak Nakan, the White-Boned Snake, represented the portal to the Lower World. In the presence of the Celestial Bird, Itzam-Ye, the representation of the divine essence of spiritual transformation, the transmigration of Pakal's k'ulel would be completed, and he would take his rightful place among the pantheon of royal Maya ancestors in the highest spiritual realm. But first he would complete his life review and the process of purification and renewal that would prepare him for his journey through the heavens.

Pakal's thoughts turned to the events that would unfold on the way to Wakah-Kan. For centuries his people had used the metaphor of a river journey by canoe to represent this time of transition—the soul traversing the Lower World (represented by water) as a canoe glides along the river. In artistic representations of this journey, the soul is accompanied by two paddlers,[11] one at the front and one at the back of the canoe. And now Pakal encountered these sacred beings—manifestations of the Divine, personifications of the mysterious, magical forces that govern the world below—who would accompany him during his time of deep introspection and critical self-evaluation in the Lower World.

Stripped of his worldly possessions and bereft of the comforts of the royal court, Pakal began his soul searching and self-revelatory process with intense determination and strong resolve. He knew his progress toward reaching Wakah-Kan depended on his ability to resolve emotional issues and unfinished business that still remained for him, left over from his earthly life. He knew his spirit would have to be cleansed, purified, and renewed in order to pass through the Wakah-Kan portal to the higher realms, and he knew that the deepest, darkest emotional currents and psychic eddies of his former life had to be brought to the surface and exorcised.

As he glided through non-physical reality, images from his former life began materializing before him. Although somewhat hazy and indistinct at first, the images intensified with crystal clarity. He saw his life unfold before him—nothing was hidden and everything had to be reckoned with. Pakal's triumphs and successes passed before his eyes, accompanied by his excesses, his hubris, his passions, and his failings. His greatest strengths and his greatest weaknesses revealed themselves along with his secrets, his innermost demons, and the darkest aspects of himself. He could not run away, he could not hide, and he could not close his eyes.

The images continued to flood his consciousness. His reactions to the images lacked the intense sensations he experienced when he was in a physical body but the impact of the events coursed through his soul and erupted from deep places within him. All the aspects of his former life—physical, emotional, mental, and spiritual—stood out in sharp contrast, calling out to him for recognition and acknowledgement. Pakal watched as the attributes and characteristics that propelled him to greatness revealed themselves to him, as well as the aspects of himself that haunted him in his darkest hours.

Images of his coronation, marriage, children's births, victorious military campaigns, political triumphs, and acts of generosity and compassion toward his subjects—all the things that had sustained him, nurtured him and given his life meaning—passed before his eyes. Incidents where his greed, rage, lust, dishonesty, vengeance, manipulation, and treachery had emerged—actions that had brought him shame, guilt, and remorse and had blocked his connection with the Divine—were present as well. All were real, all were true, and Pakal was determined to face it all, to confront and resolve those things that would hinder him on his spiritual journey.

Pakal felt himself moving through the psychic waters of the Lower World as his life review continued. The paddlers' mute but powerful presence provided the momentum that propelled him forward toward his destination, the rendezvous with Wakah-Kan. Pakal realized how easy it would be to get lost in this world, to get off track, to succumb to the temptation to take an easier way out, to find some respite in the Lower World that offered an alluring alternative to the hard work necessary to complete his transformation from the former Lord of Palenque to the Maize God. But there was no doubt in his mind that he would continue until he reached his goal—he had gone too far and worked too hard, and nothing would deter him.

Over time, the images from his life review seemed to slow and decrease in frequency and intensity. Pakal had confronted himself at the deepest, innermost aspects of his being and in the process had released old emotional patterns and karmic ties that needed to be left behind. He had completed the journey all must take and had been purified and renewed. But unlike many, he had prepared while still alive and as a result had succeeded in mastering the forces of the Lower World. He had not given up, or given in, to remain trapped in the darkness and wander the earth as a ghostly presence. And he had resisted the temptation to find a place of comfort and refuge in the Lower World rather than continue his journey to transcendence and enlightenment in the higher spiritual realms. He was ready to continue on. Recognizing their work was done, the paddlers began to lose their energetic form; their substance dissipated and merged into the ethers of the Lower World until, once again, Pakal was alone.

Prior to his death, The Keepers of the Holy Books had taught Pakal the sacred incantations that would lead him to Wakah-Kan. Pakal recalled the words and tones of the ancient chants and projected them mentally as thought-forms through the ethers of the Lower World. Suddenly, he felt himself moving forward, gaining speed, projected through time and space while simultaneously experiencing the Lower World rushing toward and past him as he remained motionless. As the last words and tones of the incantations drifted into the ethers, Pakal realized he was in the presence of Wakah-Kan.

The World Tree stood before him, a holy, ethereal being of pulsing, radiant, dazzling light-energy. Wakah-Kan shone as a brilliant beacon in the darkness of the Lower World, illuminating everything with the light that emanated from higher spiritual realms. Although rooted in the Lower World, Wakah-Kan was also a manifestation of the divine Source. Pakal had entered the Lower World through the maw of Sak Bak Nakan, the White-Boned Snake, a sacred umbilical cord emanating from the World Tree. Now, surrounded and embraced by the divine life-giving forces within Wakah-Kan, Pakal would undergo a new birth process, only this time he would be born not into the physical world, but into the higher spiritual realms.

During his journey through the Lower World, Pakal's k'ulel had been cleansed and purified. He had defeated the powers of darkness and death and emerged victorious. Now he was about to experience his resurrection and ascension to his final destination in the heavens. Shortly, Pakal would complete his ultimate transformation. On the lid of his sarcophagus, artisans had depicted him as transformed into the Maize God. Pakal's soul essence would continue as an active presence in the Otherworld serving as a counselor, intermediary, and intercessor. It would be an ever-present reality to his descendants as well as to the priests and subjects he had left behind. Just as the maize plant was a source of life for the Maya, Pakal would continue to be a source of life and sustenance for the people of Palenque.

Pakal stood, open-armed, palms outstretched, before the wondrous, awesome presence before him. The magical incantations and subsequent journey into the presence of Wakah-Kan had increased the vibrational rate of his soul-body to match the higher frequency of the World Tree. His k'ulel shuddered as the waves of energy emanating from this sacred form penetrated his energetic field. His soul was flooded with brilliant shafts of light permeating his very essence. The boundaries between his k'ulel and the sacred tree disappeared as he felt himself merging and blending with the holy presence before him. A new cycle was about to start; a destiny had been fulfilled and a life fully realized. The portal between the other worlds opened wide as Pakal was embraced by the Divine.

The scene before me dissipated as quickly as it had appeared and I was once again aware of myself sitting on the ground of the Main Plaza. It was a jarring, unsettling feeling to have left the deepest, innermost reaches of the Lower World and suddenly find myself back in ordinary reality. I wanted to remain with Pakal and witness his ascent to the higher realms, but I knew instantly that the vision I'd received was a tremendous gift, and I felt grateful for as much as had been revealed to me. I was hopeful that somehow I would experience more of the transformational process in the future and that my curiosity about the inner workings of the higher realms would be satisfied, but for the time being I was content with the new knowledge and insights I had been granted. My understanding of the Lower World had expanded and, for now, that was enough for me.

I continued to sit under the tree in the plaza for quite some time, allowing my awareness to return completely to the present and enjoying the natural beauty of the ceremonial center. During this time, the level of activity around me continued to increase as more and more tourists arrived at the ruins, making me feel increasingly uncomfortable. Realizing that I was still disoriented and a little depleted from my vision, I decided to abandon my earlier plan to spend the rest of the day revisiting the structures I had explored on my trip twenty years earlier and instead return to my hotel. That afternoon I simply relaxed and prepared for my meeting that evening with Alfonso Morales, my guide for the next three days.

Alfonso had been recommended to me by archaeologists in the U.S. He was from Palenque, spoke fluent English, had pursued a master's degree at the University of Texas in Austin, and had over thirty years' experience with Maya archaeology in Mexico, Guatemala, and Belize. He had overseen the recent excavations of Temple XIX, one of the major ceremonial structures at Palenque. The temple's dramatic and important hieroglyphic and bas relief carvings had provided critically important new information on Palenque's history, mythology, and royal rituals and on Maya cosmology in general. Alfonso's father Moises has an international reputation as Palenque's "First Guide" and had been the host of the first three

Palenque Roundtables—a series of academic conferences attended by the world's leading Mayanists to discuss and examine the latest research findings. I was looking forward to a thorough immersion in the latest Maya scholarship and a multigenerational, archaeologically-based perspective on the ancient Maya.

Alfonso's home was a short walk from my hotel. I arrived just after dinner and spent time with Alfonso and archaeologist Julia Miller learning about the history of archaeological exploration at Palenque and planning our time together. Alfonso and I would spend the next day at the ruins of Palenque, visiting key ceremonial structures and touring the new museum together. The following day we planned a full tour of Yaxchilan. After that I intended to return to Palenque by myself and then later in the afternoon to travel back to the indigenous, primarily Ch'ol Maya, community at Frontera Corozal to spend the night. From there I would travel by boat back to Yaxchilan for the day and then return to Palenque that evening.

The next four days would be quite full, but I was looking forward to being exposed to the latest academic thinking about the ancient Maya and seeing how my ceremonial experiences with indigenous elders aligned with current scholarly perspectives. This seemed to be a perfect opportunity to try to bridge these two seemingly different worlds of scholarly interpretation of academic field research and my insights from experiential, ceremonial practice.

As exciting as all this was for me, though, I found myself shaken by my encounter with Pakal. Because of my experience on the River of Ruins, I hadn't anticipated any visions or supernatural revelations, and now I didn't know quite what to make of this extraordinary encounter. Why was I shown Pakal's journey? What significance did it have for me personally? Would more revelations be forthcoming later in the trip? These were the questions I wrestled with as I prepared to meet Alfonso and thought about the other sites I would soon be visiting.

1. Although several of my friends in Los Angeles had erected tepees or built sweat lodges in their backyards, I decided to build a Pueblo-style kiva. To ensure privacy, I built my kiva inside my two-car garage. It was constructed by partitioning off one half of the garage, removing the concrete slab, excavating the area to a depth of four feet, adding retaining walls and then building four-foot-high inner walls on top of the retaining walls to achieve a total interior height of eight feet. In designing and building the kiva, I consulted with Tom Mails to make sure the finished kiva matched traditional Pueblo Indian kivas as much as possible. I did have some difficulty explaining the kiva to the real estate agent who helped us sell our house when we moved to Philadelphia, and ultimately described it in the listing as a "wine cellar."

2. Hunbatz Men gave me a copy of his new book, still a prized possession of mine, while we were together, and he wrote the following on the inside cover: *"Que la sabiduria cosmica maya haga que nuestra hermandad solar sea mas grande, dedieo con respecto este manuserito Maya a mi hermano John Kralovec, 11/16/89"*—"That the Maya cosmic wisdom will make our solar brotherhood stronger, I respectfully dedicate this manuscript to my brother John Kralovec, 11/16/89."

3. Houston and Inomata 2009: 193–95

4. Martin and Grube 2008: 165–66

5. Ancestor names are from Martin and Grube 2008: 161–168

6. Schele and Mathews 1998: 132

7. Ancestor wall figures are from Schele and Mathews 1998: 128 –129; ancestor names are from Martin and Grube 2008: 161–168

8. Grube 2006: 311–313. The ancient Maya (as well as contemporary Maya) believed individuals possessed a soul essence they referred to as k'ulel or "white flowery breath." At death the white flowery breath detached from the physical body and "entered the road" on the journey to the next world. The Temple of Inscriptions contains two references to the date Pakal "entered the road," determined by scholars to be August 28, 683 CE.

9. Schele and Mathews 1998: 110–116. On the sarcophagus lid, in the south, an image of the open maw of Sak Bak Nakan ("White-Boned Snake") depicts the portal to the Lower World. Within the portal, Wakah-Kan, the World Tree, emerges from an image of a sacrificial bowl. Itzam-Ye, the Celestial Bird, is perched atop the World Tree. Intertwined in the branches of Wakah-Kan is an image of the double-headed serpent, representing both spiritual authority and the umbilical cord connecting Pakal to the supernatural realm and the wisdom of the ancestors. An image of Pakal as the Maize God reclines on the bowl of sacrifice and is superimposed on the image of Wakah-Kan.

10. Grube 2006: 311

11. The images of these two beings appear frequently in Maya iconography. Scholars refer to them as "Paddler Gods"(Schele and Mathews 1998: 36–37, 414; Sharer and Traxler 2006: 744).

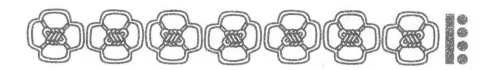

LADY XOOK'S SACRIFICE

It was early morning as I motored up the Usumacinta River toward Yaxchilan in the small cayuco with my boatman, Mayo. The brilliant tropical sun was just beginning to break above the tops of the towering canopy trees in the tropical rainforest that lined the banks of the river. It was already hot and humid on the river, and I welcomed the cool breeze and occasional spray of water. Even though I had visited Yaxchilan just two days earlier, with Alfonso as my guide, I was excited about revisiting the ruins, alone this time, because I had a particular destination in mind for a ceremony I wanted to perform. I had spent the night at a small local motel so I could meet Mayo early enough to be the first boat on the river that morning and arrive at the ruins just before the park opened.

On my earlier trip with Alfonso, we had foregone the larger, slower, covered lanchas that carried most of the tourists upriver to Yaxchilan, in favor of Mayo's smaller and much faster cayuco. When Alfonso first introduced me to Mayo, he explained that the archaeologists preferred cayucos and Mayo was the best boatman on the river. Twenty years earlier, when I'd traveled from Frontera

Corozal to Yaxchilan with the Far Horizons tour group, the cayucos that transported us had been dilapidated wooden boats with small, battered, outboard motors. But Mayo's cayuco was a modern aluminum fishing boat with a massive outboard motor that cut our travel time in half.

While sitting near the bow of the cayuco two days earlier, memories of my first visit to Yaxchilan in 1987 had come flooding back, memories so vivid and intense that it seemed as if only months, not decades, had passed since my extraordinary experiences at the ancient ceremonial center. When we reached Yaxchilan, Alfonso and I left Mayo at the river bank and climbed the steps to the trail to the entrance to the ruins. Like Palenque, visitor traffic to Yaxchilan had increased dramatically over the years. The entrance to the site had been upgraded and modernized, signage and educational plaques had been added along the paths, and many magnificent ceremonial structures had been cleared and restored.

We entered the site the same way I had in 1987, through the massive stone ceremonial structure known as the Labyrinth, and used a small flashlight to illuminate the main path through the maze of passageways until we emerged at the Main Plaza. Yaxchilan had not lost any of its beauty, charm, or majesty and it was as exciting to be in the plaza again as it had been on my first visit.

As we walked around the plaza, Alfonso began describing the extraordinary advances made during the past twenty years in deciphering ancient hieroglyphics and understanding the meaning of stone carvings on ceremonial architecture. Yaxchilan, with its many detailed historical inscriptions, had become a key to our understanding of the ancient Maya. Following the pioneering translation work done in the 1950s and 1960s by Tatiana Proskouriakoff, epigraphers such as Linda Schele, David Stuart, Michael Coe, and Nicolai Grube had been hard at work unlocking the secrets of the written language. As a result, we now had a detailed history of the city, its rulers, and their political fortunes.

Yaxchilan, which translates as "Green Stones," is the name given to the site by one of its earliest visitors, explorer Teobert Maler, but its ancient name was probably Pa' Chan, which means "Cleft (or broken) Sky." It is situated on the south bank of the Usumacinta River in the state of Chiapas, Mexico. Yaxchilan's founder and first ruler was Yoaat Balam ('Progenitor Jaguar'), who ascended to the throne in 359 CE.[1] His descendants ruled the city in an unbroken dynastic line for five hundred years until the kingdom faded into historical obscurity. Large-scale occupation of Yaxchilan ceased sometime early in the ninth century; the final inscription was recorded in 808 CE. While it thrived, Yaxchilan was one of the most powerful Maya kingdoms, rivaling major city states such as Palenque, Tikal, and Piedras Negras (twenty-five miles upriver) and dominating smaller sites like Bonampak (nineteen miles inland to the south).

As I toured the site with Alfonso, we revisited the temple-pyramids, stelae, and other monuments I had first seen over twenty years earlier. But now, with Alfonso's insights, I was able to appreciate the richness and vividness of the political and spiritual life at Yaxchilan in a way I hadn't been able to before. Alfonso pointed out hieroglyphics that named specific rulers and referenced their military conquests, political alliances, marriages, major building projects, and spiritual ceremonies. We climbed the Grand Staircase up to Temple 33, dedicated to Bird Jaguar, where Alfonso showed me ancient hieroglyphics and carved stone images of the ball game, some of the finest images in the entire Maya realm. To my dismay, the fabulous stalactite called Stela 31 had been removed from the site, but the hill and area around the temple had been cleared, revealing ancient stone stairways that continued up to a more recently restored group of temples, and other monumental structures, called the Great Acropolis, set high above Bird Jaguar's temple.

After studying the structures in the Great Acropolis, Alfonso and I returned to Bird Jaguar's temple, where I'd first encountered my ancient Maya tutelary spirit twenty years earlier. I had shared my interest in indigenous spirituality with Alfonso when we first began planning our time together and hoped I would be able to conduct a brief prayer ceremony in front of the temple if the area wasn't too crowded. Alfonso spoke to a guard at the temple on my behalf and I was granted permission to do so. I picked a spot directly in front of the temple and sat with my copal, prayer flags, and prayer ties as I prepared for the ceremony.

I could feel the presence of the ancestors and my Maya tutelary spirit close by as I sang the sacred songs and prayed in the Plains Indian tradition. I included specific prayers for our guard and his family, at his request. I was a little surprised to find that I felt comfortable and completely at home here at Yaxchilan; performing a ceremony at the temple in the middle of the jungle seemed perfectly natural. As a result of my decades of spiritual experiences and my familiarity with ancient Maya sites, my ceremonies in these settings had become second nature to me.

When I finished my ceremony I thanked the guard, who in turn thanked me for my prayers. With a bemused look on his face, Alfonso informed me that the spot I had selected for the ceremony was directly above a buried tomb chamber that had been discovered since my last trip. He showed me a picture of the temple and subterranean burial site in a reference book he had brought with him. It had been excavated and studied several years earlier, and then covered back over so that no trace of it was visible today.

We then continued back down the Grand Staircase to the Main Plaza, back toward the labyrinth. Along the way we stopped at Temple 23, the *yotoot* (house) of Lady K'abal Xook, the principal wife of Itzamnaaj Balam II ('Shield Jaguar II,' the name preferred by scholars), ruler of Yaxchilan from 681 to his death in 742 CE.

I had been fascinated with Lady Xook from the moment I first encountered her through an exhibit at the Cleveland Museum of Art in the winter of 1986. The exhibit, "The Blood of Kings," co-curated by Linda Schele and Mary Ellen Miller, had presented research findings on the ancient Maya and included material on the ritual of "bloodletting." Although bloodletting had been described by Franciscan friars during the time of the Spanish Conquest, it had been recently discovered that ancient Maya royalty and family patriarchs and matriarchs regularly shed their blood as part of their religious observances, and often documented these rituals on their public buildings for their own political and spiritual purposes. They used stingray spines, bone awls, and obsidian blades as lancets to pierce and draw blood from the lips, tongue, cheeks, or sometimes the genitals. The museum exhibit had featured images of exquisitely-carved stone lintels depicting Lady Xook in the act of conjuring ancestor spirits through letting blood by passing a cord imbedded with small obsidian chips through her perforated tongue.

It is difficult for modern people to understand or appreciate the significance of bloodletting, a practice that seems grotesquely barbaric to many people today. However, in the ancient Maya worldview, ritual bloodletting was a central element of their spiritual practices, As Linda Schele and David Freidel write in A Forest of Kings:

> Like the great metaphor of Maya life—the life cycle of maize [corn]—the continued wellbeing of the universe required the active participation of the human community through ritual. As maize cannot seed itself without the interventions of human beings, so the cosmos required sacrificial blood to maintain life. Maya life was filled with endless rituals which seem to us bizarre and shocking, but which to them embodied the highest concepts of their spiritual devotion.[2]

For this reason, the Maya rulers (referred to as Lords and Ladies by Maya scholars), offered their own blood to the ancestors and the cosmos in order to "seed" the world and maintain the connection between the human and the divine realms, assuring the continuity of life and the well-being of their people. These rituals were performed with the deepest devotion and in the purest rapture of self-sacrifice. The ecstatic trance states engendered by these sacrifices kept the membrane between the human world and the other worlds thin, and the guidance of the ancestors and the gods close by. Nowhere in the Maya realm is this ancient Maya practice of bloodletting more beautifully depicted than on two of the three lintels that originally spanned the three outer doorways of Temple 23, the yotoot of Lady Xook. The images of Lady Xook carved on the underside of the broad limestone lintels could be seen only by standing in a doorway and looking up at the sculpted surfaces.

Lady Xook was a great diviner and prophet and "one of the few women in Maya history to wield the prerogatives usually reserved for the high king."[3] Scholars now know that she was the maternal first cousin of Shield Jaguar's mother and that her father was a member of a powerful noble lineage.[4] Shield Jaguar's marriage to Lady Xook strengthened his political alliances with two important and powerful Yaxchilan lineages, and her conjuring the spirit of Yoaat Balam established his royal legitimacy and provided a political link to the founder of Yaxchilan. Temple 23 was built by him and dedicated in 726 CE to honor his illustrious wife. Lady Xook is one of only a few women in recorded Maya history who were commemorated in this way.

The lintels, referred to as Lintels 24, 25, and 26, depict Lady Xook's sacrifice and document her high position in the royal lineage and are among the most exquisite and highly regarded of all Maya stone carvings. Although the hieroglyphic texts that accompany Lintels 24 and 25 depict two different historical occasions, they can also be read as consecutive images of the bloodletting ritual itself and thus provide a wealth of insight into the ancient rite. Lintel 24 shows Lady Xook performing a ritual bloodletting by pulling a cord embedded with small obsidian chips through her tongue and collecting the flowing blood on pieces of bark paper. Lintel 25 shows her conjuring the spirit of Yoaat Balam, the founder of Yaxchilan, as the result of her bloodletting.[5] In Lintel 26, she is shown preparing her husband, Shield Jaguar, for battle.[6]

Seeing Lady Xook's beautiful Temple 23 for the first time in 1987, situated in the center of the city's largest terrace, surrounded by magnificent monumental sacred architecture, and overlooking the Usumacinta River was a thrilling and unforgettable experience. Returning to the temple twenty years later was to have an even greater impact on me because of a life-changing experience I'd had in 1990.

That summer, I danced in a traditional Plains Indian-style Sun Dance.[7] The Sun Dance is a ceremony that involves fasting, singing sacred songs, praying, and piercing the skin of the chest or back for men and sometimes flesh offerings from the arms for women. During the final phases of the Sun Dance, male dancers approach the sacred tree at the center of the ceremonial arbor. As a dancer lies on a buffalo robe, the skin on each side of his upper chest is lifted up and an incision is made, creating parallel slits on either side of the chest. A narrow, flattened piece of buffalo rib is inserted into the slits. After being helped to his feet, the dancer is tethered to the sacred tree by a length of rope, which is tied to the tree and then tied around each piece of buffalo rib. Participants then dance in place, connected to the sacred tree, until the Intercessor indicates the time has come to break the connection. One by one, each dancer then moves toward and away from the tree until he finally lurches backward, tearing the buffalo ribs free from his chest.

It was controversial at the time for non-Indians to dance and has become more so since then, but that summer there were two "open" Sun Dances, including the one I joined at Pilot Rock. The experience was one of the most powerful of my entire spiritual journey and gave me insights into the Maya practice of bloodletting that would have been unattainable otherwise. Plains Indian Sun Dancing is clearly not the same as Maya bloodletting, but they share common features: both are done in a ceremonial setting, both have elements of self-sacrifice, and both are done for the well-being of the community. Some scholars will argue that it is irresponsible to draw parallels between the ceremonies of two such unique and dissimilar cultures, but I believe we can better understand the ancient Maya by doing so.

When we arrived at Yaxchilan this time, Mayo beached the cayuco and I headed up to the ruins. Once I entered the labyrinth I used a small flashlight I'd brought with me to help navigate the sunless interior. Back home, before I left for this trip, I'd come across a drawing of the labyrinth's system of passageways and chambers[8] and had taken note of an area I thought would not have much, if any, tourist traffic. Now I found the passageway inside the labyrinth that led away from the Main Plaza, toward the northwest side of the structure, and followed it until I came to that area—a square cross-vaulted chamber with an ancient wide stone bench against one wall. I sat down on the bench and used the small shaft of light from the flashlight to explore the chamber and the passageway, which continued deeper into the labyrinth. The surface of the stone masonry walls was rough and I could make out scattered small piles of ancient rubble on the ground. I set my bag on the bench and turned off the flashlight.

I was immediately plunged into a deep and surprisingly disorienting darkness unlike anything I had experienced before. On my vision quests, even the darkest nights were at least partly illuminated by some starlight or moonlight. Inside sweat lodges, the darkness was always penetrated by the soft, rosy glow of red-hot stones that had been heated in the sacred fire pit outside the lodge and placed in the center of the lodge for the purification ceremony. And even though the darkness was absolute inside the small ceremonial house used for the yuwipi ceremonies I'd experienced on the Pine Ridge Indian Reservation, once the healing spirits departed, the room was illuminated again. But in this labyrinth, the darkness was impenetrable and enduring. None of my earlier ceremonial experiences had prepared me for the intensity of the darkness here in the inner chamber. I had to turn my flashlight back on.

The chamber seemed to be a perfect place to reflect on my experiences at Yaxchilan and offer my prayers for the Maya. I took my prayer flags, prayer ties, bowl, and copal out of my bag and prepared for the ceremony. The burning copal cast soft reassuring shadows on the stone walls. The fragrance relaxed and calmed me and I began settling into the energy of the chamber. I let my eyes follow the smoke as it drifted upward and watched as it pushed up against the dark surface of the ceiling. The ceiling seemed to be much rougher than the walls. I struggled to pick out details in the faint light until I realized that what I was looking at was not the ancient ceiling masonry at all, but a thick carpet of sleeping bats, which completely covered its surface.

My mind raced as it dawned on me that the ceilings of all the passageways and chambers were undoubtedly blanketed with bats; I had never noticed them before because our flashlights had always been focused on the ground. I knew that the Maya associated bats with the Lower World and held them in high regard. In fact, the emblem glyph of the ancient city of Copan was a bat, and ancient Copan iconography had many representations of the bat god Camazotz. But I didn't like the feeling of being deep in the recesses of the labyrinth with hundreds of bats. I just hoped that the soft light and the smoke from the copal wouldn't wake them. As uncomfortable as I was, I had chosen this place for the ceremony and I knew I needed to stay until it was finished.

I pushed myself backwards on the stone bench so I could sit cross-legged with my back against the wall, added some more copal to the glowing charcoal ember in the bowl, and watched as another plume of smoke penetrated the ethers of this Lower World. I felt myself relaxing as the fragrance of copal once again filled the chamber and I realized that the bats didn't seem to be moving. With my eyes closed, I began softly singing the Plains Indian prayer songs I had been taught for inipi ceremonies held in sweat lodges. As I sang the sacred songs, my thoughts turned to indigenous peoples everywhere and their extraordinary spiritual legacy. After completing the inipi songs, I sang the songs I had learned at the Sun Dance.

The Sun Dance songs reminded me of the actual ceremony in 1990. Vivid memories came rushing back: the sound of the drums and eagle-bone whistles; steam hissing on the red-hot rocks in the purification ceremony that prepared me for the Sun Dance; intense, unrelenting sun and almost unbearable thirst; the searing pain and rush of adrenalin during the piercing; the feeling of transcendence while dancing in the arbor, tethered to the sacred tree of life by a long rope that was tied high on the trunk and looped over the pieces of buffalo rib embedded in my chest; the unbelievable sense of freedom and power when I lurched back and broke free as the taut rope ripped the buffalo pieces out of my chest. And, the most unexpected and moving aspect of the dance for me—the look of profound gratitude in the eyes of the observers and supporters who touched and blessed each dancer with eagle feathers when we passed in front of them at the conclusion of the ceremony. As I continued to sing, I was drawn even farther back in time to when I was a young boy standing in the Field Museum, looking at an exhibit of the Sun Dance and vowing that someday I would be one of those mysterious dancers.

All of a sudden, I began to have an experience similar to ones I had sometimes during inipi ceremonies. The space around me seemed to open up. The dark confined chamber lost its oppressiveness, the walls seemed to disappear, and I felt surrounded by openness and spaciousness. It was still dark but it felt as if I were outside under the limitless expanse of the heavens. My thoughts turned to the ceremonial plaza on the other side of the labyrinth and to Lady Xook. I felt drawn farther back in time as the images of her bloodletting sacrifice—images from the underside of the lintels of her temple—seemed to open a portal to her actual ceremony one thousand years ago. I felt my heart beat faster as my vision began to unfold; I found myself standing next to the labyrinth's doorway that opened onto the Main Plaza.

In the vision, it was late afternoon and the sun was just beginning to set behind the labyrinth as Lady Xook emerged from its darkened corridors and paused next to me. She was dressed elegantly in an intricately embroidered *huipil* and her ceremonial regalia included an elaborate headdress, earrings, necklaces, and wrist cuffs. A surprisingly deep emotional and spiritual connection with her enabled me to sense what she was thinking and feeling as she stood there, waiting for the ritual cleansing and purification of the Main Plaza to begin. She felt a warm, October breeze wafting past her, brushing against her cheeks and rustling the hem of her garment. Her gaze was captured by the shifting patterns of clouds drifting over the Usumacinta River. After her time of seclusion in the darkened artificial Lower World of the labyrinth, the fading evening light seemed particularly intense, yet the softness of the clouds with their pastel colors gave her some relief from the tension of anticipation.

Her attention was suddenly brought back to the plaza by the chanting of her chief priest and the two acolytes by his side.

Even though the three of them had been with her many, many years, through hundreds of ceremonies, she always felt a rush of excitement when their chants began. The acolytes lit the large, intricately-embellished ceramic incensarios they each carried and a profusion of sweet, pungent copal smoke billowed out into the plaza. The priest and acolytes turned toward the north and started a solemn, clockwise procession around the plaza's border. As dark clouds of copal smoke poured from the incensarios, the acolytes pushed the cleansing, purifying vapors toward the center of the plaza with brilliantly-colored feather fans.

The sounds of the chants reverberated off the stucco walls of the ceremonial structures around the plaza. The ancient incantations and holy syllables mingled with the copal smoke, infusing the area with sacred energy and blessing all who had gathered to witness this extraordinary event. Lady Xook looked approvingly at the priests and acolytes who completed their preparations and returned to join her on the steps of the labyrinth. This was when she felt most alive, most complete, and almost overwhelmed by a profound sense of gratitude for the great honor being bestowed upon her.

She knew she was carried always in the hearts and prayers of the thousands who made their home here in her city. She could sense the esteem and respect accorded her by the visiting nobility, dignitaries, and others who had assembled from neighboring and distant cities. Family members and hundreds of special guests lined the perimeter of the plaza. Some stood silently, observing her every action. Some stood with their eyes closed, their bodies swaying to the rhythm of the chants. Others knelt in devotion. Many knew the chants and sang the words softly, almost in a whisper. Everyone seemed to be filled with a spirit of sacredness that kept intensifying.

Although this event was to honor the ascension of her husband, Shield Jaguar, to the Yaxchilan throne, and to legitimize his kingship, those gathered had no doubt that Lady Xook's sacrificial bloodletting would be remembered for hundreds if not thousands of years. As the city's High Priestess and principal *chilam*,[9] she was a renowned seer, prophet, and diviner. Her talents were legendary throughout the Maya realm. Enormous spiritual gifts notwithstanding, it was her humility, warmth, and unpretentiousness that endeared her to all who knew her. This ceremony would celebrate not only a seminal kingship rite, but also a return of the spirit of Yoaat Balam, who had ruled over three hundred years earlier; Lady Xook's actions would create a powerful and valuable political connection between the new king and the city's ancestral founder.

As I, in my vision, remained by her side, Lady Xook began moving slowly, following her chief priest and his acolytes as they started a second circuit around the perimeter of the plaza, with the royal party a few paces behind them. She moved gracefully and meditatively across the smooth masonry surface of the plaza, which had been given a fresh coat of stucco for this event. She felt herself swaying to the ancient sacred chants that cleansed and blessed the space within, above, and below the plaza. A breeze carried thick clouds of copal smoke up toward the heavens. And with each step, she simultaneously moved deeper and deeper into the sacred space of the Otherworld.

Lady Xook's mother, Lady Tahal-Tun—an accomplished chilam and renowned seer in her own right—walked solemnly at her other side. They were accompanied by personal attendants and acolytes bestowed with the particular honor of participating in this extraordinary ceremony. Shield Jaguar followed, along with his principal priest and attendants, accompanied by members of the royal family. For Shield Jaguar, this was to be the defining event of his kingship and he was visibly proud and self-satisfied. If Lady Xook's bloodletting succeeded in materializing Yoaat Balam from the other worlds, it would sanction Shield Jaguar's kingship and complete his initiation into Yaxchilan's ruling dynasty.

The ceremonial party completed their traverse of the perimeter of the plaza and paused where they had started at the labyrinth along the western edge. The priests' chanting ceased but the tones of the ancient sacred songs and incantations continued reverberating from the stone surfaces of the temples and altars in the plaza. Just as the last echoes faded into the heavens, the deep, throaty sounds of conch shell horns erupted from each of the four corners. The pulsing tones projected to the heavens, calling to the sacred Bacabs, guardians of the four directions. The energies within the plaza shifted and intensified dramatically. The priests resumed their chanting and sent an invitation to the other realms, calling to the spirits to join the ceremony.

Ancestor spirits, guardian spirits, and divine beings were summoned from the four directions and the Otherworld. Aspects of the Divine that guarded and protected Yaxchilan—plant, animal, and nature spirits—were called forth as well. Many who were observing or participating in the ceremony invoked their personal ancestral and guardian spirits. Some had prepared well in advance, offering their prayers and beseeching the spirits over a prolonged period before this day, while others were reaching out for the first time. The invitations traveled in sacred tones, carried to the other worlds by the smoke from the copal incense. Copal, the sacred resin that once flowed like blood in trees, was being sacrificed in preparation for the ceremony, foreshadowing Lady Xook's own sacrifice.

The chief priest and acolytes at the head of the procession turned toward the southern boundary of the plaza and began walking with slow, measured, meditative steps toward an area near the midpoint. Lady Xook, her mother, their attendants, and the rest of the ceremonial party followed closely behind. Daylight faded and twilight descended on the ceremonial center. Torches were lit to illuminate the perimeter as the party progressed toward their destination. The priests and acolytes stopped a few yards from the southern boundary. In front of them, a large rectangular area had been designated with stone corner markers and incensarios and was illuminated by torch bearers at each corner.

In the future, a temple dedicated to Lady Xook would be built on this spot to commemorate this evening's spectacular events. But tonight, all that stood in the space was Lady Xook's intricately carved, U-shaped stone ceremonial bench and behind it, a stone altar. The bench had been made for Lady Xook as a gift from her mother on the occasion of her puberty ceremony and initiation as a priestess and chilam. Its imagery held special significance for her, taken from the dreams and visions she experienced during her training. The altar had been used by her mother, grandmother, and great-grandmother, and it was imbued with sacred energies accumulated by three generations of spiritual devotions and ceremonies.

The objects for the bloodletting ritual were carefully arranged on the altar behind the bench. A stack of light tan strips of beaten bark were placed next to a large pottery bowl in the center of the altar. The bark strips would be used to catch Lady Xook's blood during the ceremony and then be placed in the bowl. A magnificently-engraved flat-bladed bone awl, incised with her name, was placed on the other side of the altar. Coiled in a circle around the blade, bowl, and bark strips was a five-foot long cord with small obsidian chips imbedded at palm-width intervals. Lady Xook would pull the full length of the cord through her tongue during her bloodletting. Her other personal ritual objects and amulets were arranged toward the rear of the altar.

The ceremonial party stopped and remained at the edge of the marked-off area. The head priest and acolytes stepped forward, followed by Lady Xook, her mother, and other attendants. Facing the altar, Lady Xook felt a surge of energy course through her body as both fear and exhilaration. She became aware of her quickening heartbeat and the moisture on her palms and forehead.

Her feet had swollen slightly and her intricately-woven ceremonial huipil clung to the perspiration on her body. In the twilight, the ceremonial space appeared to be enveloped in a faint haze of copal smoke from the incensarios. Everything was infused and alive with energy—the bench and altar were pulsing with radiant inner light.

Both the crowd assembled outside the perimeter of the plaza and the royal party were silent, yet the jungle around them was alive with the sounds of the night, frogs croaking, crickets chirping, birds calling, and an occasional screech from a howler monkey. Lady Xook closed her eyes and silently said a brief prayer to her guardian spirits as she strode to her bench, through the energy vortex that had begun to open to the higher realms. The chief priest and acolytes, her mother, and her attendants followed and took their places behind the altar. Shield Jaguar, his attendants, and members of the royal party came next and took their places along the back and sides of the ceremonial space. Those who had been waiting around the periphery of the plaza were invited to move closer.

Lady Xook moved around to the back of her bench and faced the gathered crowd. Closing her eyes, she felt currents of energy moving through her body and felt her soul essence begin to merge with the sacred energies surrounding her. Time seemed to speed up and she felt herself drifting into a dream state, suspended between the worlds. Her focus shifted from physical reality to the realm of her ancestors; she was still aware of her surroundings and the preparations that were unfolding, but she felt herself becoming attuned to the energies and vibrations of higher spiritual dimensions. Bathed in moonlight and surrounded by the delicate haze of copal smoke, she began her journey into sacred time and space.

Lady Xook felt pressure on her elbows as her mother and attendants guided her back around to the front of her bench and helped her settle into a comfortable sitting position, facing the crowd in the plaza. She felt her sandals and huipil being loosened so that her breathing and movement were not restricted. The activities surrounding the cleansing and blessing of the bloodletting implements on the altar seemed dreamlike and far away, but the familiar sound of the priest's chanting and the fragrant smell of copal incense soothed and comforted her. Her heartbeat reverberated through sacred time and space. Her journey was well underway—she was moving deeper into the other worlds and there was no turning back.

Lady Xook focused her attention on her breath, allowing long deep inhalations to fill her lungs with the warm moist jungle air. She felt the familiar tingling at the top of her head that signaled the beginning of the opening of the energy centers throughout her body. The innermost, energetic core of her physical being opened and expanded with each breath, moving beyond the confines of her physical body. She felt her soul presence merge with the sacred energy surrounding her as she continued to open and blend with the transcendent, supernatural energies of the Divine. She experienced herself as both matter and spirit, infused with the radiant light energy of the Goddess, at one with her surroundings, and at peace.

The chief priest stood in front of the altar and faced those assembled. Stretching his arm high above his head, he offered the beautifully engraved bone bloodletting awl to the heavens and the ancestors. Those closer to the ceremony were able to see the light from the Moon Goddess reflecting from the bleached, polished bone. Others perceived this reflection as the light from Venus, the Evening Star, or merely the flickering of the torchlight. The priest softly chanted a few brief prayers to complete the purification and blessing of the sacred instrument, and then offered an ancient incantation to prepare for the bloodletting. Then he slowly lowered the awl and held it gently near his heart. To be a part of this sacred event and to be of service to Lady Xook was an almost unimaginable honor, for which he felt a profound sense of gratitude.

With eyes closed, the priest began to sing a holy invocation that would conjure up Tz'at Nakan, the Vision Serpent of the Wise Ones.[10] His strong, sonorous tones reverberated off the masonry structures surrounding the plaza. The sacred syllables found their way through the ethers, penetrating to the farthest reaches of the other worlds, reaching the higher spiritual realms. The vibratory resonance of the ancient chant invoked the ethereal essence of Tz'at Nakan, summoning him from the place of the divine ancestors. A long, sinuous rift shaped like a tunnel began opening up in the other worlds as Tz'at Nakan awakened. This Vision Serpent reached out from the great beyond to pierce the veil to the world of the living.

Tz'at Nakan's gaping jaws opened majestically before the chief priest and the seated Lady Xook, his energetic body stretching like a passage back through the other worlds, his tail anchored in the realm of the ancestral rulers. Tz'at Nakan—guardian and emissary from the higher realms—provided this umbilical connection between the worlds, a holy energetic tunnel ensuring safe passage through the other worlds. In a few moments, the great serpent would convey Lady Xook to her rendezvous with Yoaat Balam; then the soul essences of Lady Xook and the founding ruler of Yaxchilan would travel through the tunnel back to this ceremonial site, emerging from the portal together.

In Tz'at Nakan's presence, the chief priest motioned for the acolyte to hand Lady Xook the bowl, which she cradled in her lap. She let her jaw relax and fall open. She felt her mother and her attendant gently pull her tongue forward, using a small piece of ceremonial fabric to keep their fingers from slipping. The priest stepped forward and carefully moved the awl into position along the midline of her tongue, halfway between the tip and the area where the membrane attached to the underside of her tongue to her jaw. Lady Xook's attention instantly returned to the plaza when she felt the point of the sharpened awl rest on her tongue. Her breathing deepened as she allowed herself to relax more deeply into the moment, letting the sensation expand to fill her entire body.

Lady Xook's mother and her attendant pulled up on the edges of her tongue as the priest pushed the awl down thorough the flesh with expert precision, stopping when the incision was large enough to accommodate the cord and obsidian chips but not large enough to cause permanent damage. As the awl penetrated her tongue, Lady Xook allowed the searing pain to reverberate through her entire body. In the same instant an extraordinary rush of ecstatic energy filled her entire being. The shock of the piercing thrust her out of her physical body and propelled her soul essence through the portal and down the gullet of Tz'at Nakan. She felt herself rushing through the serpentine tunnel at lightning speed, on a trajectory that carried her to the realm of the ancestor spirits.

All was light, all was one, and all was Divine. Lady Xook experienced herself in two realities at once. She was deep within the farthest reaches of the spirit realm; at the same time, she could feel herself hovering behind and above her own body in the plaza. She watched as the cord was threaded into her tongue and saw her body bend slightly forward to allow drops of blood to fall onto the strips of beaten bark paper in the bowl on her lap. The sensation of the cord being inserted into her tongue brought her awareness back to her physical body, but the ecstasy of the event helped her stay in the spirit realm. This was not her first journey to the ancestors in the other worlds, but it was to be the seminal event in her life as a medium and channel.

Lady Xook had known it would take enormous concentration and discipline to accomplish her task. She had become the divine intercessor between the worlds and through her sacrifice, Yoaat Balam, the founder and patron of Yaxchilan, would once again be among his people—not as a memory, apparition, or channeled presence, but as a physical presence again, bringing his descendants wisdom, guidance, and blessing. It had been almost three hundred years since his reign ended with his death, but now everyone assembled would see him; all would feel his presence and this night would be remembered for millennia. He would depart from the Otherworld with Lady Xook and materialize in the physical realm in his beloved Yaxchilan.

Preparations for this evening had been underway all year. While the royal court had planned and coordinated logistics, Lady Xook had readied herself emotionally, mentally, and spiritually. She had fasted, prayed, sought visions, and journeyed to the higher non-physical realms. Her preparations had intensified during the last calendar cycle, culminating with a three-day period of seclusion, deep introspection, and meditation. She had made a psychic contact with Yoaat Balam during that time, and their connection had grown stronger every day. She had been given a ceremonial object he had carried in life; now it would help her recognize him on the other side and guide him back to his former home.

As Lady Xook completed her journey through the body of Tz'at Nakan, she met Yoaat Balam, who had been alerted by the summoning and the awakening of the serpent. Once together, he and Lady Xook began the process of consciously merging their etheric bodies, allowing their soul essences to blend into each other. During this merging, each retained their own unique spiritual identity, yet together they formed a magnificent conjoined orb of light and energy. Once she felt this process was complete, Lady Xook turned her awareness back to her physical body and, with an extraordinary act of will, forced her physical body to pull the first segment of cord and the first obsidian chip through her tongue. As the chip passed through her flesh, waves of pain and ecstasy radiated out through her being.

The cord passing through her tongue became her lifeline to the physical realm and the vehicle for Yoaat Balam's return. As each palm-width segment of cord and corresponding obsidian chip ripped through her tongue, she felt herself drawn closer to the physical plane; the conjoined breath body she shared with Yoaat Balam moved closer and closer to the plaza at Yaxchilan, their spirit essences gaining mass and density as they moved out of the Otherworld. Yoaat Balam began to see a clear, tunnel-like path emerging onto the plaza and experienced his soul essence crystallizing into a solid form that resembled the physical appearance he had on earth.

Lady Xook continued to pull herself and Yoaat Balam back toward the human realms by drawing more of the cord and obsidian chips through her tongue. The energies surrounding the portal between the worlds continued to pulse and flow as the physical and non-physical worlds began to align for her return. From a distant place, Lady Xook heard the liquid sounds of the chanting of the priest and acolytes and saw those sounds blending with the energies of the portal. She caught the faint odor of sweet, pungent copal and watched as its fragrance blended with the sacred threshold between the worlds. With the passing of each segment of the cord and chips through her tongue, the energies in both the physical and non-physical planes intensified and moved into greater alignment; the path forward was clear and distinct.

Lady Xook's sacrifice was having a profound effect on all assembled. Many prayed silently to themselves, some wept, and many seemed to share in her ecstasy. But as she began pulling the last segments of cord and obsidian chips through her tongue, everyone's attention shifted to the magnificent sight that had suddenly formed slightly above and in front of her. A massive ball of radiant white light, tinged with a brilliant blue hue, materialized in the portal between the worlds, within the gaping mouth of Tz'at Nakan. The blended breath bodies of Lady Xook and Yoaat Balam were within the ball of light—they had returned from the higher realms to the sacred space in the plaza.

The light-energy within the orb was becoming quite dense and it was possible now to see Lady Xook's breath body within the orb, as well as the breath body of Yoaat Balam. Each remaining segment of cord and corresponding obsidian chip passing through her tongue enabled Lady Xook and Yoaat Balam to become more physically present. Lady Xook's breath body separated from the orb, first merging with the energy of her physical being and then disappearing as the last chip passed through her tongue. The diffuse light-energy of the orb continued to coalesce into the physical form of Yoaat Balam.

As Lady Xook's soul essence interpenetrated her physical being, she felt her spiritual and physical energies become aligned and balanced as a single harmonious field. She was filled with the power and presence of the Divine, a gift of grace resulting from her sacrifice and journey through the other worlds. Yet she also felt completely grounded and fully present back in the ceremonial plaza. She became increasingly aware of her physical surroundings—her feet resting on the ground, the movement of her breath, and the weight of the bowl in her lap that contained the bark strips that captured and held the blood of her sacrifice.

Opening her eyes, she saw Yoaat Balam as he stood facing her within the portal inside the mouth of Tz'at Nakan. Lady Xook's eyes met his and for the first time she seemed to fully grasp the miraculous nature of the work she had just completed. She experienced the power and grandeur of his presence and saw the gratitude and compassion in his eyes. Her extraordinary undertaking had left her feeling physically exhausted but, at the same time, exhilarated and renewed—energized from a source outside herself that now moved deeply within her.

As spectacular as Lady Xook's bloodletting had been, few in the ceremonial space were fully prepared for the event that was unfolding before them. Ancestors were a constant presence, interacting with the living on a regular basis. They were venerated by household shrines, consulted through the oracles, channeled during ceremonies, and conjured through bloodletting rituals. They were the repository for knowledge of the ways of the world, the keepers and guardians of sacred wisdom, and the intermediaries between the people and the divine realms. Communication with the ancestors and the spirit realm was essential for the well-being of all. But no one present had experienced a more perfect manifestation of an ancestor spirit than this magnificent presence of Yoaat Balam.

This triumph of belief, will, and destiny achieved by the chilam and the ancient ruler left the entire assembled group awestruck and moved to the deepest core of their beings. Many offered silent prayers; others shed tears of joy and gratitude. Yoaat Balam's visit to the physical plane would be brief. Guided by the chief priest, Shield Jaguar deferentially approached the founder, asking for the acknowledgement that would legitimize his ascension to the throne. Others in the royal party approached for a ritual blessing or healing gesture. Simply being in the presence of Yoaat Balam's energy would change their lives in wondrous ways.

Suddenly, the extraordinary scene in my vision began to fade and as much as I struggled to stay connected to the ancient ceremony, I simply couldn't prevent the images from vanishing. I felt myself pulled back forcibly into the dark interior of the labyrinth, the spaciousness of the plaza replaced by the confines of the hard stone walls surrounding the small chamber. I smelled the mustiness of the dank interior and heard the muffled sounds of visitors exploring nearby areas of the labyrinth. I had no idea exactly how long I had been sitting, but my legs were stiff and I felt a slight chill. I struggled to regain my bearings and reorient myself in the chamber. I knew that my experience of Lady Xook's ceremony was over.

I sat in silence for a few minutes. I briefly thought about trying to reenter my vision but I had a strong premonition that doing so would somehow jeopardize the gift of the insights I had been given. As I burned a small piece of copal, I offered my thanks and gratitude for what I'd been allowed to witness and prayed for the well-being of the ancestors of Yaxchilan. I repacked the items I had taken out for my ceremony and rose stiffly from the stone bench, placing a hand on the adjacent wall to steady myself as I prepared to leave the chamber. An unexpected sadness and longing overcame me as I threaded my way forward through the labyrinth. The remarkable world of the ancient Maya seemed so real, so intense, and so rich compared to my ordinary life.

Leaving the labyrinth, I entered the Main Plaza and headed for Temple 23. The ceremonial structure held a much deeper meaning for me now as a result of my vision. Although the original lintels with the carved images of Lady Xook had been removed by archaeologists (two were sent to the British Museum over one hundred years ago; the third was sent to the Museo Nacional de Antropologia in Mexico City in the 1960s[11]), I stood there superimposing my memories of the dramatic scenes on the temple's masonry and imagined how stunning it must have been when it was first dedicated. It seemed amazing to me that the lintels depicting Lady Xook's sacrifice had survived when so much of the ancient Maya civilization had been destroyed or lost over the centuries.

I wanted to perform one last prayer ceremony before I left Yaxchilan. Heading up the Grand Staircase, I continued past Bird Jaguar's temple and climbed higher to the Great Acropolis. There I found a spot on the stone risers at the rear of one of the temples, which I hoped would afford some privacy. I didn't have any other visions but I did feel the strong presence of the tutelary spirit I had encountered nearby twenty years earlier. Although I hadn't focused on him during this visit, I now realized that he had been with me the entire time. It was comforting and reassuring to be with him again at this magnificent site.

When my final ceremony was complete, I felt that my time at Yaxchilan was also complete. Although it was still early afternoon, I was ready to leave. I descended to the Main Plaza, walked to the labyrinth, and followed a direct path through the dark corridors until I emerged at the trail that led out of the ruins. Continuing on, I found Mayo waiting near the river. I explained to him that I was ready to return, but that this time I wanted to slow down and have a leisurely trip on the river back to Frontera Corozal. It was a beautiful afternoon and our slower pace on the water allowed me to reflect on the gift of the extraordinary revelation I had been privileged to receive.

Much like my earlier vision of Pakal's journey to the sacred tree of life, I had once again been led deep into the Otherworld and witnessed a stunning event that continued to expand my understanding of the spiritual realms of the ancient Maya. I was gaining important insights into the "unseen" aspects of healing and transformational processes, and even though these events had occurred over a millennium ago, I knew without a shred of doubt that these dynamics between our everyday world and the supernatural realms still exist. Mastering these dynamics would become an important aspect of my personal journey and, I hoped, a source of healing for others in this world and the next. For a moment I wondered if someday I would follow in Lady Xook's footsteps, enter the open maw of Tz'at Nakan, and rendezvous with the ancestors.

Chapter Notes

1. Martin and Grube 2008: 118
2. Schele and Freidel 1990: 19
3. Schele and Freidel 1990: 266
4. Ibid., 270
5. I found one unique aspect of Lintel 25 particularly fascinating. Thirteen hundred years ago, the artist had carved the hieroglyphics

surrounding the images of the conjuring in reverse, creating mirror images of typical text. This technique has not been found on any other Maya art work and has baffled scholars for decades. Alfonso cleared up the mystery for me by explaining that this was done so the ancestors looking down from the other world could easily read the inscriptions.

6. Sharer and Traxler 2006: 436

7. The Sun Dance I danced in took place at Pilot Rock, outside Ashland Oregon. It was a "mixed" Sun Dance and included non-Indian dancers, some from as far away as Europe. I had been to this particular Sun Dance the preceding year to observe and support friends from Los Angeles who had danced at this Sun Dance for several years. I was so moved by the ceremony that I pledged to dance the following year, and I spent the intervening time preparing in the traditional Plains Indian manner.

8. Tate 1992: 182

9. For the ancient Maya, a chilam was an individual who served as oracle, prophet or intermediary with the spirits and was highly respected in society. The term chilam is often translated as "spokesperson."

10. Artistic representations of the Vision Serpent are found throughout the ancient Maya world in sculpture and on pottery. Although images of Vision Serpents show considerable variations, all are recognizable through certain common stylistic elements. Schele and Mathews have identified Tz'at Nakan as a special Vision Serpent "that acted as a conduit for noble ancestors who enabled the succession of a dynasty." (1998: 119)

11. The British Museum. *British Museum*. 2 January 2012. www.britishmuseum.org

ROYAL CONCEPTION

It was an extraordinary feeling to be back at Tikal, all the more so because only a few days earlier I'd had no idea I would be here. I had originally planned to spend all of my three-week trip at Maya ruins in Mexico, revisiting the sites I had first seen with Julie twenty years earlier. But after a terrific week in Palenque and Yaxchilan, with a stopover in Mexico City, I'd looked forward to seeing my Maya teacher and friend Hunbatz Men in Merida. I wasn't sure exactly what he had in mind for us, but I knew my time with him would help me move deeper into the sacred realm of the Maya. Once in Merida, however, surprising events that took me in a completely unanticipated direction had ultimately brought me here to Tikal.

I had spent my last night in Palenque with Alfonso at Don Mucho's, an open-air restaurant at El Panchan, in the dense rainforest just off the road to the ruins. Alfonso's father, Moises, was also at the restaurant that evening and I had the pleasure of listening to his stories about the early days of tourism and archaeological exploration at Palenque. In the 1950s there were no tourist amenities. The ruins were reached by an old poorly-maintained gravel road and there was only a handful of visitors each day. These included politicians, presidents, prime ministers, millionaires, and renowned industrialists. Because Moises was the only guide and he also spoke English, he'd had the good fortune to spend time with many of these remarkable people. He also worked closely with the world's leading Maya archaeologists and scholars and had been at the forefront of Maya research for over fifty years. That night, Moises told me he believed "Palenque is not a place, it's a state of mind." I've thought about his comment often and it resonates with me—of all the sacred sites I've visited, there is an aura about Palenque that is extraordinarily unique and enchanting; something far beyond the ancient masonry ceremonial structures.

The next day I traveled to the colorful colonial town of Merida in the northern Yucatan peninsula. Although it was a long, tedious eight-hour bus ride, that was the most direct route and the trip gave me time to do some reading and reflect on my experiences at Palenque and Yaxchilan. That evening, Maestro Hunbatz joined me for dinner at my hotel. We reminisced about our first meeting in Los Angeles in 1990 and learned about the recent events in each other's lives. I talked about my sons, the writing I had been doing about my earlier trips to ceremonial sites in Mexico and Guatemala, and my more recent experiences with Bear Heart and Plains Indian elders. I was completely caught up in his characteristic enthusiasm and passion for the sacred sites we would be visiting and the work we would be doing together. Our plans for the next four days included a day at the ruins of Uxmal, another day at the ruins at Chichen Itza, and a visit to his Maya Ceremonial Center at Lol Be. Although we had talked about these sites and I had read what Maestro Hunbatz had written about them, this would be the first time I visited Uxmal and Chichen Itza with him by my side.

Maestro Hunbatz surprised me with an invitation to join him and a small group of indigenous Maya elders in performing a traditional Maya Fire Ceremony to bless a new park at the ancient site of Xoclan in Merida. The local Maya elders believe that in ancient times, Xoclan had been a stopping point for spiritual pilgrims headed to Uxmal or Chichen Itza. The park had recently been created to allow indigenous elders to perform traditional ceremonies and preserve their ancient spiritual practices. Maestro Hunbatz explained that Xoclan was particularly significant because the Mexican Government had forbidden indigenous elders to perform traditional ceremonies at any other ancient sites in Mexico.

The next morning, Maestro Hunbatz picked me up at the hotel at 5:00 a.m. and we drove through the city to Xoclan Park. It was a relatively short drive, so it was still quite dark when we arrived. The park contained several fifteen to twenty-foot-high mounds in shapes that reminded me of old photographs I had seen of pyramids before they were excavated and restored. We walked together in the pre-dawn darkness, and although the path we followed around the pyramidal mounds was now concrete, it was undoubtedly the same path followed by countless pilgrims over one thousand years earlier.

As the faint beginnings of the first light of day appeared on the horizon, we left the mounds and walked into an adjacent wooded area where other indigenous elders and a few participants and spectators were gathering. As we emerged into a clearing, it was immediately apparent that this was where we would hold the sunrise ceremony to bless the site and honor the ancient Maya spiritual traditions. The elders leading the ceremony, including Maestro Hunbatz, were all dressed in long white cotton pants and plain, white, long-sleeved guayaberas, a distinctive style of shirt popular in Latin America. Within the clearing, participants had clustered into small groups, each working on a particular aspect of preparations for the ceremony.

Maestro Hunbatz introduced me to h-men[1] Ildelfonso Aké Cocom and to Maestro Jesús Ortiz Pacheco, the two principal elders who were to lead the ceremony. All were members of the

Council of Maya Elders and Priests whose mission was to preserve and maintain the traditional rituals, ceremonies, and spiritual practices of the Maya. Maestro Hunbatz explained in Spanish that I was in Mexico visiting sacred sites and that I was traveling with a traditional North American Indian chanupa, or ceremonial pipe. Both men expressed their appreciation for the spiritual work I was doing at the ruins and asked me to join them at their altar for an initiation during the ceremony.

After smudging myself and my chanupa bundle with co-pal smoke from an incensario carried by Maestro Pacheco, I un-wrapped the chanupa and held it in my open palms in an offering gesture to h-men Aké Cocom, in the manner I had learned from North American Indian elders. H-men Aké Cocom motioned to me to approach him and as I bowed my head he proceeded to bless me in the traditional Maya fashion—dipping a small, sanctified bundle of ceiba leaves representing Ya'axché, the sacred tree, into a bowl of consecrated water he was holding in his other hand, and then sprinkling the water on my head and shoulders. After the blessing he motioned for me to place my pipe with the other Maya ritual objects on an altar that had been prepared on the ground just outside the circle. Remaining behind the altar, I watched one group prepare the circle for the Fire Ceremony itself, while anoth-er group at the edge of the clearing used copal smoke to cleanse and purify the conch shell horns to be used during the invocation.

In the center of the clearing, a perfect circle approximately six feet in diameter had been etched on cleared, smooth ground. The boundary of the circle had been enlarged to form a shallow trench, which was completely filled in with successive layers of ground tree bark (signifying the earth), sugar (symbolizing joy), and water (symbolizing purification). Inside the circle, groups of thin, tapered, ten-inch colored candles were arranged at the points representing the four cardinal directions, while a fifth group of candles was placed in the center. Each individual group contained fifty-two candles—the number representing the Maya solar year—arranged in a circular pattern with the wicks touching at the center and the bodies of the candles radiating outward like spokes. Red candles, representing the fiery glow of the morning sun and the place of birth and new life, were arranged in the east. White candles, representing wind and rain and signifying the place of the ancestors, were arranged in the north. Black candles, representing night, darkness, and the lower realm, were arranged in the west. Yellow candles, representing the path that leads out of the earth at death, were arranged in the south. Green candles topped with a bundle of green leaves, representing the sacred Ya'axché tree at the center of creation, were arranged in the center of the circle.

Twenty participants, including the Maya elders, formed a wide circle around the trench and candles and turned to face the rising sun. At a signal from h-men Aké Cocom, four assistants blew conch shell horns in unison, sending long, sonorous tones ringing through the park. The horns were accompanied by the beating of *tunkuls*, ceremonial drums, which provided a deep, rhythmic cadence to the proceedings. Maestro Pacheco circled the group with a large canister of burning copal, releasing billows of the sweet, pungent smoke. The toning of the horns, the rhythm of the drums, and the clouds of smoke seemed to meld together in a universal offering to the heavens.

Facing the rising sun, h-men Aké Cocom began an invocation from his place behind the ceremonial altar. With eyes closed and arms raised he greeted the sun, giving thanks for the new day and praying for the continuation of the earth's bounty and blessings. He prayed for the Maya ancestors, the living Maya, and the Maya yet to come, and he prayed for the well-being of all the participants. He prayed to the powers and spirits of each of the four cardinal directions, as well as the powers and spirits above and below. As he spoke, I felt the energy from the circle expand outwards, engulfing the participants and filling the sacred space surrounding the entire ceremony, which had been created by the energetic vibrations of the horns, drums, and copal.

Each group of candles was lit one by one, and prayers and blessings were offered by h-men Aké Cocom, Maestro Pacheco, and Maestro Hunbatz. I was then asked to add my prayers and blessings, which I did in the Lakota language. We offered our prayers and blessings for the health and well-being of the Maya, for the preservation of their sacred spiritual traditions, for the sacred site of Xoclan, and for the new ceremonial center at the park. We prayed for peace and harmony among all peoples and all nations and for the health and well-being of our families, friends, and communities. As flames from the burning candles leapt skyward, molten masses of liquid wax pooled in each of the sacred directions where the candles had been placed, creating a colorful mandala within the circle. Before the last flames of the final group of candles died down, all the remaining participants—those who hadn't spoken before—had an opportunity to come forward and add their personal prayers.

Standing at the edge of the ceremonial circle, I could sense the presence of the ancestors, their prayers added to ours. I was struck by the similarities between the ceremony I had just experienced and those I had participated in with North American Indians. There were some superficial differences of course; the words were spoken in Spanish and Mayan, the colors associated with each sacred direction differed a little, and copal was used instead of sage, cedar, or sweet grass. But the prayers were the same, the ancestors were present as they always were, and we were surrounded by holiness, suspended in sacred time and space, recreating a ceremony that was thousands of years old.

I didn't want the ceremony to end; to share an experience like this was such a gift, and to stand at the altar with Maestro Hunbatz and the elders was such a privilege, that I found myself hoping the sacred fires created by the candles in the circle would just keep burning and never go out. I soon realized, however, that even though the candles couldn't burn forever, the sacred fires they represented would never truly go out as long as we kept them alive through ceremony and in our hearts and minds.

When the last flames had disappeared, h-men Aké Cocom gestured to all that the hour-long ceremony had ended. I took my chanupa off the altar and walked a short way to a wooded area, where I sat, rewrapped my chanupa, and placed it back into my bag. I spent several minutes just sitting there, shaded by the trees, relishing the warm moist air and savoring the odor of copal that still lingered in the area.

I was stunned by the synchronicity surrounding this event. When I made my original plans I had no idea that I would have an opportunity to participate in this ceremony. I could easily have missed it if I had arrived in Merida a few days earlier or later, and had I known about it beforehand, I would have planned my entire trip around it. As I was thinking about this, I was approached by a reporter for the local newspaper who had observed the ceremony and was preparing an article for the next day's paper.[2] I was able to provide him with some information about the ceremony and in return he offered to provide me with copies of two pictures he had taken of me participating in the ceremony. Although I didn't know it at the time, the newspaper article about the ceremony that I carried with me for the remainder of the trip would be extraordinarily helpful at Tikal and Copan.

Maestro Hunbatz and I drove back to my hotel in downtown Merida and I spent the rest of the day by myself, exploring the beautiful colonial city. I found the Casa de Artesanías Ki-Huic, a store with a wonderful selection of handicrafts by artisans from the Yucatan. Later I walked to Amate Books, where I had the good fortune of meeting the bookstore manager, archaeologist Kai Del-vendahl. Kai provided helpful insights on the Maya ruins I hoped to visit on my trip, and he also mentioned that the Mexican government had forbidden ceremonies at ancient Maya ceremonial sites and suggested I travel to Guatemala or Honduras where such ceremonies were still allowed. That afternoon I started to make plans to travel to Tikal (in Guatemala) and Copan (in Honduras) rather than remain in Mexico after my next three days with Maestro Hunbatz.

The next day, we visited the ancient ceremonial site of Uxmal, the "Place of the Eternal Moon." At the Pyramid of the Magician, Maestro Hunbatz talked about the Moon Goddess, Ix-Chel, the feminine aspect of the Divine, and the initiation ceremonies that were held in the temples here. He explained the association between the Goddess and the sacred waters in rivers and lakes, and we talked about my vision of Ix-Chel at the lake at Coba twenty-five years earlier. Later, during our tour of the ruins, Maestro Hunbatz explained the Maya understanding of "duality." "It is important to understand," he emphasized, "that all things existing on our Mother Earth contain both 'spirit' and 'essence' and everything comes into the world first 'spiritually' and then 'physically.'"

I told Hunbatz about my experience of the Divine emanating from within all things during my vision quest on the Pine Ridge Indian Reservation and asked if that was the duality he was talking about. "Exactly," he replied. "Now you have personal knowledge and true understanding that Hunab-Ku or God is within all things. It is the greatest of tragedies that for so many today, God is believed to be 'outside' of us or 'out-there-somewhere-else,'" he continued, "and this has resulted in so many people being disconnected from the giver of life, feeling lost and losing their connection to life itself."

The following day we began at Chichen Itza. Standing in front of the temple-pyramid El Castillo, also known as the Temple of Kulkulkan, Maestro Hunbatz explained that the Maya concept of sacred geometry "was expressed through the design and construction of ceremonial centers, temple-pyramids, and other ritual structures."

I asked him to tell me more about how they actually did that. "For example," he replied, "the temple-pyramid in front of us has precisely-calculated dimensions based on sacred ratios. The angles of the sloped sides of the pyramid, the nine platforms comprising the body of the pyramid, the total number of steps from the base to the top, and the alignment of the pyramid to the sun, moon, and cosmos were all carefully planned by master architects and priests."

I asked, "Is that why we're able to see undulating patterns of light forming the image of Kulkulkan [the Feathered Serpent] crawling down the pyramid during the equinoxes?" "Precisely," he said. "But that is only a small demonstration of the true genius of the ancient Maya. The entire pyramid itself is a sacred calendar and astronomical observatory."

Maestro Hunbatz then proceeded to explain the relationship between sacred geometry, architectural alignment, astronomy, and the Maya calendar systems. He helped me develop a much clearer understanding of the unbelievably sophisticated and complex Maya system of multiple interrelated calendars, including the 260-day Tzolk'in calendar, the 365-day Ha'b (solar) calendar, and the 584-day Venus calendar, as well as the concept of the Long Count and the Calendar Round. Another fascinating insight he shared was that El Castillo has an exact mirror image that exists, energetically, underground, directly beneath the physical structure itself.

Later that afternoon on our way back to Merida, we stopped at Lol Be (Path of Flowers), Maestro Hunbatz's Maya Ceremonial Center. As we walked the grounds, viewing the beautiful gardens, dwellings, and ceremonial areas, I was impressed by what he had already accomplished and inspired by his vision for the future—to create a center that will restore the Maya Itza cosmic wisdom as it was lived, in its science and religion, some thousands of years ago. He also envisioned an international residential community at Lol Be consisting of students, adepts, and spiritual teachers, with classes, ceremonies, and a "Path of Initiation" occurring year-round. Before we left, I conducted a brief Plains Indian-style prayer and blessing ceremony for Maestro Hunbatz and presented him with a set of prayer ties I had prepared for this occasion as a gesture of gratitude.

The next morning, I went with Maestro Hunbatz to meet with the Dean at the University of Mesoamerica to discuss their interest in courses Maestro Hunbatz was offering through his Cosmic Mysteries School, which included teachings on the ancient Maya calendar, the secrets of Chichen Itza, the mysteries of Uxmal, and Maya celestial wisdom. That afternoon I returned to my hotel and completed preparations for my trip to Guatemala and Honduras.

The more I thought about the ruins at Tikal and Copan, the more eager I was to get there. My trip to Tikal in 1987 had been fantastic. The site itself was the most dramatic and awe-inspiring I had ever encountered, the ancient sacred architecture was stunning, and the surrounding rain forest with its abundant wildlife was spectacular. But it was the opportunity to visit Copan that really excited me. Copan was the site of the Stela H, which I'd seen in a drawing as a young boy, and it was that drawing that had started my fascination with the Maya. It was hard to believe that in a few days I would be there in person. In fact, it seemed strange that I hadn't thought of visiting Copan before.

On my last night in Merida, I had dinner with Maestro Hunbatz in an outdoor café near the center of town. I was fascinated by what I learned from him that night about the politics of Mexico and the plight of the indigenous Maya. Both the Maya and the indigenous tribes in North America had suffered similar fates—the Maya at the hands of the Spanish, the North American tribes as a result of the "Westward Expansion" three hundred years later. During the Spanish Conquest in the 1500s, Maya ancestral lands had been confiscated, their culture suppressed, and every attempt made to completely destroy their religious traditions. Millions died of diseases brought by the invaders. Today, the indigenous Maya face on-going discrimination, political oppression, and economic hardships. As I listened to Maestro Hunbatz and thought about the discrimination, poverty, and hardships I'd witnessed facing indigenous peoples in the States, I was struck by the universality of the human experience and our shared humanity.

The next morning, I took an executive-class bus to Cancun, flew from there to the city of Flores in Guatemala, and took a taxi straight from the airport to Tikal where I had booked a hotel room right at the ruins. It felt great being back there, almost like a homecoming of sorts. I felt exhilarated by the expansiveness of the site, the breathtakingly beautiful temple-pyramids, the lush rainforest foliage, the towering trees, and the abundant birds and wildlife. But I was particularly excited about the prospect of performing a ceremony, a vision quest, in this amazing setting. Much to my relief, even though twenty years had passed since my last visit, the site seemed to have changed little—it had escaped the overdevelopment and quasi-theme park atmosphere of Chichen Itza. Electricity at the hotels was still sporadic, and the nights peaceful.

My first morning at Tikal started at 4:00 a.m. for a sunrise tour to the top of the colossal Temple IV, Tikal's largest pyramid. It was thrilling to watch the sky slowly light up in magnificent yellow, orange, and red hues and then to experience the spectacular tropical sun as it exploded above the dense rainforest canopy, emerging from behind the majestic temple-pyramids to the east of us. It was a perfect beginning to what turned out to be a perfect visit to Tikal. The ruins were more crowded than when I was first there, but much less so than in Mexico. I spent the rest of the morning and early afternoon with a guide, studying the stunning structures that comprised Tikal's ceremonial center: the Great Plaza, the North Acropolis, and the Central Acropolis that archaeologists believe was Tikal's royal palace.

Since my last visit, scholars had learned that Temple I, the Temple of the Great Jaguar, on the eastern border of the Grand Plaza, had been built as the mortuary pyramid of Jasaw Chan K'awiil I, one of Tikal's greatest rulers. The temple-pyramid is now believed to have been built by his son Yik'in Chan K'awiil ('K'awiil who Darkens the Sky'), who was inaugurated as king in 734 CE.[3] Jasaw K'awiil's large, richly-furnished burial chamber was discovered beneath the pyramid by archaeologists in 1962. On the western border of the plaza, Jasaw K'awiil had constructed Temple II (the Temple of the Masks) as a memorial for his principal queen and mother of his heir, Lady Lachan Unen Mo' ('12 Baby Macaws').[4] And recent advances in deciphering the hieroglyphics found on the temples, stelae, and altars in the North Acropolis, on the northern border of the plaza, resulted in an astonishingly complete history of Tikal's ruling dynasties for thirteen hundred years beginning in 350 BCE.[5]

One of the most interesting areas I visited in the Central Acropolis that afternoon was a structure known as the Palace of Chak Tok Ich'aak, one of Tikal's early kings. Within the palace is a courtyard that scholars believe was the site of ceremonial dances involving *wayob* (the plural of way), the Mayan term for companion spirits, which usually took the form of wild animals. Contemporary Maya use the term *nagual* to describe this spirit companion. In *The Code of Kings*, Linda Schele and Peter Mathews write that "According to Maya belief, all human beings have spirit companions with whom they share their souls. Adepts, using the dance and trances, transformed into their spirit companions to access the power of the supernatural world."[6] Artistic representations of masked dances involving humans and wayob have been found throughout the ancient Maya world.

Toward the late afternoon, I left the ruins and headed back to my hotel room to prepare for the ceremony I would perform that evening. Although it was probably the most heavily visited area in the ruins, I knew without a doubt that I wanted to do my vision quest in the Great Plaza, with its spacious open setting bordered by the most magnificent and inspiring temple-pyramids in the entire ancient Maya realm. I was fascinated by what I'd learned about the latest research on the ancient Maya concept of wayob, and excited about the conclusive link the research established with the universal shamanic practice I'd experienced with Michael Harner and North American Indian elders involving animal spirit companions. As I prepared for the ceremony, I found myself hoping some of the secrets of the ancient traditions would be revealed to me that evening and that I would come to a fuller understanding of their meaning and significance.

The brilliant hues of a glorious tropical sunset were just beginning to appear on the horizon as I paused at a large tree behind the Temple of the Great Jaguar before entering the Grand Plaza. A warm, moist breeze wafted through the air and the melodic cries of weaver birds resounded off the ancient stone masonry of the pyramids and temples around me. It had always been a thrilling experience to enter the sacred ceremonial precinct, and this time was no different.

After asking the ancestors at Tikal for their blessing and guidance, I gathered the items I had brought for the ceremony and stood to enter the Grand Plaza. When I turned the corner of the massive stone base of the Temple of the Jaguar and saw the entire plaza area, I was relieved to see that it was relatively deserted. I placed my ceremonial items in the center of the plaza, in an area I had chosen earlier, and carrying my bowl of burning charcoal and a small bag of copal, I walked back to the entrance of the plaza.

Following the practice I had seen in my earlier visions at Tikal and Yaxchilan, I placed a large amount of copal on the burning charcoal and started walking slowly along the perimeter of the plaza. Using a large turkey feather I had found earlier in the day, I pushed the billowing copal smoke out toward the center of the plaza and up to the heavens while I sang Plains Indian prayer songs and spirit-calling songs in honor of the Maya ancestors. When I reached the place where I had started, near the base of Temple I at the southeast corner of the plaza, my smudging was complete. I turned and headed back to my vision quest site.

I prepared my site using four votive candles to mark the corners of a large (four-foot by eight-foot) rectangle, which I aligned perfectly with the cardinal directions and the orientation of the plaza. Standing within this rectangle, I unrolled my string of four hundred and five multi-colored prayer ties and laid them on the ground, following the rectangular pattern marked by the candles to form the boundary of my questing site. I placed the four prayer flags at each corner, each with a different color to represent the four directions, and a blue and green flag at two of the corners.[7] I lit the four candles at the corners of the site. Finally, after placing a large chunk of copal on the charcoal in my bowl, I smudged the perimeter and interior of my rectangular space and then sat cross-legged in the center, facing north—the direction of the ancestors.

It was twilight when I finished my preparations for the vision quest. Gazing out at the ceremonial complex, I was overwhelmed by the beauty of my surroundings: the peaceful energy in the plaza, the magnificence of the temple-pyramids around me, and the beauty of the twilight evening. It was a breathtaking experience. I closed my eyes, brought my awareness to my breath, and for a few minutes simply allowed myself to blend with the energy around me. I had no idea what to expect—one never does on a vision quest. The experience could be something miraculous or something seemingly mundane. Either way, I knew it would have some meaning or significance. I reminded myself that I simply needed to remain open, receptive, alert, and aware.

As the night unfolded, my emotions shifted and I realized I was feeling anxious and fearful. The energy in the plaza at night was incredibly powerful and unbelievably intense. The North Acropolis was directly in front of me, a massive grouping of ancient royal tombs—a burial site that had been excavated by archaeologists. My thoughts turned to harrowing stories I had read of night-long spiritual initiations in India at burial sites and charnel grounds. I sensed the presence of ancestor spirits everywhere around me and I hoped that all would go well.

I had been on many vision quests before, but nothing quite like this; I had never felt so completely alone and vulnerable. Knowing I was one thousand miles and one thousand years away from home, unprotected in the middle of the Guatemalan jungle, was profoundly disturbing. None of the sites in North America where I had vision quested before had the intensity of energy or potential physical and psychic danger of Tikal. Wildlife, including jaguars and poisonous snakes, abounded in the jungle around me and could easily stray into the plaza at night. At the time of my trip, American tourists were being harassed and sometimes kidnapped in Mexico and Guatemala. And I had no idea whether the dark, threatening energy I had encountered in Coba twenty years earlier might also exist at Tikal.

For a moment I thought this was a horrible mistake, one I might pay for dearly. It took all the mental discipline I had to stay focused on my purpose and not panic. Breathing deeply, I was comforted somewhat by the knowledge that the park guards were aware that I was in the plaza and would undoubtedly check in on me at some point. Earlier in the day I had met with the park manager and had received permission to stay a little later in the ruins and to perform a ceremony in the plaza. He had agreed after I showed him a copy of the newspaper article on the ceremony at Xoclan in Merida, with my picture. I also knew that my tutelary spirit from Yaxchilan and other spirit guides were present, helping me.

I reminded myself that events on my trip had unfolded in such an unexpected manner that it seemed as if I were destined to end up here. On one level, I was starting to feel safer and more protected, reassured by the presence of my personal spirit guides and the sacred energies I'd experienced before on other quests. But fear was ever-present, waiting to erupt whenever my focus wavered or my thoughts drifted away from my spiritual purpose. I burned more copal and softly sang two vision quest songs. I finally began to calm down, accept my fear as part of my vision quest experience, and allow myself to open to receiving whatever might be revealed to me.

As the night deepened, I felt the energy around me begin to shift, somewhat like the changes in atmosphere I had experienced with the opening of sacred portals to the Otherworld. The energy in the entire plaza seemed to begin vibrating and pulsing at a higher frequency. The boundaries between the physical world and the realm of spirit seemed to dissolve, and the past seemed to merge with the present. As I sat there, I remembered the words I heard twenty years ago as I descended from top of the Temple I. "You can come here as a tourist or you can come here as a priest but you can't be both." I was clearly here this time as a priest. However, I was beginning to wonder if I was really "here" now, or at some time in the distant past.

A vision began to unfold before me—a royal ceremony in the plaza that seemed almost like a memory. The full moon, born in the east, had begun her ascent: a graceful, majestic arc rose from the eastern horizon on a trajectory that would pass directly over the midpoint of the Great Plaza of Tikal. Her journey this night would coincide with the spring equinox, and somehow I knew that the ceremony I was about to witness had been meticulously planned around her journey. The sun had already descended in the west, signaling his daily death and subsequent journey through the lower realms. Together, the sun and moon traveled the never-ending cycle of birth, death, and rebirth, moving as one in a cosmic dance through time and space.

As she rose over the shoulder of the Temple of the Great Jaguar on the eastern boundary of the Grand Plaza, the moon's radiance began to waken and transform the sacred setting and ceremonial preparations occurring in the plaza far below her. The plaza and surrounding structures—pyramids, temples, ball court, and other buildings designed for the royal court and royal residences—had been constructed to align perfectly with the four cardinal directions. The magnificent pyramid-tombs of the royal ancestors occupied a propitious location just north of the plaza. In addition, the ceremonial center had been positioned so as to ensure that at key times, the sun and moon would pass directly over the midpoint of the plaza. Tonight would be one of those times.

The light from the moon intensified as she became visible over the top of the roof comb adorning Temple I. The presence of Ix-Chel, the Moon Goddess, became palpable to a royal party that had assembled on the plaza for the ceremony. As she moved closer to the zenith of her journey, the moon's radiant light-energy flooding the plaza began animating the ceremonial structures below, as if the Goddess Ix-Chel Herself was imparting the breath of life. The stones of the sacred architecture in the ceremonial complex, which had seemed so solid and immutable in the light of the sun, were softening and opening in the light of the Moon. In Ix-Chel's presence, the plaza was being transformed into a portal to the Dreamtime and structures that were "asleep" earlier in the day were now coming to life.

The royal party formed a large circle around the area that marked the exact midpoint of the ceremonial complex—the center of Tikal, the center of the world, the center of the cosmos. As the moon continued her journey, pulsing beams of radiant light-energy converged at the center of the plaza, focusing laser-like at a point around the whirling mass of an energy vortex condensing around a portal opening to the other worlds. The veil between the physical and non-physical realms had been pierced, and waves of high frequency energy now radiated out from the center of that portal vortex. In the opening to the portal, in the center of the vortex, within a space of calm and crystal clarity, the Goddess Ix-Chel materialized suddenly in physical form.

Her physical manifestation was breathtaking, even for those who had been in Her presence before; radiant beauty, compassion, and unconditional love poured from the core of Her being. All assembled were transfixed and humbled by Her grace and the gift of being in Her presence. The Holy Goddess, Sacred Mother, manifestation of the Divine Feminine, She stood on the smooth stucco surface of the Great Plaza in fully human form. Through this incarnation, She brought balance, harmony, and peace to all beings. Thus embodied, She held the space that allowed the complete and perfect alignment of the physical and spiritual realms.

Her eyes were soft and gentle as She gazed at those assembled in the plaza. Her body appeared to be pulsating as She oscillated between solid physicality and Her higher ethereal, energetic form. She was surrounded by a magnificent aura of crystalline white light, tinged in azure blue. Her outstretched arms and upturned palms beckoned, welcoming all in Her presence. Simply experiencing Her dazzling countenance had a transformative effect on everyone; a deep sense of holiness, calm, and inner peace pervaded the plaza. Some of the assembled party were standing silently in her presence; some prayed softly, expressing the profound gratitude they felt for this extraordinary opportunity; some wept gently. All heard Her say in a strong, clear voice, "You are my beloved."

In my vision, I sensed that earlier in the evening, at twilight, as the sun set in the west and the moon rose in the east, preparations for the ceremony had been underway in the two temples facing each other on the eastern and western boundaries of the plaza. Now, my perspective shifted and I experienced myself standing next to a man I knew to be King Yik'in Chan K'awiil, one of Tikal's most notable builders and greatest military heroes.[8] He was sitting on a stone bench against the rear wall of the innermost room of Temple I, the temple-pyramid of the Great Jaguar. The King sat patiently, his back resting against the smooth stucco wall of the sanctuary, looking out through the temple doorways across the plaza to Temple II, the Temple of the Masks, at its western boundary. He felt at ease and content, resting in the sacred space that surrounded him.

Closing his eyes, he focused his attention on his heartbeat and the rhythmic flow of his breathing. The sounds of the soft chanting of his chief priest reverberated off the walls of the small interior spaces of the three temple chambers, and seemed to mingle with the odor of copal as clouds of the fragrant incense rose from the incensarios carried by the other priests in the sanctuary. Shortly, he would join his queen, Lady Shana' Kin Yax'chel Pacal ('Green Jay on the Wall')[9], on the plaza for the ceremony that would open the doorway between the worlds and prepare for the conception and birth of their son, the next ruler of Tikal. For now, he was grateful for the small amount of privacy the sanctuary afforded and the respite from the burdens of his responsibilities as Tikal's king.

The last tones of the sacred chants of the priests faded into the twilight as they finished their preparations in the inner chambers and moved outside the temple to take positions on the four corners of the platform at the top of the pyramid that served as the temple's base. Each priest, their backs to the corners of the temple, faced one of the four non-cardinal directions and proceeded to pass a sacred conch shell horn through the copal smoke that poured from their incensarios. To those below who were looking up, the pyramid appeared to be shimmering in the moonlight, the perfect manifestation of the sacred mountain (*"witz"*) it was built to be. In perfect unison, soft musical tones joined to form a long, dynamic crescendo as the four priests called to the heavens through the conch shell horns.

Sound waves pulsed and radiated toward the heavens—calling, beseeching, and summoning the great cosmic forces to the sacred spaces of the holy mountain. Supernatural energies penetrated the seemingly solid stone masonry of the temple and roof comb, transforming them into a porous matrix that opened to receive the energy of the sound waves and began to vibrate in perfect synchronization with the oscillations from the conch shell horns. An inner glow began emerging from the stone and stucco matrix of the roof comb; light and sound waves pulsed upward toward the heavens, and the temple and roof comb were transformed into beacons, channeling the energy of the higher spiritual realms into the Great Plaza.

The King emerged from the inner sanctum of the temple and stood just outside the doorway, facing west toward the Temple of the Masks at the opposite end of the plaza. It was almost time for him to descend from the sacred mountain and join his queen and the others assembled at the portal to the Dreamtime, which Ix-Chel had opened at the center of the plaza. He sang his personal sacred song, calling forth his way or spirit animal, the jaguar, and felt its strength, power, and spirit surge through his body. Raw, powerful jaguar energy coursed through his entire being, transforming him into the great Jaguar King—protector of the people, master of the forces above and below.

296

Directly across the plaza, in the inner sanctum of the Temple of the Masks, the Queen was undergoing a deep and profound spiritual transformation of her own. Sitting on a smooth stucco-covered stone bench at the back of the innermost chamber, she had positioned herself behind the exact center of the temple doorway which was perfectly aligned with the path of the rising moon. As the moon cleared the top of the Temple of the Jaguar, the rays of its light—from the heart of the Goddess, from the core and essence of Ix-Chel's inner being—reached through time and space to pierce the darkness of the inner sanctum where the Queen sat, and bathed the entire space in dazzling, supernatural moonlight.

The Queen had known what to expect and had been preparing for this encounter since she took her place inside the temple. Breathing deeply and rhythmically, she relaxed her body, calmed her mind, and allowed her energy field to open and receive the gift of light and life from the Divine Mother. As she sensed the energy in her body pulsing and aligning with the vibrations from the moon, she felt herself being led gently into a deeper experience of the Dreamtime.

With Ix-Chel as her guide, she allowed herself to drift further into the supernatural realm of the Goddess. The small torches that had been lit earlier in the four corners of the inner sanctum flickered as a gentle breeze wafted through the temple, causing their warm soft light to dance on the temple walls. The fragrant aroma of the copal and the gentle sounds of the sacred songs sung by the priestesses soothed the Queen as she drifted between the physical and non-physical realms. She continued to let her body release, sometimes swaying gently and gracefully with the currents of energy, sometimes twitching slightly as her energy aligned with the higher vibrations. As she allowed herself to open to and receive the spirit of the Goddess, she felt Ix-Chel entering her energetic and physical bodies until she and Ix-Chel were "one" and the Queen had been transformed into a manifestation of the Goddess.

Kneeling on the floor of the temple in front of her, two priestesses ritually washed her hands and feet with water that had been sanctified and blessed earlier in the day. When they were finished, they pushed the pottery basin of water under the stone bench and stood gracefully, facing the Queen. They bowed with their hands folded in prayer and turned to leave the temple through the central doorway. Outside the temple, they joined two other priestesses who had been waiting for them. Moving in perfect unison, they each walked toward one of the four corners of the wide pyramid platform that supported the summit shrine and took a position next to the large cylindrical incense burners placed at each corner.

The priestesses knelt and carefully unwrapped the fist-sized corn husk bundles of copal lying next to the incense burners. They quickly placed the balls of sticky copal onto the glowing charcoal that had been lit earlier in the evening. Large dense plumes of fragrant smoke drifted up to the heavens. Hanging from a lanyard around each of their necks was a small bone whistle made from the long wing bone of the macaw. Bending toward the smoke, they passed their whistles through the copal smoke, blessing and purifying the sacred instruments. After each of the whistles had been smudged, the priestesses stood, faced outward toward the non-cardinal directions, and brought the whistles to their lips.

The melodic high-pitched tones from the macaw bone whistles pierced the night and mingled with the deep, rich conch shell tones coming from the Jaguar Temple at the opposite border of the plaza. The musical tones from the whistles called out thorough time and space, guiding the Queen back from the other worlds and out of her trance-like state, bringing her awareness back to the temple and the sacred space at the peak of this holy mountain to the west of the Grand Plaza. The whistles continued to call out through the night, drawing in the spirit of the sacred macaw, beckoning the spirits of the ancestors, honoring the Moon

Goddess, and transforming the energy at the temple-pyramid into the sacred mountain.

As her attention was drawn back to the temple, the Queen became aware once again of herself sitting on the stone bench at the rear of the inner sanctum, and she felt her physical body flooded with pulsing, vibrant, Divine energy. Opening her eyes, she saw the hand of an attendant extended toward her, and taking that hand, she stood up slowly. She looked out through the main doorway of the temple and saw the Jaguar Temple in the distance, with her husband standing at the edge of the wide platform in front of the summit shrine. She saw the sacred pyramid mountain pulsing and shimmering in the Moonlight. Guided by her attendant and filled with wonder, awe, and gratitude, she walked through time and space to the edge of the pyramid stairs.

The priests with conch shell horns and the priestesses with macaw bone whistles let the blended sounds of their final tones fade into the night. Distant echoes drifted through the ethers as the last pulsing, reverberating sounds settled and dispersed in the Otherworld. Absolute silence descended on the plaza and in the opening created by the silence, a stunning figure emerged from the shadows inside the Jaguar Temple—a man wearing a magnificent jaguar pelt that wrapped around his body and closely covered his back and portions of his chest, arms, and legs. The jaguar's head was positioned on top of his own, with its upper mandible resting on the crown of his skull, as if his face were emerging from the jaws of the sacred animal.

At the same time, across the plaza, a figure emerged from the Temple of the Masks—a woman wearing a resplendent gown of macaw feathers wrapped around and fitted closely to her body, and a train of feathers trailing down her back. Once through the temple doorway, she extended her arms to reveal rows of feathers extending down, forming glorious, lustrous wings that fluttered in the soft tropical breeze. These figures, *wayob* impersonators of the King and Queen, took their places beside and slightly behind the rulers at the top of the stairs of the pyramid-temples, with the brilliant white jaguar teeth flashing and iridescent feathers sparkling in the moonlight.

The King and Queen began a slow, graceful descent down the steep, high steps of the sacred pyramid mountains, followed by their jaguar and macaw wayob. On the Great Plaza below, the circle the royal party had formed around Ix-Chel and the energy vortex opened and expanded, filling the plaza to the base of each temple, with gaps where the temple-pyramid steps rose up from the plaza floor. Ix-Chel remained in the center, perfectly aligned with the midline of the pyramids. As the rulers and their wayob descended the steps, deep resonant drums began to beat a slow, pulsing cadence, mimicking the sound of a beating heart, the rhythm of the cosmos, and the heartbeat of the universal soul.

Stepping down onto the smooth stucco surface of the plaza, the King and Queen began to walk toward each other in slow, measured, deliberate steps, following a direct path that led to Ix-Chel in the center of the plaza. Behind them, their jaguar and macaw wayob danced in and out of the shadows created by flickering light from torches that lined the perimeter of the plaza. Synchronizing their graceful, fluid movements to the cadence of the drums, the Queen's macaw *way* bobbed, wove, and soared while the King's jaguar *way* prowled, stalked, and preened. The wayob danced and spun in arcs and circles around the King and Queen, the exuberant ebb and flow of animal essence commingling with the direct, purposeful movement of the rulers.

As the King and Queen drew near Ix-Chel, they moved to the south and then met and turned to stand side-by-side, facing Her and the sacred necropolis that formed the northern boundary of the plaza. Synchronizing their steps to the rhythm of the drums, the royal party moved toward the center of the plaza to form a smaller circle around Ix-Chel, the King and Queen, and the wayob. When the new circle was formed, all except Ix-Chel danced in place to the cadence of the drums with light, stomping footsteps, as if the smooth stucco surface of the plaza were a massive drumhead and the dancers' feet were beaters. Each step and every drumbeat reverberated across the surface of the plaza with increasing intensity.

The force of the dancers' steps beat against the stone and stucco matrix of the surface of the plaza, creating a resonance within the seemingly-solid structure and setting in motion an alchemical process that began to transmute matter into spirit. Each percussive thrust sent shudders of energy downward through the plaza floor, penetrating the pores and crevices in the limestone blocks and earth and then moving sideways through interstices and seams in the rocky substrate. The original energy vortex and portal to the Dreamtime at the center of the plaza began to expand slowly as the vibrational field of the plaza was transformed through the sacred dancing and drumming. The heartbeat-like rhythm pushed waves of energy outward from the center.

Ix-Chel stood, calm and poised in the center of the plaza, in the center of the circle, in the center of the vortex, in the center of Dreamtime. She remained almost motionless except for a gentle movement of Her chest that created the impression of Her heart beating and Her breath flowing. Arms still outstretched, Ix-Chel motioned for the circle of dancers to begin moving in a slow, deliberate, counterclockwise fashion. The dancers' footsteps struck harder on the surface of the plaza as they moved around the King and Queen, as well as their wayob jaguar and macaw, causing the energy vortex to intensify and sending pulsing waves of energy farther outward from the center.

Sound waves from the drums and feet, light waves from the moon, and energy waves from the dancers coalesced and came to a crescendo, opening etheric fissures and intensifying the transformation of the stucco, stone, and earth beneath the circle of dancers. The physical form of the surface of the plaza that had seemed so solid and impenetrable only hours before began to disappear like mist rising in the morning sun, revealing its ethereal, energetic matrix. At a sign from the Moon Goddess, the drummers and dancers stopped abruptly. Faint echoes reverberated and died as the plaza was enshrouded in a profound silence disrupted only by the dancers' breathing. The dancers appeared motionless, suspended within the energy vortex.

With an upward movement of Her hands, Ix-Chel sent the vortex rippling farther upward toward the heavens, and then with a downward movement She pushed the vortex deeper into the Lower World. A magnificent cylinder of energy extended from the heavens above to the depths of the unseen realms below and enclosed the ceremonial party. Next, from a still-point at the center of the vortex, a bright flash of light and a percussive explosion of energy shot out in all directions, piercing the walls of the cylindrical vortex. The churning energy radiating from the still-point vanished suddenly, leaving a purer, crystal-clear energetic void defined by the dense tropical air.

Above the ceremonial party, the moon was perfectly positioned at her zenith. Below, the sun was revealed in the Lower World in direct alignment and celestial opposition to the moon. Energy from the Mother and Father merged and blended in perfect balance, harmony, and unity. Suspended within the emptiness of the cylindrical space, the King and Queen turned to face each other and grasped hands; their wayob did the same. Together they surrendered to the great cosmic forces, above and below, that washed over them. From high above, from Kumuk' lu'um, the "door to heaven" or center of the sky, transparent sheets of pure, rich, liquid, crystalline energy radiated out toward the King and Queen, carrying the newborn soul of their future son.

The Queen's energetic body instinctively opened to prepare to receive the gift of the soul of the future ruler of Tikal. Journeying from spiritual creation to spiritual conception, from Kumuk' lu'um to the Queen's womb, the soul found its way to its destiny at Tikal and completed a spiritual conception that preceded and opened the way for the physical conception that would soon follow. Ix-Chel raised Her hands, palms facing the royal couple, and offered a silent benediction. This was the culmination of years of preparation and the moment all had waited for, the blessing from the Holy Mother for the new mother and the soul that would become her son.

The air was still, the night was quiet, dazzling starlight filled the heavens, and peaceful calm pervaded the plaza. Finishing her benediction, Ix-Chel raised Her head. Her body, glowing and shimmering in the warm, moist tropical air, began to rise from the surface of the plaza, toward the heavens. As Ix-Chel's body began to lose its solid form, the physical world around the ceremonial parties reclaimed and re-manifested itself. Dense jungle air moved into the cylindrical void at the center of the plaza. The stucco, stone, and earth substrate of the plaza regained its physical form and mass. The sun disappeared below as he continued his journey through the Lower World. Particles of light energy danced in the space where Ix-Chel had stood only moments before.

After Ix-Chel departed, musicians positioned on the lowest of the three tiers surrounding the pyramid of the Temple of the Masks began playing for the royal party. The joyful celebratory sounds of horns, drums, pottery flutes, and gourd instruments filled the plaza and ricocheted off the sacred architectural monuments. From the southern border of the plaza, two small groups of attendants bearing two royal litters approached the ceremonial circle and the royal couple. A passage through the circle formed by the ceremonial party opened, allowing the litter-bearers to approach the King and Queen. The litters were lowered and each of them found a comfortable position for their short journey out of the plaza to the royal residence.

The ceremonial party formed a processional line and moved from the plaza toward the chambers where the King and Queen would spend the night physically consummating the spiritual conception that had just occurred. Music from the plaza continued to fill the night air, reverberating off the hard stone and stucco surfaces of the ceremonial and residential structures. A soft breeze wafted through the processional. Bird calls and the grunts of howler monkeys pierced the night. Ix-Chel continued Her celestial journey, dipping below the roof comb of the temple atop the pyramid mountain in the west. The magic lingered as the first rays of dawn broke the horizon.

The vision of the conception ceremony started to fade for me with the image of the first rays of dawn breaking the horizon. For a few moments I experienced the same disorientation and disappointment I had felt as my visions ended at Palenque and Yaxchilan—disorientation resulting from leaving the visionary realm and returning to the present time and disappointment that the vision had to end. But these sensations were quickly replaced by wonder and awe at what had been revealed to me. The manifestation of Ix-Chel was familiar to me from my experience at Coba decades earlier, and the dance of the wayob was familiar to me from my work with Michael Harner and North American spiritual leaders. But the process of spiritual conception I had witnessed in the vision was something completely new to me and totally unexpected.

I was still trying to process what had just occurred when I noticed the bobbing beam of a flashlight coming toward me from the far western boundary of the plaza near the base of the temple-pyramid. As the light drew nearer, I realized it was one of the park guards I'd seen earlier in the day. I assumed he was coming to check on me and to ask me to leave the ruins and, frankly, I was to glad to see him. I felt drained from the intensity of the vision and from the emotional energy I had expended simply being alone in the plaza at night. It was also an enormous relief that I wouldn't have to hike back out of the park alone in the dark. When the guard reached me I explained I needed just a few more minutes to give closure to the ceremony, and he respectfully moved a short distance away to let me finish.

I burned a small piece of copal, offered my thanks for what I had been allowed to witness, prayed for the well-being of the ancestors of Tikal, and expressed my gratitude to those who had kept me safe during my vigil, including the tutelary spirit who had first contacted me at Yaxchilan on my first visit decades earlier and had accompanied me here. I carefully repacked the items I had taken out for my ceremony, and rose stiffly. I joined the park guard and we left the plaza along the northern boundary, passing the ruins of the royal necropolis. I could feel the strong presence of ancestor spirits around me and it seemed as if I saw them moving out of the corner of my eye as we walked past the ancient royal tombs.

That night, as I recorded the vision in my journal, my memories were so clear and intense that it seemed as if I had never left the plaza. My body was still tingling, and I continued to feel engulfed by the same aura of profound holiness I had experienced in Ix-Chel's presence. I tried briefly to interpret the events during the ceremony and draw some conclusions about what I had witnessed, but I was still in such a liminal space that it was impossible for me to do so. Once my journaling was complete, I closed my eyes and let the physical sensations and thoughts continue to wash over me like lucid dreams in the twilight of sleep.

The next morning, I made arrangements with one of the park guides to take a private tour of the tunnels the archeologists had excavated decades earlier to study the insides of the pyramids. The ancient Maya built newer, larger pyramids on top of older standing ones, since the energy vortexes were already in place. Archaeologists created interior tunnels to enable them to study older substructures without dismantling the newer pyramids. The tunnels were dark, dank, only about five feet high, and very narrow—I had to stoop down and turn my shoulders to get through the passageways. As my guide led me through the tunnels by flashlight, we encountered dozens of flying bats, giant centipedes, enormous cockroaches, tarantulas, and scorpions. But the reward for the experience was seeing ancient hieroglyphics, stone carvings and stucco masks on temple walls that had been buried for millennia.

I spent my last full day at Tikal visiting ceremonial structures I hadn't seen previously and savoring the beauty of my surroundings. But I found myself in somewhat of a daze, continually preoccupied with thoughts of my vision quest. At both Palenque and Yaxchilan I'd had historical references and insights related to Pakal and Lady Xook that provided some context for my visions. Here, except for my vision of Ix-Chel at Coba decades earlier, I had no antecedents for the conception ceremony I had just witnessed. Nothing I had studied about the ancient Maya or other ancient civilizations and world mythologies referenced this type of ceremony or sacred couplings. This vision had come to me completely "out of the blue," not as the result of anything I'd felt or dreamed or heard or read or knew, and I still didn't know quite what to make of it.

As I thought about this, I remembered the realization I had had twenty years earlier in the presence of the World Tree at the cave at Balankanche, that we emerge from the Divine as a spiritual essence, a soul destined to enter the womb, and are then born in a physical body. I recalled my journey with the Celestial Bird at Palenque, to the place in the higher spiritual realms that is "the source, the center of the crossroads, the core of the sacred Tree of Life, the womb of the creator, the place where life begins and the circle starts." I also thought about my recent conversation with Maestro Hunbatz and his comment that everything starts with the spiritual and then is manifested physically.

By the end of the day I still didn't know if the events I'd witnessed in my vision were common throughout the ancient Maya realm or unique to this one incident at Tikal. But I did come to accept the fact that, as Maestro Hunbatz had explained to me earlier, the "higher dimensional frequency" at Tikal had allowed me to receive spiritual wisdom from the higher realms. It also became clear to me that the ceremonies I had performed at this sacred site, including the one twenty years earlier in the inner sanctum of Temple I—the location where I encountered Yik'in Chan K'awiil in this most recent vision—created an "affinity" that had enabled me to receive an extraordinary revelation.

Chapter Notes

1. The Mayan term *h-men* (or "doer") is generally used to refer to a shaman but is also used to describe one who is a Daykeeper (a person who keeps track of the meaning and quality of days, according to the Maya calendar), diviner, seer, healer, spiritual leader, or indigenous priest.
2. The article, by Emanuel Rincón Becerra, appeared in the *Diario de Yucatan* on Sunday, May 20, 2007. The article is titled "Ritual de raíz maya honra al astro rey: Peculiar ceremonia en un antiguo sitio de Xoclán en Mérida."
3. Sharer and Traxler 2006: 400
4. Martin and Grube 2008: 46
5. Ibid., 43
6. Schele and Mathews 1998: 83. The concept embodied in the Maya word way is also referred to by Maya scholars as a "co-essence." Sharer and Traxler characterize the decipherment of the way glyph as providing "one of the most important insights for understanding the ancient Maya belief systems (2006: 147)." Contemporary Maya throughout Mesoamerica

share this belief system, often using the term nagual to refer to supernatural spirit companions. The concept of a supernatural spirit companion is also a fundamental, universal belief of other indigenous, shamanic cultures worldwide, throughout history.

7. This arrangement was somewhat different from the one I used during my vision quests in North America. Although the Maya use candles in ceremony, they are not used in Plains Indian ceremonies and prayer flags are tied to small, cut-off tree branches and used to mark each corner of a vision quest site.

8. Martin and Grube 2008: 48

9. Authentic Maya. *Tikal's Dynastic Line*. 28 January 2011. www.authenticmaya.com

CONSECRATION
OF THE MAIZE

COPAN

COPAN DEPARTMENT, HONDURAS – 2007

The ancient Maya city of Copan was built in a river valley along the Copan River in western Honduras, near the Guatemalan border. Although it lacks the grand monumental ceremonial architecture of Tikal, and was much smaller (Copan's population in its heyday was one quarter the size of Tikal's), it is the site of extraordinary artistic treasures that comprise the greatest in the entire Maya realm. In addition to its distinctive architecture, Copan is famous for its magnificent artwork that includes breathtakingly beautiful sculpted stone stelae, exquisitely carved stone hieroglyphic stairways, and stunning sculptures of supernatural deities and ancestors conjured from the other world.

Although I didn't know much about the specifics at the time of my visit, I had read that the hieroglyphics deciphered at Copan and the images in the ancient artwork that had been decoded provided unparalleled insights into the ancient spiritual realm of the Maya. I was also looking forward to visiting Copan because

309

Alfonso Morales had suggested I look up a friend and professional colleague of his, Luis Reina, who lived in the adjoining pueblo; Alfonso and Luis had worked together for many years on the archaeological excavations at Copan.

During the three-hour bus ride from San Pedro Sula, we drove through the lush, fertile Copan River Valley, passing tobacco plantations, coffee farms, and hot springs. The valley was at an elevation of two thousand feet, so it was a relief to leave behind the dense and sometimes oppressive humidity of the steamy jungle sites in Guatemala. The morning after our arrival I walked from the village to the ruins. When I arrived at the park I enquired about Luis but was told that he was in the country visiting relatives (it was Sunday, his day off) and wouldn't return until Monday. Rather than head directly for the ruins themselves, I decided to stop at the on-site Copan Sculpture Museum, an attractive new building that seemed to emerge organically from its surroundings. The entrance to the museum was framed by a stylized representation of the open jaws of a serpent, reminiscent of the Vision Serpent. The entrance led directly into a long, dimly lit, gently curving serpentine tunnel that created a wonderfully realistic impression of journeying from the contemporary world into the sacred realm.

Storyboards along the walls described the tunnel as a representation of a natural cave that, according to ancient Maya beliefs, provided access to Xibalba, the mythological Maya Lower World. The descriptive panels also introduced the famous *Popol Vuh* legend: the story of how the primal ancestral Maya Hero Twins descended into Xibalba, their trials with the Lords of the Lower World, and their eventual ascent to the celestial cosmos. Just beyond its end, the darkened tunnel opened dramatically into a large, two-story, sun-filled atrium surrounded by stunning displays of ancient Copan stone and stucco sculpture that included re-creations of temple facades; gigantic three-dimensional carvings of killer bats, water birds and stylized macaws; life-size figures of ancestral warriors and mythical deities; and hieroglyphic reproductions. As I struggled to absorb all the treasures the museum held, my attention kept coming back to the structure dominating the center of the atrium.

Before me was the most incredible building I had ever seen. The three-tiered edifice, obviously created for ceremonial purposes, rose over forty feet and measured sixty by forty feet at its base. It was covered with boldly sculpted, highly stylized, otherworldly figures that I later learned included fanged vision serpents, other world deities such as the Celestial Bird, Cauac (also referred to as "The Witz Monster"), and Yax K'uk' Mo' ('Radiant First Quetzal Macaw'), the founding ruler of Copan. The temple was painted bright blood red with brilliant green, yellow, and white highlights. It was so colorful and the sculptured images so vibrant and lifelike that the structure seemed almost alive with writhing serpents, flying birds, menacing monsters, and resurrected ancestors.

The structure before me was an exact, meticulously crafted replica of an ancient temple-shrine known as Rosalila. The actual building had been discovered accidentally by archaeologist Ricardo Agurcia when he was excavating beneath Temple-Pyramid 16 (also referred to as Structure 16) in Copal's ancient acropolis. Rosalila had been buried intact within the much larger Temple 16. This was a stunning discovery because the ancient Maya typically destroyed older ceremonial buildings when newer ones were built in their place.

Even more remarkable than the discovery of the building was the manner in which it had been preserved. Usually, the Maya ceremonially "decommissioned" a temple-pyramid and removed the artwork from the outside of the structure before constructing the new temple on top of it. However, the treatment of Rosalila had been different. Rosalila's interior had been carefully filled with clay and rocks, and its sculpted outer panels had been covered with a thick coat of white stucco before the entire structure was buried within the newer temple. Ricardo Agurcia has observed that "Rosalila was a living being, charged with spiritual force. It was wrapped in a white mantle and buried with due ceremony and offerings of great value. In life it was a sacred mountain that provided access to the world of the dead." [1] He also noted that "[t]he embalming of the temple in white finds its counterpart in mortuary practices that remain in use among the contemporary Ch'orti Maya."[2]

In *The Code of Kings*, Linda Schele and Peter Mathews observe that the ancient Maya conducted dedication rituals that allowed them to bring their ceremonial buildings to life and prepare them for use by human, spiritual, and supernatural beings.[3] They note that "[o]ne purpose of dedication rituals was to put *k'ulel* or soul force into buildings" and that "[t]his soul force was ever more powerful with usage."[4] Their research had confirmed my previous experiences that ancient ceremonial buildings contained portals through which ancestors and deities materialized into the physical world. I hadn't realized that "spiritual beings left residual energy in the buildings and the objects that opened the portals" and that the most intense k'ulel was found in very old buildings where very sacred rituals were performed.[5]

Archaeologists believe that Rosalila was built by Copan's tenth ruler, Moon Jaguar, after 520 CE and used by three rulers for over one hundred years until its termination sometime around 655 CE. [6] Other excavations have revealed that Rosalila had been built on top of much earlier structures that included two elaborate royal tombs. The oldest and deepest buried tomb was filled with royal jade, symbolic of sovereign authority, and is believed to have belonged to Copan's founder and first ruler, Yax K'uk' Mo' ('Radiant First Quetzal Macaw'), who died sometime around 437 CE. A later tomb, the richest Maya female burial place found to date, was discovered above his and is presumed to be that of his widow. Although her name is not known, scholars refer to her as "The Lady in Red" because her skeleton was found covered in rich hematite and cinnabar pigments.

The more I learned about Rosalila, the more enthralled I became with this architectural and spiritual masterwork. The building is composed of three levels, or as Agurcia has observed, "three bodies."[7] The first and lowest level of Rosalila contains the main temple structure. The interior walls of the original building are covered with a heavy layer of soot from the ceremonial use of copal and smoke from the burning of torches. During Rosalila's excavation, archaeologists found numerous ceremonial objects inside, including seven pottery incense burners (two of which were placed on carved stone jaguar pedestals), flowers, chert knives, ceremonial scepters, shark vertebrae, jaguar claws, and stingray spines used in ritual bloodletting.[8]

On the outside, the lowest level is adorned with bold, richly-sculpted representations that include K'inich Ajaw (the Sun God) portrayed as the Celestial Bird, and masks representing Copan's founder, Yax K'uk' Mo', being conjured from the Lower World. Anthropomorphic images emerging from vision serpents adorn the lower walls, and massive serpent heads with images of deities emerging from their jaws form the building's lowest corners.[9] The sculpted imagery and ceremonial items clearly identify this section of the temple as a representation of a sacred cave and a path to the other worlds. The images of Yax K'uk' Mo' and the proximity of his tomb beneath the structure document his supernatural presence during ceremonies.

An enormous mask of Cauac, the Witz Monster, dominates the walls of the narrower second level. Agurcia has observed that in this sculpture, "its brow is split, and scrolls that end by cradling a young ear of maize merge from this cleft."[10] The four corners of the second level are formed by massive serpent heads whose bodies descend from the upper, third level. The upper level itself, the smaller and narrower of the three, contains three small rooms connected by two narrow passageways. Together, the second and third levels comprise the roof comb of the entire temple structure. The presence of the mask of the Witz Monster identifies Rosalila as a sacred mountain (*"witz"*), while representations of incense burners confirm Rosalila as a "house of smoke" or temple.[11]

The spiritual symbolism of Rosalila's architecture and iconography, viewed as a whole, is incredible almost beyond belief. Although described as a sacred mountain, a place of creation and the birthplace of the sacred maize, to me the combination of witz and serpent images, along with the depiction of a young ear of maize, identify Rosalila as a manifestation of Sustenance Mountain or Yax Hal Witznal, the "First True Mountain."[12] I also came to believe that the interpretation of the imagery from the Temple of the Jaguar at Chichen Itza applies to Rosalila as well: both display images of "[t]he snake in the mountains [which] represents a conduit from the supernatural world into the human world—a kind of vision serpent" and also a "birth canal."[13]

I was stunned with what all this seemed to be communicating about the purpose and function of this ancient structure. Maize was so central to the life of the ancient Maya that they referred to themselves as the "people of the maize" and Rosalila seemed to be at the very heart of their most sacred mysteries. The temple was the living embodiment of First True Mountain, the source of life-sustaining maize for the Maya. The sacred crop was birthed on the summit of Yax Hal Witznal, and was brought forth from the higher spiritual realms into the human world through the umbilicus of the supernatural serpents. Inside the sacred mountain, deep within the sacred cave, Copan's founder, Yax K'uk' Mo', was resurrected from the other worlds to preside over the divine gift of maize to the Maya.

I spent three hours in the museum that day. Most of my time was spent at the Rosalila reconstruction, and the rest viewing the other exhibits of spectacular stone and stucco sculptures that included supernatural beings conjured from the other worlds, witz masks, *waybil* (god houses), images of killer bats (the emblem glyph of Copan), and other architectural works of art. Early that afternoon I left the museum area and walked toward the Great Plaza of Copan, beyond the entrance to the ruins. I found a semi-secluded area outside the plaza and stopped among the trees to prepare to properly enter the sacred site. I burned copal, smudged myself, offered a few short prayers to the Maya ancestors and their living descendants, and then walked directly across the grassy plaza until I found Stela H.

Standing in front of this magnificent stela, the freestanding, monolithic stone carving of Copan's thirteenth ruler, Waxaklajuun Ubaah K'awiil ('18 Rabbit'), was an electrifying experience. Although Frederick Catherwood's nineteenth century lithograph of the monument was hauntingly beautiful, seeing the actual stone masterwork was absolutely breathtaking. I immediately recalled in minute detail the moment I had first encountered Catherwood's drawing. I remembered the chills that had swept through my body as the ancient ruler's magnificent visage and elaborate ceremonial regalia seemed to leap off the page of the picture book in my hands. It was as if his image had called out to me, awakening what seemed to be an ancient, forgotten memory.

But Catherwood's striking drawing paled in comparison to the actual monument before me. The sculpted image of Waxaklajuun Ubaah K'awiil, dressed as the Maize God in his full ceremonial regalia, was over seven feet high, three feet wide, and three feet deep. The carved representation of his ceremonial headdress extended the sculpture's height to over eleven feet. The entire surface of the limestone slab was comprised of intricately-wrought carved images that depicted not only Waxaklajuun Ubaah K'awiil, but also supernatural deities, serpentine images of the twisted cords of the cosmic umbilicus that carried souls between the physical and non-physical realms, and wayob (animal spirit companions) conjured from the Otherworld.[14]

There on the grassy plaza, underneath a crystalline blue sky, Waxaklajuun Ubaah K'awiil was as present to me through his sculpture as if he had been standing there in person. The space around me seemed to expand, time seemed to slow down, and the sounds of other visitors seemed to drift off into the distance. I stood there transfixed, mesmerized by the presence of the ancient ruler. I realized my legs were shaking and tears were running down my cheeks. Somehow, decades after our first encounter, I had found my way back to Waxaklajuun Ubaah K'awiil and I knew something profoundly important was unfolding for me; I knew there was a reason for my being there.

I spent a leisurely time studying the other monumental stelae in the plaza and then ventured deeper into the ceremonial site. Unlike most other Maya sites, where limestone had been the primary building material, here at Copan, green and buff-colored volcanic tuff predominated. Although archaeologists believe that the ceremonial structures were once brightly painted (much like Rosalila), today they have an incredibly beautiful greenish patina that gives them an aura of enchantment. Copan's altitude and proximity to the river have resulted in trees and lush highland foliage that envelope the site and give it an unmatched natural beauty.

Walking through the ruins, I passed breathtakingly beautiful architectural masterpieces that included the Ball Court, the Hieroglyphic Stairway, and the Temple of Inscriptions. Eventually I made my way to the East Court (also known as the Court of the Jaguars) and found the entrance to the underground tunnel that led to the original Rosalila, entombed within the pyramid that supported Temple 16. My heart was racing as I covered the short distance through the tunnel into the base of the pyramid, bringing me face to face with the excavated portions of Rosalila on public display. Signs along the tunnel walls helped orient visitors to the various architectural elements and provided a reference to the replica in the museum.

Although the tunnel was cramped and dark, it was thrilling to see portions of the actual temple in person, including an original stucco mask of the Yax K'uk' Mo' as the Sun God and a double-headed serpent with an anthropomorphic face emerging from its jaws. Knowing that the tomb of Copan's founder Yax K'uk' Mo' as well as the tomb and offering chamber of his wife were farther below me (although not accessible to visitors) made the experience all the more exciting. The ruins were relatively deserted that day so I had ample time to spend within the Rosalila tunnel and another called the Jaguar Tunnel that was also open to the public. By the time I had finished the second tunnel tour, I'd had enough for one day and decided to walk back to the hotel.

That night I had an incredibly difficult time sleeping as I struggled to make sense of the unexpected correspondences I was seeing between Maya maize and North American Pueblo Indian corn ceremonialism. The symbolism of Waxaklajuun Ubaah K'awiil depicted as the Maize God on Stela H and the Yax Hal Witznal imagery on Rosalila had helped me to more fully appreciate the role maize played at the very center of the heart and soul of ancient Maya spirituality. According to their spiritual traditions, the Maize God was the First Father of world creation and the Maya were originally created from maize dough. Maize was a primary component of their diet and they depended on it for their livelihood. It became clear to me that understanding this maize symbolism was the key to understanding who the ancient Maya were.

With this awareness, my thoughts turned immediately to the Pueblo Indians of the American Southwest. I had learned from the writings of Hopi Indian scholar Barton Wright that the Hopi, as well as other Pueblo tribes,[15] believe that corn is their "Mother"[16] and the source of their livelihood. The Hopi and other Pueblo tribes have developed elaborate ceremonies designed to elicit supernatural assistance to ensure an adequate harvest. The Hopi believe that "God and nature are one" and that "[e]very object possesses a spirit or animus of its own that can be coerced to intercede for the Hopi in this dual world of the natural and the supernatural."[17] I was realizing that the ancient Maya and Pueblo cultures shared surprising similarities regarding maize and corn.

I also began thinking about Rosalila's role as a sacred cave and portal to the other worlds. As I did so, my thoughts turned to the Pueblo Indian altars at the Field Museum and the ancient Anasazi ceremonial kivas at Chaco Canyon. The altars were used inside subterranean kivas for rituals that involved accessing the Otherworld for supernatural assistance and blessings during sacred ceremonies related to the annual planting and harvesting of corn. The Pueblo peoples are also the living descendants of the ancient Anasazi Indians whose kivas at Chaco Canyon—places like Casa Rinconada—are the precursors to contemporary pueblo kivas.

Lying in bed that night I kept thinking about this possible kinship between the ancient Maya and Pueblo peoples. I couldn't help feeling there were underlying universal realities they both recognized and shared that were expressed through their spiritual and ceremonial traditions. It felt as if I were coming full circle on a spiritual journey that had started for me as a young boy in the Field Museum and had led me here to Waxaklajuun Ubaah K'awiil. It seemed he had first beckoned to me when I was five years old and was continuing to guide me.

Rosalila was built some five hundred years before Casa Rinconada. The exhibits in the Field Museum were based on observations of Pueblo ceremonies that occurred almost seven hundred years after Casa Rinconada was abandoned. It was hard to comprehend a relationship between peoples separated by one thousand two hundred years and almost two thousand miles, yet the resemblances were inescapable. Quite unexpectedly, I found myself struggling to come to terms with the strange coincidence that the two cultures I had been most fascinated with since childhood shared analogous perspectives concerning maize and corn. I wondered if there might be something about the Pueblo rituals that would provide some insight into the ancient Maya.

The replicas of the Pueblo ceremonial altars and ritual practices in the Field Museum, created over one hundred years ago, were based on ethnographic research sponsored by the museum. My thoughts kept returning to one dramatic exhibit in particular; it was the re-creation of a ritual for renewing the world and sanctifying seed corn to promote better growth of the crops. The sanctification rites took place in an underground kiva and were the climax of a nine-day ceremony that occurred annually, immediately after the winter solstice. The exhibit, which used mannequins attired in authentic ceremonial regalia to represent Pueblo priests, was based on multiple observances of the ceremony by ethnographers between 1893 and 1900.

A special altar had been constructed at the rear of the kiva for the ceremony. The reredos (back screen) consisted of two six-foot high posts, about four inches wide and one inch deep, spaced four feet apart. A horizontal beam almost four inches high, one inch deep, and five feet long capped the two posts. Spanning the space between the two vertical posts were six horizontal slats, two inches wide by one inch deep, equally spaced from the top to the midpoint of the reredos. On the ground between the vertical posts, carefully tied bundles of ears of corn had been stacked in a large mound that reached almost to the lowest horizontal slat. The bundles belonged to families who would be planting corn crops the following spring, and had been placed on the altar by the priests performing the ceremony.

In front of the altar, extending toward the center of the kiva, a coating of sand had been placed on the floor, creating a "sandfield" containing sacred objects for the ritual blessing. *Pahos*, small cane-shaped prayer sticks representing ancestors whose spirits would be summoned from the other worlds during the ceremony, had been inserted into clay bases and placed along the sandfield.

In the exhibit, two priests were depicted in the act of sanctifying the corn. One, identified as the Star Priest, held a large, circular image of the Sun. Beside him was a large framed vertical screen with an image representing Müy'ingwa, the Corn God (also referred to as the God of Germination). The complex ceremony involved chanting, prayers, and other ritual acts that continued throughout the night. At the completion of the ceremony, the bundles of corn were brought up from the kiva and spread out on a blanket in the plaza where the women who had originally prepared them for blessing retrieved their particular bundles. As a child, I had been particularly fascinated and profoundly moved by this exhibit; now the memories flooded back to me with crystal clarity.

My thoughts turned to another, much more recent experience. Several years earlier, I had spent months building a detailed replica of another type of Pueblo ceremonial altar. The idea for building the altar came from one of the workshops I had attended, given by Tom Mails. I decided to build an altar to use in personal ceremonies to help me realize certain results in my personal and professional life, much as the Pueblo peoples used altars in ceremonies to manifest an abundant harvest.

During my research in preparation for building the altar, I encountered a detailed colored rendering of a Pueblo altar in the *Twenty-third Annual Report of the Bureau of American Ethnology* (circa.1901–1902), which particularly appealed to me. I was able to draw plans and construct an exact replica. The altar consisted of a large vertical wooden back screen composed of six boards—each one four feet high, eight inches wide, and one inch deep, fastened together to form a single piece. A stylized representation of the sun rested atop the left outer board while a stylized representation of the moon rested atop the right outer board. The four center boards had scalloped tops representing clouds, with paintings representing rain below. In front of the back screen was space for a sandfield, with two pairs of additional vertical boards of the same dimensions positioned along each side. One pair had a representation of a spirit being with a dragonfly image painted below. The other pair had a star shape carved at the top; the left one represented Venus as the Morning Star and the right one represented Venus as the Evening Star. The image of a cougar was painted below each star. Additional details included carved representations of serpents and a celestial bird.

As I reflected on the Pueblo altars and ceremonies that occurred inside the kivas, my thoughts kept returning to Rosalila. Ancient Maya pyramids were built as "sacred mountains" and their corresponding temples built as "caves" providing a path to the Lower World. Subterranean Pueblo kivas are Lower World sanctuaries, containing portals to the other worlds, where the conjuring of ancestors and kachina spirits occurs during ceremonies. I began to see Rosalila as a magnificent fusion of the Pueblo kiva architecture and altar iconography. The striking similarities between the ceremonial structures and sacred imagery of both peoples, as well as the parallel roles that maize and corn played in their mythologies and worldview, led me to conclude that the ancient Maya and Pueblo peoples shared fundamentally similar spiritual truths.

One other fascinating piece of information occupied my thoughts that night. Shortly before leaving on this trip I had read an article in a scientific journal that provided new evidence of a direct connection between the ceremonial practices of the ancient Maya and Anasazi peoples. For years, archaeologists had recognized the similarities between ancient ball courts, platform mounds, and certain construction techniques discovered in the American Southwest and those in the ancient Mexican and Maya realms. In Chaco Canyon, archaeologists had also discovered other Mesoamerican goods, including copper bells, cloisonné, and feathers from scarlet macaws (a species native to Mexico and found in the Southwest). Recently, researchers had found residues of Mesoamerican cacao inside pottery cylinder jars in the Pueblo Bonito ruins at Chaco Canyon. This discovery documented Chacoan ceremonies' use of unique sacred pottery of Maya-inspired design in connection with the drinking of cacao—a ritual practice common among the ancient Maya.[18]

The cacao residues found inside cylinder jars contained a specific chemical composition found only in cacao from the Maya areas of Belize, Guatemala, and Honduras. The jars—vase-like cylindrical containers typically two-and-a-half times as tall as they are wide—were a classic Maya ceremonial shape not found elsewhere in the Southwest. In addition, they were decorated with complex symmetrical serrated patterns instead of the simpler banded patterns found on indigenous Anasazi pottery.[19] We now have evidence that rituals performed by Chaco practitioners at Pueblo Bonito between 900 and 1200 CE followed Maya ceremonial patterns, or that Maya practitioners may have performed rituals at Chaco Canyon during this time, or both.

One of the reasons I struggled that evening to make sense of my strong impressions regarding a possible link between the ancient Maya, ancient Anasazi, and Pueblo peoples is that I had never found any significant references to the American Southwest by any Maya scholars. It had always puzzled me that in twenty years of research I had only come across one single reference. Scholars of North American indigenous cultures have frequently suggested possible connections between North American and Mesoamerican Indian communities, but that has not been the case with Maya scholars. I was becoming more and more convinced of a strong connection between these cultures did exist. I hope that someday, someone will study this in more detail.

I woke early the next morning, despite having gotten very little sleep, and after a quick breakfast decided to walk back to the ruins. At Yaxchilan, my experience with the Plains Indian Sun Dance had helped me appreciate at least some aspects of ancient Maya bloodletting rituals. Now, I hoped my experience with the Pueblo Indians would help unlock some secrets of ancient maize ceremonies.

When I arrived at the ruins I went directly to the museum and inquired about Luis. In a few minutes he emerged from his office and greeted me with a big smile and a warm handshake. His sister had spoken to him the day before about my being here and he had adjusted his schedule so we could spend a little time together. We talked about my interests in the ancient Maya, the journey I had been on for the last two-and-a-half weeks, and my particular interests in Copan. As we toured the Museum together, Luis provided background information on the construction of the museum, the exhibits, and in particular, the reconstruction of Rosalila. He shared with me some of the history of the archaeological investigations at Copan—it is one of the most extensively studied of all Maya sites—and we talked at length about Alfonso and the work they had done together on Copan's excavation tunnels.

The extensive use of tunnels to study the sequence of building that occurred over centuries is a defining characteristic of the archaeological investigations at Copan. The tunnels here totaled over two miles in length, a dramatic contrast to the smaller, limited, poorly maintained ones I saw at Tikal. As was common practice, the ancient Maya buried older structures with wet-laid fills before building newer, grander structures over them. As a result, archeologists have been able to tunnel into the fills and reveal the older underlying substructures. While time-consuming and labor-intensive, this process prevents the destruction of underlying architecture that occurs when open trenches are dug for exploration purposes; it eliminates the need to completely dismantle and desecrate entire pyramids and temples to study successive levels of superimposed buildings or to search for hidden tombs, as occurred at the North Acropolis at Tikal.

At Copan, archaeologists have discovered that the area known today as the East Court had actually been built-up "layer cake" fashion over hundreds of years, as earth and stone platforms elevated its surface. The courtyard's original surface was actually several meters below its current level. This build-up began with the construction of the tomb of Yax K'kuk' Mo'. At a later time, his wife's tomb was placed within a platform constructed at a higher level, and even later the base of Rosalila was constructed on a platform at a still higher level. Temple-pyramid 16 (also referred to as Structure 16) was constructed on the highest level of the courtyard, the one we see today. All of the structures surrounding the courtyard as it exists today encapsulate older ceremonial buildings and, archaeologists speculate, possibly undiscovered tombs.

After Luis and I had spoken for a while, he took me to meet Professor Oscar Cruz, the Copan regional director for the Instituto Hondureño de Antroplogía e Historia (IHAH). Professor Cruz was a recognized expert on the ancient Maya and had played a major role in the successful completion of the museum project. We spoke at length of his academic interests and the ongoing archaeological work at Copan. When I mentioned my work with the Maya and showed him a copy of the newspaper article with pictures of me participating in the Fire Ceremony in Merida, Professor Cruz told me about local Maya shamans who still conduct ceremonies here in the ruins. He also told me the specific location where these rituals occur and gave me permission to perform a ceremony while I was there.

Both men had busy schedules and our meetings ended sooner than I would have liked, but I was grateful for the time I'd had with them, and Luis and I were able to make plans to meet for dinner that evening. As I walked toward the ruins from the museum, I continued to struggle with thoughts that had kept me up the night before. I stopped in a grove of trees before entering the Great Plaza, burned copal, said a few short prayers for the Maya ancestors, and asked for help and guidance during my time at the ruins that day. I also asked the spirits to help me find a place to conduct a longer prayer ceremony later in the day; I was hoping to have some private time as I'd had at Tikal, even though I knew from my earlier conversations with Professor Cruz that I couldn't stay late after the park closed.

As I entered the Great Plaza, I realized that something had shifted for me in a profound way during the last twenty-four hours. I began seeing the ruins in a completely different way. Instead of just traces of red painted on the stelae, I could imagine them bright red like the painted surfaces of Rosalila; the sculptured imagery on the stelae seemed to come to life as well, and I could see the symbolism of maize everywhere. I remembered observing the kachina dances on the Hopi Indian reservation and marveling at the precision of the dancers and the beauty of their colorful masks and ceremonial regalia; every movement, every image, every accoutrement had a clear meaning for everyone in the community.

And so it must have been here as well. Waxaklajuun Ubaah K'awiil presided over the plaza, resplendent as the Maize God, on display for all to see and admire. There could be no doubt about his primal role as First Father. Moving farther into the ruins, I passed the Ball Court. I had seen many such structures over the years at several different ruins, but it was as if I were seeing a ball court for the first time. I recalled Linda Schele and Peter Mathews' observation that the ball game itself was a reenactment of the Maya creation and origin myths and that "[t]he Maize God died and was reborn in the ball court."[20] Once again, the maize symbolism struck me dramatically in a way I hadn't appreciated before.

Continuing on, I passed the magnificent Hieroglyphic Stairway and then scaled the stairs that led up to the area of the ruins that included the Acropolis and the East Court. When I reached the top of the stairs, I was standing beside the temple on top of Temple-pyramid 22 (also referred to as Structure 22), the Temple of Meditation. This temple, built some two hundred years after Rosalila, contains a beautifully sculpted doorway and abundant sculptural and hieroglyphic images that, like those at Rosalila, also identify it as a representation of the primordial Yax Hal Witznal, the "First True Mountain of Creation," or "Substance Mountain." Although architecturally and artistically it is much different from Rosalila, the temple is arguably one of the most dramatic expressions of Yax Hal Witznal in the Maya realm.

From the vantage point of the temple, I looked out across the sunken East Court, ancient Copan's original plaza, toward the massive Temple 16. Rosalila was nestled out of sight within its interior, and the tombs of Yax K'uk' Mo' and his wife were deep inside the earth beneath Rosalila, and well below the current grade of the courtyard. As I gazed at the area, I tried to imagine Rosalila in its full splendor and glory standing as it once did as the centerpiece of the royal acropolis. I imagined the structures around me— built much later than Rosalila—dissolving like mist evaporating in the morning sun to reveal the radiant temple as the center around which the spiritual life of the ancient city revolved over one thousand five hundred years ago.

I could easily imagine Rosalila—the living embodiment of the First True Mountain of Creation and a portal between the worlds—at the very heart of Maya spiritual life at Copan. My thoughts returned to the Pueblo Indians and the kachina dances I had witnessed years earlier in Arizona. I wondered if the ceremonies at Rosalila might have shared any similar elements. In the Pueblo ceremonies, men from the villages, attired in spectacular regalia and wearing dramatic masks, impersonated kachina spirits who had been summoned from the Otherworld to provide supernatural help with the season's corn crop. After emerging from the underground kivas, the kachina spirits danced to the beat of drums and tones of sacred chants in the open plaza, surrounded by the community.

Kachina dancers appeared bare-chested, wearing knee-length dance kilts of white homespun cotton embellished with two striking vertical embroidered panels decorated with stylized symbols in black, green, and red, representing clouds, lightning, rain, the rainbow, and life. Tied around their waists were broad white homespun cotton sashes with embroidered end panels containing stylized representations of mountain lion teeth, tracks of the War God, and blossoms of squashes, melons, and flowers. Dramatic body paint was used extensively to represent specific supernatural powers. Ceremonial dance moccasins, leather arm bands, and various types of necklaces (including turquoise, coral, shell, corn, horn and sometimes mountain lion claws) were also worn, and dancers carried large gourd rattles they shook rhythmically to accompany the singing of sacred songs. A fox fur pelt hung from the back at the top of the kilt and extended downward with the fox tail almost touching the ground. The most striking items of the dance regalia were painted leather helmet masks representing the specific supernatural kachinas the dancers were impersonating. The masks, which covered the dancers' heads, included various symbols representing an abundant harvest (corn, rain, lightning, etc.), animal powers (wolf, buffalo, deer, etc.), and celestial bodies (sun, moon, stars, etc.).

As my thoughts returned to the present, the ancient stone structures around me reemerged and in my mind's eye Rosalila withdrew into the interior of Temple 16. Although I loved being at the temple and close to the East Court, I was anxious to see the other locations in Copan where I had been told the contemporary Maya shamans still performed ceremonies. And I hoped to conduct a prayer ceremony myself in the ruins later that afternoon. Although I had intended to do so at a site that was still being used by the contemporary Maya, Rosalila and the East Court were intensely compelling. Something was beckoning me to this particular place, reaching out through the ages to touch a place very deep inside me. I knew I would return here when the time came to do my ceremony.

I turned, descended the steps back down the pyramid, and headed toward the Great Plaza. Before I reached it, I took a side path Professor Cruz had mentioned, and followed it to a secluded wooded area away from the main ruins until I came to a large monolithic stela. I was in an area a distance from the main paths that led through the ruins, at the edge of an ancient sacbe that had once been used to enter the sacred ceremonial center of Copan. The stela had been erected by Waxaklajuun Ubaah K'awiil to mark the end of the first period of his reign. While not as dramatic as the others he had erected in the Main Plaza, the hieroglyphics on the monument delivered an important message, linking Waxaklajuun Ubaah K'awiil to rituals performed two hundred sixty-six years earlier by Copan's founder, Yax K'uk' Mo'. At the base of the stela in front of me, I could still see faint traces of a Fire Ceremony that had been held on the recent equinox.

I spent quite some time undisturbed in this shaded, semi-secluded and serene setting, thinking about the last twenty-four hours and recording my impressions in my journal. The writing helped me organize my thoughts and make sense of the seemingly random insights I had been experiencing. My knowledge of the striking similarities between the spiritual worldview and ceremonial practices of the ancient Maya and the indigenous peoples of North America had allowed me to enter the sacred realm at Copan with ease and comfort. I had found that while the specific rituals differed, the same eternal truths were being expressed. The ceremonies I performed in ancient Maya settings, like those I performed at sacred sites in North America, moved me closer to a universal Divine presence. I finished my journaling early that afternoon, returned to the hotel to get my things for the ceremony, and then walked back to the ruins. I went directly to the East Courtyard, the Court of the Jaguars, where I had decided to do my ceremony.

I descended the steps next to Temple 22 leading into the sunken courtyard, and at the bottom I paused briefly to say a silent prayer and ask permission from the spirits to enter. I walked over to a park guard standing near the entrance to the tunnel that led to Rosalila, showed him a copy of the newspaper article from Merida, and explained the prayer ceremony I wanted to perform. With his consent, I placed a small ceremonial blanket on the ground along the midpoint of the eastern boarder of the courtyard, took my ceremonial items out of my bag, and prepared a small altar on the blanket. After lighting a piece of charcoal and placing it in my bowl, I added copal and smudged myself with the fragrant incense.

I tried to imagine the route ancient priests would have taken to enter the courtyard when performing ceremonies, and my attention was drawn to a narrow passage at the southeastern corner that led out of the East Court. Cradling the bowl with the smoking copal in my hands, I stood up and walked toward the passageway defined by a low stone wall along its eastern border and by the base of Temple 16 along its western border. I followed the passageway out of the courtyard until I reached its end at the far side of Temple 16. I turned, paused, placed more copal on the burning charcoal, and said a few more prayers, asking for blessings and guidance from the ancestor spirits. Imagining how ancient ceremonies would have been conducted, I then retraced my steps along the passageway and reentered the East Court. Much as I had done at Tikal, I walked slowly in a clockwise direction around the perimeter of the courtyard. As I walked, I sang Plains Indian prayers and spirit-calling songs and used a feather to smudge the perimeter of the courtyard with copal smoke. When I was finished, I walked back to my ceremonial blanket and sat at the eastern boarder of the courtyard, facing west.

Except for the guard facing the entrance to the Rosalila tunnel, I had been alone in the East Court since my prayers began. But now I could see dozens of spirit beings entering the courtyard from the south and taking positions along its perimeter. I was quite familiar with multiple spirit encounters at night and limited spirit encounters during the day, but the numbers of spirit beings (there seemed to be around forty or fifty) and the intensity of their presence surprised me. Though I felt some anxiety, I quickly realized that none seemed threatening and I was able to relax and continue praying. I found myself sinking deeper into the energy and spirit of the ancient ceremonial plaza and my heartbeat quickened as I opened to receive any guidance, insight, or revelation that might be granted me.

As I prayed, I continued to add copal to the charcoal. After each round of prayers, I paused to watch the veil of smoke from the copal drift upwards toward the heavens or I looked toward Rosalila. From behind the translucent copal vapors, the ancient ceremonial structures around me seemed to shimmer, mirage-like in the late afternoon sun, their physical boundaries yielding to reveal an inner spiritual essence. I allowed my breathing to become slow and deep as I continued to open myself to the energy in the courtyard. Suddenly, I felt the ground beneath me give way and felt myself dropping down below the surface of the courtyard, much like the experience I'd had many years before inside Casa Rinconada, the great kiva at Chaco Canyon.

I knew I was still in the East Court, but realized that I was moving into sacred time and space, experiencing the courtyard as it had been when it was the Main Plaza at Copan, shortly after the reign of Yax K'uk' Mo'. I experienced myself coming to rest on an older elevation of the courtyard several meters below where I had been sitting just moments before. Temple 22 behind me, as well as Temple 26 and other buildings in my field of vision, began losing their physical substance and eventually vanished like wisps of smoke, only to be replaced by smaller, older, phantom structures I didn't recognize. Temple 16, to my left, had disappeared as well, its former location shrouded in a dense fog.

As this was occurring, the numerous ancestor spirits that had gathered around me earlier appeared less like phantoms, as if they had taken on physical bodies. The immediacy of their presence startled me and I experienced pangs of anxiety regarding this transformation. After taking a few deep breaths to calm myself, I realized I still felt safe and could continue to allow the vision to unfold. However, the experience was still unsettling enough that I periodically pulled my attention back to present time and space to maintain a connection to physical reality.

Off to my left, in the space formerly occupied by Temple 16, Rosalila began to appear, emerging from the shadows of the other worlds as if a veil had been lifted to reveal an amazingly beautiful apparition. I turned my body slightly to the left so I was directly facing this magnificent temple. As I continued to look, the once translucent structure became increasingly opaque, metamorphosing into a numinous form unlike anything I had seen before. It looked like the replica in the museum and the stonework seemed to have characteristics similar to the original ancient masonry. But the temple itself seemed to have a startlingly organic aliveness. It was like a living, breathing being filled with life force and awareness.

As Rosalila came into sharper focus and my impressions gained greater clarity, the surrounding space in the ancient plaza seemed to open up and become more expansive. The ancestor spirits around me had taken on physical bodies as real as any I had encountered in everyday life. Preparations for some sort of ritual seemed to be underway. The level of intensity of activity around me and the tangible excitement in the air gave me the distinct impression of being at the epicenter—both physically and spiritually—of a great ceremonial event unlike any I had observed, or participated in, before. The energy surrounding the occasion was electrifying; an atmosphere of holiness was pervasive and palpable.

I turned my attention away from the preparations occurring around me and focused once again on Rosalila. I was still struggling to fully accept my sense of the vividly animated temple. At the same time, because the temple seemed so organic, I was terrified to think that if I were to go over and touch the building it might feel warm and fleshy. From where I was sitting, I couldn't see into the temple; there were no doors facing me. But I could tell that a ceremony was occurring inside. Clouds of copal smoke were flowing out of the temple's window openings, filling the plaza with a pungent fragrance. I could also hear chanting coming from the temple's interior.

Rosalila appeared to be enveloped by a massive cylindrical energy vortex radiating several meters from the building itself. The vortex also extended downward to embrace the burial chamber of Yax K'uk' Mo', who had "entered the road" to take the journey to rejoin his ancestors, some one hundred years before Rosalila was built. The burial chamber itself seemed to be an integral part of the ancient architecture, linked through stone and earthworks to the masonry substance of the temple and now energetically linked through the vortex that also extended heavenward, above the temple's uppermost third level and roof comb. The roof comb seemed to connect Rosalila to the Upper World while the burial chamber connected it to the Lower World.

Suddenly it dawned on me that I was in the presence of the actual "First True Mountain of Creation;" this human-made structure had transformed into the supernatural mountain. To the Maya, mountains and caves are living beings and here, through the spiritual genius of the ancient Maya, Rosalila had been created and brought to life to serve the needs of the people of Copan. Through prayer, ritual, and the visitation of the ancestors, k'ulel— "soul force"—had saturated Rosalila's stone and stucco structure until it had become a living, conscious being. Rosalila seemed both male and female, primordial father and mother, embodying the attributes of the Sun God in the sky above and the Goddess below in the sacred cave-like womb within the temple.

I realized that Rosalila was the crown jewel of Copan, a magnificent expression of "Substance Mountain," a majestic tribute to the founder, a dramatic symbol of the physical and spiritual preeminence of the city, and a stunning beacon of hope to all. Rosalila served as the bridge between the physical realm, the Upper World, and the Lower World, channeling supernatural powers and providing a portal to access the wisdom, guidance, and assistance of the ancients. And now, within its hallowed chambers, an ancient ceremony was occurring to ensure the survival and well-being of all of Copan. It was becoming clear to me that the thoughts I had struggled with over the past twenty-four hours had been preparing me for what was about to be revealed.

In the next instant of my vision I knew I was witnessing a ceremony to sanctify the maize seed at the beginning of an annual growing cycle. I understood that bundles of maize ears, saved from the previous year's crop, had been brought to the temple from around the countryside over the past several days. Pilgrims carrying small bundles of life-giving maize had traveled to the temple on ancient sacbeob, as part of a reverent and joyous procession to the center of the universe, the *axis mundi*, the place where heaven and earth would be united and the Maize God would dance to bless their crops. They had traveled prayerfully, reverently, some in silence, some singing softly, and some speaking in hushed tones. This was a new beginning, a time of resurrection and rebirth.

I sensed that the maize bundles had been carefully stacked somewhere within the temple, although I wasn't sure if they were in the main chamber or in the small rooms on the uppermost third level, at the very top of the sacred mountain. The ceremony underway inside the temple seemed to be building in intensity, the activity on the physical human plane occurring simultaneously with the activity in the Lower World and the celestial realms. The vibration field within the vortex was becoming stronger as the three worlds came into alignment. Pulsing waves of energy radiated out in all directions. Rosalila's physical body was shifting as well, adjusting to the changing energy patterns and opening to receive the supercharged force flowing throughout the vortex.

As the energies of the three realms continued to align and balance, Rosalila's physical structure acted to channel the forces into an energetic octahedron composed of two opposing four-sided energy pyramids, one pointing toward the heavens, the other pointing toward the Lower World. The two pyramids shared a common energetic base—oriented to the four cardinal directions—at the same level as Rosalila's structural base. The apex of the upper energy-pyramid rose from the shared base to a point in the air past the top of the upper roof comb. The lower pyramid descended downward from the shared base to a point below the tomb of Yax K'uk' Mo'.

Once the energy pyramids were fully formed, the tip of the upper pyramid began acting like a lightning rod, attracting and absorbing celestial energy from the Upper World that entered the energetic pyramid like lightning bolts. The tip of the lower pyramid acted in a similar fashion, attracting and absorbing the energy of the Lower World. The penetrating energies from the opposing realms coalesced in a pulsing sphere whose core was positioned at the center of the base of the two pyramids. One half of the hemisphere of the pulsing core protruded up from Rosalila's base while the other half extended below. This supercharged sphere continued to grow in intensity, sending pulsating, spherical waves of energy out from its core.

Although I wasn't completely certain, it seemed to me that the priests inside the temple were sitting in a circle around the perimeter of the energy sphere. I could hear chanting inside the temple, as clouds of copal smoke continued to billow from open vents in the temple walls. I tried to sense what the experience must be like for the priests inside but couldn't as nothing in my personal experience had come even remotely close. I was certain, however, that the sphere was actually a portal beginning to open, and that the portal seemed to rest inside the jaws of the gigantic Otherworld serpent represented in full relief on the sculpted corners of the temple.

Directly behind the gaping jaws, I could now see the body of the serpent forming an energetic tunnel, a supernatural umbilical cord, along which ancestor spirits could travel between the worlds, from the celestial realm to the temple itself. To my amazement, someone or something was about to emerge from the serpent's mouth, through the spherical portal, and into the temple chambers. I realized that my heart was racing and my breath was short as I sat in awe and fear. Although I had witnessed this phenomenon before at Yaxchilan with Lady Xook, the intensity and vividness of the event unfolding before me took me completely by surprise. I knew it was somehow related to the maize ceremony occurring inside the temple and to the mythology of the sacred mountain where maize had originated, all involving the Celestial Bird and the Sun God. Perhaps I was about to witness the resurrection of the founder of Copan, Yax K'uk' Mo' himself.

At that moment, the frenetic energy subsided and a startling calmness descended, as if everything and everyone were suspended in time and space, at the still-point in the center of a spiritual storm. I could see an orb of light moving through the body of the serpentine tunnel that stretched out into the other worlds. Within moments, rays of brilliant, dazzling light from the orb began to emerge from the serpent's mouth and then, like the sun breaking over the horizon, the orb emerged from the mouth of the serpent like a glorious tropical sunrise. The radiant orb shone at the center of the temple, in the exact center of Copan, like the sun shining at the center of life.

Soft ripples of energy began to disrupt the surface of the sun-like orb inside the temple as a translucent form became visible within the orb. The form became increasingly opaque, eventually recognizable as Yax K'uk' Mo', resurrected as his avian way, Quetzal Macaw. Yax K'uk' Mo' seemed vividly alive and magnetically present within the orb. He had returned from the higher realms, bringing the Sun, the source of life. And there, inside the sacred cave at the heart of the sacred mountain, he began to dance, bringing his blessings for the future of his people. He was resplendent in ceremonial regalia, luminous Quetzal feathers trailing from his outstretched arms, fluttering with his graceful movements.

He danced as both Yax K'uk' Mo' and Quetzal Macaw, a manifestation of the Celestial Bird at the center of creation. He was both Copan's first ruler and the archetypal First Father who brought maize to the Maya people. He danced as Sun God and Maize God, the symbolic representations of divine essences that sustained and nurtured life. Yax K'uk' Mo' had been resurrected as Yax Hal Witznal to aid in the resurrection and transformation of maize seed from the previous year. Through his dance, his k'ulel (soul force) would impregnate the seed corn, ending its period of dormancy, filling it with divine life. Soon, the seed corn would be awakened and ready for planting so the cycle of life could start anew.

As each slow, rhythmic footstep touched the temple floor, k'ulel from the other worlds flowed into and through Yax K'uk' Mo', into and through the portal, penetrating the physical realm and Rosalila. The cosmic dance intensified the radiance of the solar orb and amplified the divine energy present during the ceremony. Prayers from the priests joined those of other ancestor spirits conjured earlier from the other worlds. Together, their energy mingled with the holy incantations being carried toward the heavens on the smoke from the copal incense. The center of the temple, at the heart of Copan, had been transformed into the center of the sacred mountain at the heart of the world—the place of all creation within the heart of the Divine.

I was completely enthralled as Yax K'uk' Mo's danced; life was beginning anew, the world was reborn, and the great cosmic cycles were continuing to unfold. I suddenly realized that the portal and solar orb had vanished into the ethers, revealing Yax K'uk' Mo' in crystal clarity dancing on the temple floor. The energy of his movements had intensified and the impact of his rhythmic footsteps was creating energy fissures erupting like lightning bolts within the vortex around Rosalila. I looked toward the top of the pyramid and noticed that the roof comb at the upper levels of the temple was acting like a metaphysical lightning rod, drawing and focusing the numinous flashes of primordial, cosmic, creative life force into the temple.

I was witnessing the ritual that summoned the cosmic forces that drew life into the temple to impregnate the seed corn—a ceremony reenacting the primal creation of maize on Sustenance

Mountain. The soul or spirit of the maize had departed with last year's harvest[21] and now a miraculous rebirth was about to occur. Life force would soon saturate the maize kernels, awakening and resurrecting them.

These resurrected maize seeds would be planted in the fields in the spring and grow into fully mature maize plants, the divine presence permeating the kernels, ears, and body of the sacred plant. Once summoned from the higher realms, the Maize God, representing the spiritual essence of maize, would remain until the harvest and then depart until He was resurrected the following year. The people would have the divine gift of maize for their sustenance and well-being and the cycle of birth, death and rebirth would repeat all over again. I was at the very heart of one of the greatest spiritual mysteries.

I immediately thought once again of my journey with Itzam-Ye, the Celestial Bird, over twenty years earlier. In some way I didn't fully understand, Rosalila now inhabited the same space Itzam-Ye had taken me to in the spirit realm. At this moment, the Upper World, Lower World, and physical world had merged and all three realms were united with Rosalila, the Center of the Universe, the place of divine creation. The ceremony I was witnessing was occurring at the place where life begins and ends, where the circle starts and finishes, where the cycles come and go, a place both source and destination.

I sat spellbound as my vision continued to unfold. Swirling cloud-like masses of transcendent cosmic gasses coalesced around the Universal Center. The translucent k'ulel-infused vapors, saturated with the life and soul force of the Divine, were being drawn toward the still point of creation. For a moment the transcendental energies appeared to thin, and I could see the ears of maize from the previous year's crop enshrouded by the supernatural forces at the center. Divine life and soul force penetrated each kernel and moved deeper into the core of each ear, saturating every cell. Moving deeper still, k'ulel streamed toward an infinitesimally small microcosmic point within the atomic structure of each ear.

The divine essence infused and then merged with the physical structure of the maize as the corn was transmuted and the Maize God—the unique expression of the Divine, clothed in the physical body of the grain that grew on the leafy stalks that fed the Maya people—was manifested. The kernels, imbued with sacred power, glowed with divine radiance that emanated from the spirit, soul, and life force within them.

Like an infant, the resurrected seed maize seemed both miraculous and fragile. My thoughts turned to the Maya classic, the *Popol Vuh* or "Book of Counsel" written by a Maya scribe in the mid-1500s during the Spanish Conquest. The book records the ancient Maya oral traditions regarding the creation of the world and the exploits of the Hero Twins. When I had been at Palenque with Alfonso Morales earlier on my trip, we had spoken about the maize symbolism in the *Popol Vuh*. Alfonso suggested that the battle with the dark forces in the Lower World by the Hero Twins could be interpreted as a metaphor for the potential perils facing the vulnerable maize seed during germination.

Reflecting on Alfonso's comments, I recalled the accounts of Pueblo Indian corn ceremonies I had read about years earlier. During the ceremonies, Pueblo priests enacted rituals inside underground kivas designed to keep the corn seeds safe during the underground germination period and to ward off destructive forces of drought, disease, insects, birds, and other animals that could damage or kill the nascent corn. I thought about the parallels between the Hero Twins fighting for survival in the Lower World and seed corn germinating underground. As I considered the importance of the Pueblo priest's prayers and rituals to protect the seed corn and ensure an abundant harvest, I realized I had not seen this in my vision and wondered if something similar might have occurred at Rosalila but had not been revealed to me.

The act of divine creation evaporated in my vision to reveal a scene of the Maya priests inside Rosalila, praying and chanting over the carefully stacked bundles of ears of maize. With hands extended in a gesture of blessing, the priests surrounded the bundles, arms outstretched, open palms facing the ears of maize, and performed a ritual "laying on of hands." Yax K'uk' Mo' stood behind them, adding his prayers to theirs, bringing blessings and k'ulel to the ceremony along with the other ancestor spirits and supernatural beings summoned into the chamber. The annual consecration and sanctification of the seed maize concluded just as the sun broke the horizon to the east and the first light of dawn streamed into the temple.

Priests carried the bundles of ears of maize with their resurrected kernels out of the temple and into the courtyard in front of Rosalila. The pilgrims who had brought the maize to Rosalila from their villages had been waiting patiently, prayerfully, for this moment. They moved reverently toward the bundles as the priests carefully placed them on blankets spread out in front of the temple. As the priests held up the bundles, each tied with a unique distinctive cloth band, pilgrims stepped forward to receive their own bundles. The priests acknowledged each pilgrim and offered a prayer for a bountiful harvest; the pilgrims in turn expressed their deep gratitude to Yax K'uk' Mo', the other ancestors who were present, and the priests.

By midday, the courtyard had emptied and the pilgrims were on the sacbeob, returning to their villages. The priests inside Rosalila had completed rituals to enable Yax K'uk' Mo' and the other ancestor spirits and supernatural beings to return to the other worlds. And now a vigil began that would last until the maize seed had defeated the dark forces in the Lower World and

had risen safely to complete its transformation into the fully rip-
ened kernels on silky-tasseled ears hanging from the leafy stalks,
and ceremonies would continue at Rosalila throughout the entire
growing season until the corn was ready for harvesting. Farmers in
the villages prepared for the planting season by invoking the protection and blessings of their ancestor and guardian spirits. Ancestral fields (*milpas*) were prepared to receive the resurrected kernels
through ritual, prayer, and careful tending.

As my vision of the consecration ceremony ended and the
images from the past faded, I was left with the same sense of the
excitement, hope, and optimism that must have accompanied the
ceremony some fifteen hundred years ago. The gift from the Divine,
the dawn of a new year, the beginning of a new cycle, the blessing
from the founder of Copan, and the presence of the ancestors all
seemed to coalesce into a magnificent spiritual tapestry reflective
of the rich, colorful life of the ancient Maya. And through all of
this, Rosalila had stood in the center of Copan, at the heart of the
ceremony, a silent, vigilant sentinel. As the ancient images continued to recede, the structures in the East Courtyard regained their
present-day form and Rosalila disappeared from view.

The area around me that had been so animated and alive in
my vision now seemed empty and deserted. The guard was still in
the courtyard with me but the park had closed and I was the only
visitor left inside. For a few moments I watched the soft shadows
cast by the late afternoon sun moving across the ancient stone masonry beside me. The setting was perfect, breathtaking and beautiful. And yet, after the vividness of my vision, everything seemed a
little dull and muted.

I decided to stay as long as I could and see if I could recap-
ture some of the magic I had experienced from my vision. Looking around the perimeter of the courtyard, I realized the ancestor
spirits who had joined me when I first arrived were still with me.

Although not as vivid as they had been in my vision, their presence was very intense nonetheless.

As I looked at them, something quite unexpected happened. It became clear to me that they wanted me to leave the ruins immediately. Communicating with me telepathically, they insisted it was time for me to go. I didn't sense any disapproval or dissatisfaction on their part—they seemed to be pleased with the ceremony I had performed in the plaza—they simply wanted me to leave now.

I was incredibly conflicted. It had taken me decades to finally find my way to Copan and there wasn't anywhere else in the world I would rather have been at that moment. Yet I knew better than to ignore the wishes of the spirits at a sacred site. The thought flashed into my mind that maybe I could pretend I didn't really see them, or pretend they weren't really there at all. But I knew that wouldn't work. I knew I couldn't fool the spirits and that I really did need to leave. The ancestors instructed me to leave the courtyard the way I had entered, from the south, and to walk directly through the park without stopping or looking back.

I quickly repacked my ceremonial objects, stood up, and started walking toward the southern passageway behind Temple 16. The guard noticed I was leaving and rushed over to me with a surprised look on his face. He had clearly expected me to stay longer and, as we spoke, he made sure I understood that it was all right if I did. I thanked him and continued on. As I walked through the passageway, I had the distinct impression that the spirits had remained in the courtyard. I remembered several North American Indian sweat lodge ceremonies where medicine men told me that spirits who visited often stayed behind after the ceremony had finished. It seemed the same here.

I was still anxious as I left the park and headed for my hotel. I hoped I had conducted myself in a respectful and responsible manner in the eyes of the ancestors, and that nothing bad would happen later that evening. The walk back was pleasant and calming for me. My concerns began to diminish as I got closer to town, and by the time I had reached my hotel I was sure everything was going to be all right. At dinner, Luis and I picked up our conversation where we had left off earlier in the day. As we sat in the open-air upstairs dining room of the restaurant, Luis shared colorful stories about the people and personalities behind the local archaeological activities and Sculpture Museum. It was a beautiful, warm tropical evening and the dining room had a spectacular view of the mountains surrounding the Copan Valley. The moon was almost full and as the evening progressed, brilliant stars emerged in the darkening heavens. I found myself wishing I had more time to spend at Copan, but unfortunately this was my last evening here. In the morning I would take the long bus ride back to San Pedro Sula, where I would spend the night before flying back to the States the next morning.

As I lay in bed trying to fall asleep that night, images from my trip kept flooding my consciousness. I could barely believe the extraordinary good luck I'd had on the trip and how incredibly fortunate I had been. Hunbatz Men, the Maya elders in Merida, Alfonso, and Luis had all opened doors for me in ways I could never have anticipated.

I did finally fall asleep, but sometime in the middle of the night I awoke in a panic, sensing that someone else was in my room. It took me a few moments to realize that this feeling was the same as the one I had experienced years earlier in Yaxchilan when I first encountered my Maya tutelary spirit at the ruins. Now he was here with me again; I was relieved it was someone familiar and not an ancestor spirit from the ceremony earlier in the day. However, I was certain he was with me now *because* of that ceremony. I had never experienced him quite the way I was experiencing him now, extremely present and more three-dimensional than I was used to. But more importantly, I sensed he was what I could only describe as "pleased."

As he stood before me, he let me know telepathically that he had come to talk to me about the ceremony at the courtyard. He wanted me to know the spirits were happy with how I had conducted myself and that I had done a good job—not perfect, but good enough. Being asked to leave quickly had been a test of sorts, a way for the spirits to determine how aware I was and how respectful of their wishes I would be. He let me know I had done exactly the right thing and that as a result I had earned their trust. The spirits would welcome me back in the future and were willing to reveal more to me. As he told me this, I knew from his countenance that I was moving into a deeper, richer level of understanding and awareness of the ancient Maya and the deeper universal spiritual truths they understood and lived. In the morning I would be leaving Copan and returning to San Pedro Sula for a flight home. But at that moment, it felt as if this magical ancient realm were my true home and I had been accepted into its spiritual family. I knew then, without a doubt, that I had been chosen to share the gifts of wisdom they had given me through my visions.

CATHEDRAL OF ST. PETER THE APOSTLE
SAN PEDRO SULA, HONDURAS — 2007

The light from the late afternoon sun shone through the stained glass windows casting soft, colorful shadows on the pale yellow plaster walls of the Sanctuary. Although less than sixty years old, the peaceful, serene Cathedral of St. Peter the Apostle had an almost timeless quality; I felt welcomed and comforted. I had wanted to visit the cathedral, situated at the west end of the Central Plaza in San Pedro Sula, as my last stop in Honduras before returning to the United States. The three-hour bus ride from Copan earlier in the day had seemed almost interminable, and I was weary from the past three weeks of travel and intense emotional experiences at the ruins. I was hoping the cathedral would provide a brief refuge before I reentered my demanding, hectic twenty-first century life.

As I looked around the Sanctuary, I was impressed with its soaring spaciousness and the relative simplicity of the cathedral's interior architectural style. The building did not have the grandeur or richness of many of the great European cathedrals but it seemed a perfect expression of the local environment and blended wonderfully into the neighborhood. The openness of the structure, the brightness of yellow plaster walls, the light that streamed through the stained glass windows, and the soft breezes from the large doors that opened onto the plaza at the end of the nave and transepts helped me experience an emotional and mental expansiveness matching my surroundings.

Sitting in a pew near the central gallery, I looked up to study the enormous oversize portraits painted high above me on the upper wall of the central cupola. The images were both familiar and somewhat foreign at the same time. I immediately recognized the four portraits, San Mateo, San Marcos, San Lucas, and San Juan, as the four apostles I knew as Matthew, Mark, Luke and John. Beside each figure was their winged counterpart: angel, lion, ox, and eagle. Looking over to a small chapel off the narthex, I saw a large female statue dressed in flowing robes with a banner draped over her shoulder identifying her as Nuestra Madre, the figure I knew as Mary the mother of Jesus.

While I was comforted by my intimate knowledge of the ceremonies that occurred here and by my familiarity with the architecture and iconography, the fact that everything was in Spanish and I was in a foreign country shifted my frame of reference just enough to allow a fresh insight to come to me. This was the spiritual world I had grown up in and the lens through which, as a child and young adult, I had viewed the sacred realms and the ultimate reality. But now I was reminded that I had experienced a far different reality through my studies with indigenous elders and experiences at the ancient ceremonial centers of the Maya. The world would never look, or be, the same to me again. Among the many new truths I came to embrace were that God (Hunab-Ku, Wakan Tanka) was in this world and available to all, the Divine Feminine was an active equal presence, the other worlds and higher spiritual realms were readily accessible, and a spiritual quest could lead to an encounter with the Divine in this world, not just the next.

While I was staying at Tikal earlier in my trip, I visited the nearby town of San Jose to meet with local Maya elders. During one conversation, I asked how it was possible for contemporary Maya to preserve their spiritual traditions while surrounded by the pervasive influence of the Christian Church. I was told that traditional Maya—those who had not abandoned their spiritual heritage—protect their ancestral beliefs and blend them with Christian religious observances (anthropologists refer to this as "syncretism"). Christian saints are seen as representing Maya deities, the Christian cross represents the World Tree, the Christian resurrection is a reminder of the rebirth of the Maize God, and religious observances are tied to the Maya calendar. "Traditional Maya may worship in a Christian setting," the elders told me, "but all the time they are thinking Maya."

I looked up at the cupola and saw the apostles—ancestors accompanied by their way animal co-essences (angel, lion, ox, and eagle)—looking down from the Upper World; I looked over and saw Nuestra Madre—the Goddess, our sacred Earth Mother—with her open palms offering a blessing; I closed my eyes and gave thanks for the astonishing spiritual pilgrimage that was just ending and the equally extraordinary spiritual journey that I knew was just beginning.

1. Agurica Fasquelle 2004: 111
2. Ibid., 102
3. Schele and Mathews 1998: 48
4. Ibid., 48
5. Ibid., 50
6. Agurica Fasquelle 2004: 103
7. Ibid., 102
8. Ibid., 104
9. Ibid., 107–109
10. Ibid., 109–110
11. Ibid., 110
12. In *The Code of Kings*, Schele and Mathews describe the basic imagery associated with Yax Hal Witznal, "First True Mountain (43)." Different scholars studying Rosalila at Copan have arrived at various interpretations for the serpent imagery on the upper structure. They "have been variously interpreted as symbols for the sides of the sky, smoke produced by the burning of incense to attract dark clouds and the precious water they shower upon the earth, and representation of *chijchan*, serpents still revered by the nearby Chorti Maya (Fash 2011: 43)." In *Maya Cosmos*, Freidel, Schele and Parker describe Temple 22, "Temple of Meditation," a structure built some two hundred years after Rosalila, as "Copan's version of the 'First True Mountain of Creation,'" due to the beautifully detailed and magnificently executed sculptured images and hieroglyphics that adorn the Temple (149). I believe the serpent images on Rosalila identify it as an earlier representation of Yax Hal Witznal.
13. Ibid., 217
14. Ibid., 154–156

15. The contemporary Pueblo Indians are comprised of approximately nineteen tribes in the Southwestern United States that share similar cultural, political, social and spiritual practices; they include the Hopi Indians in Arizona and the Zuni Indians in New Mexico.

16. Mora 1982: 17

17. Ibid., 17

18. Crown, Patricia and W. Jeffery Hurst. "Evidence of Cacao use in the Prehispanic American Southwest." *Proceedings of the National Academy of Sciences of the USA* 106 (2009): 2110–2113

19. Washburn, Dorothy K., William Washburn and Petia Shipkova. "The prehistoric drug trade: widespread consumption of cacao in Ancestral Pueblo and Hohokam communities in the American Southwest." *Journal of Archeological Science* 38 (2011) 1634–1640. These researchers conducted a similar analysis using a different experimental method with a larger and more diverse pottery sample. As a result of their study, the researchers "propose the existence of extensive trade and interaction among the peoples of the American Southwest and Mesoamerica." They found that "similarities in [pottery] vessel contents, form and features" are the result of "direct and extensive interactions between" the American Southwest and Mesoamerica. They also believe that "one possible interpretation is that [cacao] was traded for Southwestern turquoise." By 900 CE, turquoise was in high demand in Mesoamerica, replacing jade as the most sought-after luxury mineral. The researchers note that Neutron Activation analysis has matched turquoise from New Mexico with turquoise found in Chichen Itza and in the Yucatan. They believe that at the height of the Chaco civilization, (900–1150 CE), there was "long distance activity that tied together the American Southwest and the Mesoamerican states."

20. Schele and Mathews 1998: 73

21. Maya scholar Simon Martin has observed that "[n]umerous ethnographic sources describe the soul or spirit of corn, and even the idea that such a spirit must leave the cob before it is harvested (Martin 2006: 159)."

AWAKENING

Thirty years ago you came as a seeker, a novice,
an initiate—today you have returned wakened.
Your true journey is just beginning.   — Maya Elder

CAVE AT OXKINTOK
YUCATAN, MEXICO – 2015

I paused for a moment at the top of the steeply inclined path leading downward to the entrance of the ceremonial cave at Oxkintok. It was hard for me to believe that it had been thirty years since I had first descended into the depths of the cave at Balankanche near Chichen Itza and had first encountered the ancient Maya. At the time, I had very little knowledge of their spiritual traditions, but my experiences inside the cave had given me a glimpse of a stunning sacred world I never knew existed and started me on a miraculous path of self-discovery and personal healing. In the years since then, I have been exposed to ancient shamanic secrets and profound wisdom teachings that have been astonishing, exhilarating, empowering, and a few times, terrifying. Now, I was about to undertake another descent, but this time with much greater insight and understanding.

Caves like Balankanche and Oxkintok were powerful and highly revered by the Maya as ceremonial sites because they were, both figuratively and literally, the womb of Ix-Mucane, the sacred Earth Mother. These large-domed grottos deep within the Earth served as physical representations of the generative, life-giving powers of Ix-Mucane, but more importantly, if one is humble, open and receptive, they make it possible to directly encounter Her spiritual essence as well. A small group of us, led by two Maya shamans, had come to this remote cave to participate in a ceremony for purification, healing, and personal transformation.

Like Balankanche, this cave had been used by the ancient Maya for sacred ceremonies for at least two millennia. Archaeologists discovered that the nearby ceremonial center of Oxkintok had been established as early as 600 BCE and was actively in use until the 1500s, when the site was abandoned sometime during the Spanish Conquest. Caves located near ancient ceremonial centers throughout the Maya realm always played a major role in the spiritual life of the community. Some, like Oxkintok, are still used today and may have been used in secret for hundreds of years following the Conquest. My excitement was building by the minute as other members of the group ahead of me disappeared into the cave.

The womb-like quality of the cave and the presence of the Great Mother were on my mind as I reached the large opening at the bottom of the trail. Before entering, I paused a moment, as the shamans had instructed everyone in our group to leave an offering, connect with the spirits of the "elementals" (nature spirits) and ask for permission to enter. My heart was beating fast as I peered through the opening into the cave and caught a glimpse of the limestone formation of stalactites and stalagmites, which I immediately recognized as the World Tree similar to the one at Balankanche. I passed through the arched opening and continued to descend a short distance, climbing over limestone rocks until I reached the floor of the cave.

The shamans had entered earlier and had begun the ritual purification and blessing. As I stood near the entrance I watched as sunlight streaming in through the mouth of the cave illuminated the thick plumes of copal smoke drifting toward the soaring ceiling from their incensarios. The smoke seemed to dance in the light as it spiraled upward, eventually finding its way to the apex where ancient Maya artisans had painted sacred hieroglyphics and pictographs. Although worn and faded, these symbols seemed to come alive. I felt chills ripple through my body as I sensed the presence of ancestor spirits, moving in the shadows, arriving to join us in ceremony.

I took a seat on a boulder close to the area where the shamans were constructing a traditional Maya altar on the ground and closed my eyes to reflect on the purpose of the ceremony. Earlier, one of the shamans had explained to us that caves represent unconscious aspects of our inner selves that are hidden in darkness—parts that need to be acknowledged and healed if we are to live a fully realized life. He explained that in this ceremony, we would connect with the sacred Earth Mother and ask Her help as we confronted old thoughts, feelings, and beliefs that limited us and needed to be released. Through Her, we would connect to our higher spiritual nature—the aspect of self closest to the Divine—and in the process, experience healing and transformation.

I was grateful to have been able to return to Oxkintok, thrilled to participate in another Maya ceremony, and excited for this opportunity to continue my personal and spiritual growth, this time with Ix-Mucane. As I sat on the boulder, I anticipated an insightful, memorable experience but I had no sense that anything truly extraordinary was going to unfold for me. Over the years, premonitions had often preceded my visions or otherworldly encounters, but nothing alerted me to the fact that I would soon have the most remarkable encounter of my entire spiritual journey.

My anticipation increased as I carefully observed each aspect of the shamans' preparations. A large diamond-shaped background had been formed on the ground, comprised of four smaller diamond-shaped colored cloths (black, white, red and yellow) positioned so each point faced a cardinal direction, edges touching to form the larger, single diamond. A large gourd with water had been placed at the center of the diamond and four smaller gourds, each with water from the larger gourd, had been positioned in the center of the smaller diamonds in each of the cardinal directions. Corn, for offerings, had been placed on the altar as well as other ceremonial objects including drums, rattles, and conch shell horns.

When the preparations were complete, we were invited to form a circle around the altar. The shamans, each carrying a pottery incensario, moved among the group smudging each of us with thick, fragrant smoke from the burning copal. Sharp, penetrating tones of the conch shell horns pierced the interior of the chamber; drums and rattles summoned the spirits of the ancestors; and invocations were made in Spanish and Mayan, offering prayers to Hunab-Ku, divine Father and Mother. As the shamans opened a portal to the Otherworld and guided us through the liminal space in the depths of the holy grotto, we were transported to another dimension to connect with the Earth Mother.

Although my first encounter with Ix-Mucane had been at Balankanche, I had felt her presence at dozens of sacred caves I had visited over the years. Some of the caves had been small and relatively modest. Others, including the cave systems at Loltun and Bolonchén, were spectacular monumental labyrinths with miles of underground passages. Regardless of the size of the caves, all possessed Her indwelling spirit. But now, I felt Her presence as never before. I caught my breath as I realized the hard limestone cavern had been transformed into the soft, warm, nurturing womb of the Great Mother. Farther back in the shadows, the massive stone trunk of Wakah-Kan, the World Tree, was glowing with an inner aliveness, radiance, and animation. I was filled with an unimaginably deep sense of peace, safety, and maternal love.

The shamans motioned for the group to follow them a short distance farther into the interior of the cavern, toward the World Tree. I paused so I could be the last one in line—giving me a little more time for reflection. The shamans stood close to the World Tree as one by one each person was beckoned to it to make a personal request to Ix-Mucane for healing and to receive a blessing from the shamans in Her presence. During the earlier ceremony I had been thinking about my request, but now, unanticipated memories erupted and forced me to abandon my original plan.

I felt myself traveling back in time to when I was a young boy. I recalled my struggles to cope with my alcoholic father and his abusive behavior. Feelings of hopelessness, despair, self-pity, fear, self-doubt, and shame—all constant companions growing up—resurfaced with surprising intensity. The feelings were accompanied by thoughts that I wasn't safe, I wasn't good enough, nobody cared about me, and I'd be abandoned and rejected. These feelings and thoughts were not a revelation to me. I had first encountered them during a vision at the Las Pinturas pyramid-temple in Coba thirty years earlier and on subsequent vision quests, retreats, and at Adult Children of Alcoholics (ACOA) meetings. Healing these patterns had been a major focus of my spiritual journey and although there were times when they still surfaced somewhat, they didn't have the power or control over me they'd once had.

In the darkness of the womb of the Earth Mother, these thought patterns surfaced once again with their original intensity. Deep, almost overwhelming feelings of sadness and grief erupted—my tears were flowing and my body was shaking almost uncontrollably. Yet as these thoughts and feelings emerged, I felt them leaving my body, sloughing off in some type of emotional and psychological "molting" I had never experienced before. They accumulated at my feet as if I had shed my old skin and was now emerging to start a new life.

Once these patterns had emerged and been discarded, I found my thoughts traveling farther back in time. Unexpected memories surfaced of the time immediately after my birth. I had been born prematurely and spent my first days alone and isolated in an incubator. Through it all I had felt abandoned and terrified I might not survive. Back in the present, I was aware of the line shortening as, one by one, others joined the shamans at the Tree. I was still flooded with emotions and sobbing as my turn arrived. For a moment I considered foregoing the ceremony and just going off to regain my composure, but when I was beckoned I found myself going to the Tree.

At that point everything had taken on a dreamlike quality. I could feel one of the shamans steadying me from behind with one hand on my shoulder and another on the top of my head. The other shaman was standing in front of me, praying in Mayan while using yaxche leaves to sprinkle water on me as a blessing and baptism. My thoughts continued farther back in time and I found myself in the womb of the Earth Mother even before I had entered my mother's womb. I felt their two wombs joined, superimposed, as I was gestating simultaneously in Her womb and my mother's. As I stood at the Tree, my focus drifting between my teacher, the Maya shaman, and Ix-Mucane's womb, I became aware of a brilliant golden light inside me, radiating throughout my body. The light, which seemed to emanate from the Earth Mother, filled the core of my being.

Suddenly, the light within me erupted and I became the light. I experienced the sensation of rushing towards the Earth Mother, the source of the light, but as I reached Her and then passed through Her, I realized the true source was farther beyond. I immediately knew that not only was the source of the light the Divine, the light itself actually was the Divine presence.

I felt myself merge and become ONE with the Divine and then, for a moment, I *was* the Divine.

Memories of my experience at Balankanche came flooding back. I recalled my revelation thirty years earlier that we emerge from the Divine as a spiritual essence, a soul destined to enter the womb and then to be born in a physical body. Wakah-Kan is the conduit, the mystical link, between our higher spiritual nature and our everyday self in the physical world. At Balankanche I had first learned that this transformation process took place in the womb of the sacred Earth Mother, the Divine Feminine. Through Her we come into the world from the Source and through Her we can find our way back to the Source. At the time, I had a vague understanding of those insights. Now, I had experienced their absolute truth. I realized that things would never be the same for me again.

As my awareness returned to the cave and the Sacred Tree, the shamans stepped aside and I turned to place my hands on the Tree. The emotions had subsided but I was still trembling. As surprising and transformative as my direct encounter with the Divine had been fifteen years earlier on the Pine Ridge Indian Reservation, I had never imagined I would experience what the Maya term "awakened consciousness." I was humbled, awestruck, and filled with gratitude. I silently offered prayers to Hunab-Ku, Ix-Mucane, and Wakah-Kan, and to the shamans and all who had guided me, helped me, and kept me safe during my amazing spiritual journey. Taking a deep breath, I slowly turned and walked back to rejoin the group around the altar.

The shamans led the group in a final round of prayers and expressions of gratitude to the spirits, sacred beings, elementals, powers of the four directions, and the Heart of the Sky and Heart of the Earth. We all drank the water from the gourds and each of us gathered corn from the altar and sprinkled it around the cave as an offering. The altar was carefully taken apart and the sacred objects were wrapped and packed away. Before leaving, I was invited to sing a Lakota (Sioux) prayer song as a last honoring of the ancestors.

As I climbed back out of the cave I thought about my Awakening and what a complete and shocking surprise it had been. I never imagined that someone like myself, a middle-aged man from the Midwest, living a traditional American life with a family, career, and civic responsibilities, could have an experience like this. If I had known what was in store for me, I would have doubted this was possible, and my uncertainty and disbelief might have prevented me from having the experience.

The drive from the cave back to Merida, where we had been staying, had an almost dreamlike quality. I was feeling overwhelmed by the intensity of my encounter and still struggled to absorb all I had experienced. I had been pushed deeper and further spiritually than I had ever gone before. And although I trusted the veracity of my experience, it was still almost beyond my ability to comprehend. I was comforted knowing that the group would be together for another week and we were headed to other spectacular ancient ceremonial centers. I was confident my thoughts would clear, and more would be revealed as the trip progressed and I participated in additional ceremonies. I was particularly looking forward to our last stop, Palenque, where we would have three days of teachings and ceremonies.

WEST COURTYARD OF THE PALACE, PALENQUE
CHIAPAS, MEXICO — 2015

Although the breathtaking stucco bas relief sculptures and masonry work of the West Courtyard of the Palace had deteriorated somewhat, everything looked as I remembered it from my first visit thirty years earlier. Even though I had returned to Palenque many times since,

I had not revisited the West Courtyard, or another structure, the Temple of the Foliated Cross. In both locations I had experienced powerful visions and spirit encounters but during each subsequent visit I had been told by the spirits to avoid these two areas. I never understood why, but I had known enough not to violate this admonition.

When our group had arrived at Palenque the day before, one of the shamans from Oxkintok who had traveled with us led us in ceremony to honor the ancestors and spirits at the site and ask their permission and blessing. We then entered the ceremonial precinct and headed toward the Main Plaza, the Temple of Inscriptions, and the adjacent, more recently excavated, Temple VIII and the Tomb of the Red Queen. Crossing the plaza, I felt not only surrounded by the presence of the spirits, but welcomed in a way I had not experienced before. Suddenly, I had the premonition that this visit would be different from my other trips here. I immediately thought of the West Courtyard and the Temple of the Foliated Cross and wondered if I might be permitted to finally revisit them.

Suddenly, I heard a Maya ancestor spirit say, in a clear and distinct voice: "Thirty years ago you came as a seeker, a novice, an initiate—today you have returned Awakened. You have come full circle. Although you have crossed a major threshold, your true journey is just beginning." The words seemed to reverberate through time and space and I began to lose track of where I was or what I was doing. For a moment, I experienced myself simultaneously walking into Palenque for the first time, standing at Wakah-Kan in the cave at Oxkintok at the moment of my Awakening, and now standing in the plaza in present time. Tears welled up as I recognized the truth of what the ancestor spirit told me and I was flooded with a feeling of gratitude and joy.

Even though it wasn't stated, I knew the ancestor spirit had given me permission to return to the West Courtyard and the Temple of the Foliated Cross. My excitement grew with the thought of once again revisiting the sites I had desperately wanted but not dared to revisit during my other trips to Palenque—the sites that had been the source of some of my most transcendent experiences and profound revelations.

It was noon on the second day of our Palenque visit when I finally had the opportunity to visit the West Courtyard. I quickly made my way through the complex of buildings that comprised the palace, choosing a route that led past the Palace Tower toward the courtyard's southwest corner. Upon emerging from the tower, I walked a few steps until I was standing exactly where, in my vision thirty years earlier, I had seen the spirit of a priest begin a procession around the courtyard's perimeter. I was relieved to find that even though Palenque was filled with visitors, I was the only one here at the moment. Fortunately for me, because it is small and unimposing compared to the surrounding structures and barely mentioned in the guidebooks, the West Courtyard is not a popular destination.

The day was overcast with a light, soft rain falling intermittently. On a clear day, a brilliant tropical sun would have flooded the courtyard, making it blazing hot and obscuring the stucco sculptures that lined its sunken walls. Now, the light grey haze softened its features and shadows highlighted the sculptures of ancestors, supernatural beings, serpents, and peccaries. The brilliant emerald green color of the thick mat of rain-moistened grass covering the floor of the courtyard stood out in sharp contrast to the subdued and muted shades of gray of the ancient stone masonry and stucco. For a moment I had the distinct impression that the rain had been responsible for a ritual cleansing and purification of the magnificent setting.

Closing my eyes, I took a deep breath, said a silent prayer to the ancestors, and allowed myself to open to the energy of my surroundings. Intense memories of my first visit immediately resurfaced. In vivid detail, I recalled the original procession of twelve men and women, led by a chief priest, majestically moving along

360

the perimeter of the courtyard. In his hands, the priest held the spiritual essence of Itzam-Ye, the Celestial Bird, my guide on a journey to the Center of Spiritual Creation. Now, I sensed myself at the head of a similar procession; many of the same ancestor spirits were with me, and I knew I was meant to lead this procession along the same route I'd witnessed thirty years ago. Taking another deep breath, I opened my eyes and started walking forward, emulating the demeanor of the original group.

Following the path created by the broad capstones on the courtyard wall, I covered the seventy-five foot west wall, turned right for the thirty-foot length of the north wall, and then right again, traveling along the east wall. About fifteen feet before reaching the southeast corner of the courtyard, the capstone path ended, creating an opening for a set of four wide and deep stone steps down the four feet to the grass-covered courtyard floor. I turned right and descended the steps. The procession followed me. At the bottom of the steps, I again turned right and walked a few feet until I reached the recessed, throne-like stone seat built into the courtyard wall. I sat as I had thirty years earlier, pushing back to rest against the stone wall, and I looked over to the procession that had followed me and had now assembled on the courtyard floor to my right, facing me.

Closing my eyes, I took a deep breath and became aware of a deep calm and peacefulness enveloping the entire structure. I could feel the air's moisture on my skin and smell its clean and fresh scent. For a moment I couldn't tell whether I was back in the courtyard in 1985 or here now in 2015, or both simultaneously; each experience blended into the other seamlessly. The courtyard seemed alive with the same sacredness I had experienced in 1985. The stone and stucco sculptures seemed to pulse once again with vibrant, radiant energy. Suddenly, the rectangular courtyard with its four-foot-tall walls seemed to metamorphose into a large pool filling with pure, fluid, crystalline energy. I felt immersed in that energetic field.

As I opened my eyes and looked out across the courtyard, I saw that the crystalline energy filling the courtyard to the top of the wall was radiating upward and mixing with the ambient energy above. As this process unfolded, a spherical vortex began to form in the center of the courtyard with the lower half of the sphere growing down below the plane of the top of the courtyard wall, and the upper half growing above the plane. The vortex continued to expand, filling with dazzling white light that increased in intensity and brilliance until the sphere was a magnificent, radiant, translucent orb approximately ten feet in diameter. At that point the sphere stopped growing and a form began to manifest within it.

The orb now possessed a womb-like quality and I sat enthralled by the mystery of the spiritual being that was emerging. Although the form had an avian essence similar to the Celestial Bird I had experienced in 1985, as the shape continued to define itself, I realized the luminous being was a glorious white quetzal bird with its characteristically spectacular train of tail feathers. But then the form morphed again into a Divine Feminine presence bathed in the same radiant white light. While the feminine presence had some of the characteristics of the Moon Goddess, Ix-Chel, I could tell she was not Ix-Chel. As I sat contemplating the identity of this spiritual being, it continued a slow oscillation between her manifestation as a quetzal and as a Divine Feminine presence.

A blinding flash of insight sent shivers through my body as I realized I was in the presence of Lady Sak K'uk', a former ruler of Palenque and the mother of Palenque's most famous king, Pakal I. Slowly, I began to understand my vision as I recalled that Lady Sak K'uk's name in Mayan meant 'Resplendent White Quetzal'.

I sat transfixed, in a state of wonder and awe, marveling at the beauty and mystery of this encounter. Although I was vaguely familiar with Lady Sak K'uk' through my teachers and my research on the ancient Maya, nothing in my earlier visits to Palenque had given me any indication that I would encounter her. I was mystified by her presence here, eager to know its significance and curious about what would happen next. Images flashed through my mind of other Maya spirit encounters where I had been given specific information or shown sacred ceremonies. I was hoping something of a similar nature would occur now but at the same time I realized I would be completely content if I experienced nothing more than her astonishing presence.

Before I had a chance to reflect any further on the purpose and meaning of her materialization before me, I felt my thoughts drawn, almost involuntarily, to her countenance. As I gazed into her eyes, I felt my awareness of my physical surroundings fade as my total attention became riveted on her. And then she spoke—her words flowing towards me like liquid energy in a dreamscape, moving through time and space to reach deep into my consciousness. "We have forgotten who we are. We have forgotten why we're here. We have forgotten how to live a life of balance and harmony."

I was stunned. Her words reverberated in my consciousness and throughout my entire being. I had never before received a transmission like this. For a moment, I experienced myself hearing these words as though I were sitting before her when she was alive—fourteen hundred years earlier. At the same time, I knew she had come from the distant past to deliver a message to me in the present, one that I was destined to hear. I started to feel anxious and disoriented as I lost my spatial and temporal bearings, but somehow the truth and insight of her words provided a focus that comforted me. As I sat there, immersed in her energy and lost in her pronouncement, I realized this was the answer to a question that had plagued me for some time.

Not quite a year earlier I had retired from a career in business to devote myself full-time to finishing this book and beginning a new career as a writer, lecturer, and workshop leader. During the intervening months I had struggled to decide the direction and focus for my teaching. After studying and training with indigenous shamans and spiritual leaders for thirty-five years I had a wealth of experience, knowledge, and insight to draw from. But now, with Lady Sak K'uk's help, a clear path opened for me. I realized that at the start of my spiritual journey thirty-five years earlier I didn't know who I was or why I was here or how to live a life of balance and harmony. Now I realized that millions of others struggle with the same issue. My spiritual journey had helped me find answers to life's most basic and profound questions, and I was now able to help others find answers for themselves as well.

Ever since my vision quest on the Pine Ridge Indian Reservation in 2000, I had understood that we are truly spiritual beings and aspects of the Divine Source. But as a result of my recent Awakening at the cave at Oxkintok, I had gone beyond an encounter with the Divine to experiencing Oneness with the Divine and I now *knew* this reality. With this experience I was certain I could help others understand and hopefully achieve their own Awakening. It had allowed me to discover my own higher calling and soul's purpose—not in a way that required me to withdraw from the world, but instead in a way that meant I could bring my unique skills, gifts, and passion into whatever endeavors I undertook.

I also realized now that living a life of balance and harmony was not so much a matter of achieving "work-life balance" (although it is important to work towards this goal) or trying to live a completely "natural" lifestyle (although this is helpful as well). Achieving balance and harmony involves discovering our true selves and being in the world in an authentic way that honors our deepest spiritual attributes. When we know who we are, our sense of isolation disappears and we feel connected to our lives and the world around us. When we know why we're here, we discover a new sense of meaning and purpose in our lives. And with this knowledge we begin to make better decisions in all aspects of our lives, which brings us a greater sense of inner peace and harmony.

Slowly, my awareness began to return once again to the courtyard. I felt the limestone blocks against my back and the grassy floor beneath my feet. Lady Sak K'uk' was still a beautiful and remarkable apparition before me—fully present, here and now, in this physical world. As I continued to gaze at her I could see the energy surrounding her in the orb begin to shift and I felt a pang of sadness as I realized that the portal would close soon, and she would return to the higher realms. The incredible gift of her wisdom and insight filled me with a deep sense of gratitude. I was reluctant to see her depart and wished her teaching could continue. But my disappointment was alleviated by a premonition that she would be with me again when I visited the Temple of the Foliated Cross.

Lady Sak K'uk's form, which had seemed so solid only a few minutes earlier, now resembled a fine mist that began to dissipate and then finally disappear. The crystalline energy that had filled the courtyard structure earlier was now receding, like water draining from a swimming pool. I glanced to my left to see if the figures in the procession were still present and although they were, their forms were becoming less distinct as they too departed with Lady Sak K'uk'. The sky had brightened somewhat and the dreariness of the day was lifting, but the setting felt empty now with their departure.

I reluctantly stood up, paused, closed my eyes, and said a short prayer of thanks for the gift of the amazing vision and transcendent teachings. Turning to my right I walked the few steps to the stairs that led out of the courtyard, climbed to the main palace level, and then headed down the corridors through the complex of buildings, to rejoin the group near the entrance of the park. The day had brightened and rich hues from the rainforest surrounded me, but the physical world paled in comparison to the unimaginably incandescent presence of Lady Sak K'uk'. As I walked through the ceremonial center, my regret over the end of my encounter with Lady Sak K'uk' was tempered by my excitement about returning to the Temple of the Foliated Cross the next day.

TEMPLE OF THE FOLIATED CROSS, PALENQUE
CHIAPAS, MEXICO — 2015

Memories of the ceremony I had performed at the Temple of the Foliated Cross years before returned with surprising vividness— the sweet pungent odor of copal, prayers for Palenque's lost souls, the portal to the spiritual realms that opened above me, and the passing of spirits to the other worlds. The thoughts sent shivers through my body. Because the initial experience had been so much more profound and intense than I had ever imagined, the thought of returning made me somewhat anxious. At the time, I had been shaken by the enormous responsibility of the task I found myself performing and if I had known what was in store for me, I might have lacked the confidence to proceed. But, as had been the case with other encounters, I found the resolve and inner strength I needed and was able to persevere and accomplish things I never would have thought possible.

Over the years I had often wondered why the spirits had asked me not to return to the Temple of the Foliated Cross after I'd performed a ceremony there. I'd finally concluded that through the ceremony, the space where the transmigration of souls had occurred had become hallowed; returning prematurely would have been a desecration. I had no idea what was in store for me here now, but I was open and willing to allow events to take their own course.

366

Standing at the base of the pyramid now, my heart was already racing, and I was about to begin my climb to the temple on top. Unlike many of the ceremonial structures at Palenque that had been meticulously restored, this pyramid looked much as it had when it was first discovered—a large rocky mound covered in dense jungle foliage. Scattered remnants of the original masonry had been exposed in a few limited areas, but none of the original crisp geometric forms, expertly-crafted masonry tiers, or precise architectural details had been restored. A relatively narrow path surrounded by moss and manicured jungle grasses meandered up the pyramid's face. The rest of the structure was engulfed in towering trees, dense shrubs, and massive broad-leafed ferns.

Although the temple-pyramid hadn't changed over the years, the number of visitors had continued to increase. As I made my way up the path to the top, I saw dozens of individuals climbing up and down the pyramid and stopping on top to look at the temple. Whatever I would be doing, it was clear that I wouldn't be alone. I knew I wanted to do a ceremony but it was going to be difficult to have any privacy, and burning copal and blowing conch shell horns at these sites were both strictly forbidden by the Mexican government. I finally decided to sit at the far southeast corner of the temple, facing the jungle, with my back to the center of the temple platform.

As I settled into this position, I closed my eyes, took a few slow deep breaths, and opened to the energy around me. I mentally recited an invocation to Hunab-Ku, Ix-Chel, Ix-Mucane, and other spiritual powers and sacred beings of the ancient Maya. As I did so, I became aware of the presence of Lady Sak K'uk'; the awareness was not quite as vivid or profound as at the courtyard, but her presence was nonetheless unmistakable. As she materialized before me, her arms outstretched with her palms facing me, I knew she was here to guide me through a ceremony, although at that moment I had no idea what it might be.

As I looked down, I noticed the area at my feet was covered with rubble, including larger fragments of stone blocks that had once been part of the temple structure. I realized I could discretely burn small pieces of copal in the crevices between the blocks without attracting attention. Looking back up to Lady Sak K'uk', I was guided to burn thirteen pieces of copal, one piece for each of what she said were the thirteen "heavens" of the Maya. I wasn't completely comfortable having other people around, but no one seemed to be paying attention. As small, faint wisps of smoke from the copal began rising toward the heavens, Lady Sak K'uk' began to chant an incantation I couldn't hear well or understand. An energy vortex began forming above my head and I knew a portal would soon open to the other worlds.

Thirty years earlier, following the instructions of the spirits, I had created and opened a portal to the other worlds by reciting a prayer nine times while burning nine pieces of copal. During that ceremony, the souls passing through the portal had *descended* to the heavens, making their way to the Lower World to begin their journey through their next life. The energy in that portal initiated a downward trajectory into Dreamtime. Now, the energy in this vortex had a dramatically upward thrust. Lady Sak K'uk's invocation and the thirteen pieces of copal were creating a portal to the higher spiritual realms. I was enthralled by the prospect of her invocation conjuring a supernatural manifestation that might appear through this opening to the Upper World.

As smoke was released by each piece of burning copal, Lady Sak K'uk's own form became more solid and the force of the energy in the vortex increased. Suddenly, I found myself pulled up into the energy vortex and through the portal. A wave of terror raced through my body. This was not at all what I had expected and the abruptness and intensity of the event shocked me. But I quickly realized that Lady Sak K'uk' was journeying with me, and her presence calmed and soothed me.

Glancing down, as I felt myself rushing upward toward the heavens with Lady Sak K'uk', I could see my physical body, sitting on the stone platform beside the temple, rapidly receding below us. The sensation was almost identical to my out-of-body journey with the Celestial Bird at the West Courtyard thirty years earlier and I was excited about revisiting my previous destination, the "Center of Spiritual Creation." But to my amazement, as we reached that place we continued moving upward to an even higher realm. I was stunned and amazed. For some reason I had always assumed there was nothing beyond the Center, but now a vast new realm was opening up to me. The Maya concept of thirteen heavens was taking on a whole new meaning.

Shortly thereafter, our movement slowed and then stopped, and I floated with Lady Sak K'uk,' suspended in this expansive ethereal space. As I looked down and saw the Center of Spiritual Creation far, far below me, I became completely disoriented and overcome with a vertigo so intense that I felt nauseated. I quickly shifted my gaze to Lady Sak K'uk', seeking her reassurance. Her radiant countenance comforted me immediately and the feeling of vertigo began to subside. It had taken me years to become comfortable with journeying and learning how to work with the energies at the Center of Spiritual Creation since my initial experience, and I realized it would also take some time for me to become comfortable returning to this realm. The question that immediately came to mind was: "Where am I?"

As soon as the question arose, I began to experience Lady Sak K'uk' communicating with me telepathically as if she had read my mind and was now responding. I learned from her that I was on the Plane of the Ascended Masters. She explained that my Awakening had allowed me access to this higher spiritual realm. Rather than being the final step in my spiritual journey, my Awakening was just the beginning and, as had been the case for seekers throughout the ages, my real journey was about to start.

Her "statements" seemed to echo through time and space, causing a shift in my awareness that filled me with a deep peace and sense of gratitude. Ever since it occurred, I had been struggling to understand and process my Awakening experience at the cave—Why had it happened? What did it mean? What do I do now? Suddenly, all the questioning, uncertainty, and doubt that had been troubling me faded. In Lady Sak K'uk's presence, I realized there was nothing I needed to figure out, nothing I needed to resolve, and nothing in particular I needed to do. My journey was continuing; my learning was ongoing. And although I had no idea exactly where this journey would take me and what I might encounter in the future, the thought of continuing to deepen my knowledge and understanding was thrilling. I vowed then that I would soon return to this spiritual plane.

Just then, the energy around me started to shift and I felt myself being pulled back into the vortex towards the portal at the temple. Lady Sak K'uk' remained behind as I began my descent. Soon I was back in my body and became acutely aware of the stiffness in my back and the hardness of the masonry rubble under my legs and ankles. The sounds of other visitors outside the temple came into sharp focus and I felt an urge to leave as quickly as possible. I closed my eyes again for a moment to say a brief prayer of thanks to Lady Sak K'uk' and the other Maya spirits and then rose, turned, and climbed down to the bottom of the pyramid. From there, I turned and crossed the Main Plaza, headed for a small restaurant just beyond the park entrance where I knew the shaman would be waiting.

When I arrived, I was relieved to find him sitting at a table by himself. He was wearing a crisp, white Oaxaca-style shirt, with two narrow, colorfully embroidered panels running the length of the front, and new blue jeans. As always, his calm, confident, self-assured bearing and worldly demeanor set him apart from the frenetic activity surrounding us. During the preceding two weeks I had been quite impressed as I watched him move effortlessly between the ethereal world of ceremony and the pragmatic demands of his life at home in the urban hustle and bustle of Merida, Mexico. Watching him as I approached the restaurant, I thought anyone meeting him for the first time would never imagine he was a gifted shaman and ceremonial leader but rather assume he might be a university professor, doctor or possibly even a diplomat.

The shaman greeted me with his customary warmth, a big smile, and a knowing look. I was grateful to have some time alone with him before the rest of the group joined us. We talked about the progress I was making on my book and my plans for teaching and leading groups to sacred sites in Mexico in the future. We talked about the importance of continuing to be open to inspiration from the higher spiritual realms. We talked about my Palenque visions and how they related to my Awakening experience at the cave at Oxkintok. Most importantly though, we talked about my newfound focus for my teaching, and how my Awakening would enable me to teach from personal experience and help others find what I had found.

During a pause in our conversation, I looked out to the parking lot that bordered the restaurant and noticed other members of the group approaching. I took the opportunity to ask him one last question, one that had been on my mind for decades but that I'd never asked my other Maya teachers. I asked him why I, a white American who grew up in the suburbs of Chicago, was able to have these extraordinary visionary experiences at these ancient ceremonial centers. He looked at me, paused, and then with a wry smile said "because you showed up." I realized immediately that part of my mission now was to help others to learn how to show up as well.

TERMINOLOGY

AMERICAN INDIAN AND INDIAN Throughout this book, I generally use the term Indian, rather than Native American, when referring to indigenous peoples. Although Native American is the common term used in popular culture, and one many believe to be the favored description, it is not the term endorsed by the majority of indigenous peoples. Referencing specific tribal affiliations (e.g. Muskogee Creek, Lakota, Hopi, Maya, etc.) is preferred, although, when a general designation is required, the term Indian, or American Indian, is used. Indigenous authors, journalists, and activists—as well as other governmental, political and social organizations—follow this convention. Some examples include the American Indian Movement (AIM); the National Museum of the American Indian (NMAI); the Bureau of Indian Affairs (BIA); and Indian Country Today Media Network (ICTMN), a national news source about native peoples in North America.

BCE and CE Throughout this book I use the term BCE (Before the Common Era) rather than BC (Before Christ) to reference dates prior to the birth of Christ. I use the term CE (Common Era) rather than AD (Anno Domini) to reference dates following the birth of Christ.

CHANUPA The Lakota term for the sacred prayer pipe used in their unique Chanupa ceremony to convey prayers to the Great Spirit (see, Wakan Tanka) and other spiritual beings. Sacred pipes have been used by indigenous cultures throughout the world, with each culture developing a specific ceremonial style. Prehistoric pipes found in connection with ancient North American Indian ceremonial centers have been determined to be over fifteen hundred years old.

DIVINE AND DIVINE FEMININE Many names are used to describe the Ultimate Reality, depending upon the cultural or religious frame of reference. Some call this Source, the Absolute, the One God, Brahman, Great Spirit, Allah, Ultimate Mystery, or other names. I use the term Divine throughout this book to describe this transcendent and immanent reality. I also use the terms Divine Feminine and Goddess to reference the feminine, maternal aspect of the Divine, thereby reflecting the universal belief shared by indigenous peoples, Gnostic Christians, and other mystical traditions that the Divine is both male and female, both Father and Mother.

HANBLECHIA The Lakota term for their unique style of a spiritual ceremony often referred to as a Vision Quest. Versions of this ceremony are common to native peoples throughout the Americas, including the Maya, and are practiced by indigenous cultures throughout the world.

HUNAB-KU The Mayan term for the Divine. Spanish missionaries, writing at the time of the Spanish Conquest in the sixteenth century, noted Hunab-Ku was incorporeal and could not be represented artistically.

374

INIPI The Lakota term for their unique style of a spiritual ceremony often referred to as a Sweat Lodge or Purification Lodge. Versions of this ceremony are common to native peoples throughout the Americas, including the Maya.

K'UH The Mayan term for the invisible, sacred quality—the Divine—inhabiting all things in the universe
(see also "Hunab-Ku").

K'ULEL The Mayan term for soul essence, generally translated as "white flowery breath body."

LAKOTA SIOUX I often use the term Lakota Sioux when referring to the Lakota Indians. While Lakota is the appropriate tribal designation, the term Sioux is not. The term Sioux, derived from the French and Ojibway languages, was initially used in a pejorative manner to describe the Lakota peoples beginning in the eighteenth century. I have included the term Sioux because it has become firmly embedded in popular culture and allows many readers to identify the unique cultural characteristics of the Lakota peoples. When I use the term Sioux, I put it in parentheses following the term Lakota. The Lakota peoples migrated to the Great Plains during the mid- to late-seventeenth century where they were a dominant presence until their defeat by the US Army during the Great Sioux War of 1877. They were subsequently confined to government-established reservations, predominantly in South Dakota but also in parts of North Dakota and Nebraska.

LOWER WORLD AND UPPER WORLD All shamanic cultures, including the Maya, share a common conception of a universe composed of three realms of existence. These include our physical world and two non-physical realms—the Lower World and Upper World. Alternative terms are frequently used to reference these three realms. The Lower World is sometimes referred to as the Underworld or, in Maya mythology, Xibalba; the Upper World is sometimes referred to as the Overworld; the physical world is sometimes referred to as the Middle World. Some Maya scholars also refer to the Upper World and the Lower World collectively as the Otherworld. Throughout this book, I use the terms Lower World, Upper World and Otherworld.

MAYA AND MAYAN The term Maya is appropriately used as a noun or adjective to describe the people and their culture (e.g. Maya art, Maya architecture, ancient Maya ceremonial centers, the Maya communities etc.). The term Mayan is used as a noun or adjective in reference to the Mayan language. Although this convention is often not followed in popular culture, this is the approved usage endorsed by government, scholars and other professionals. For an introduction to the Maya people and their culture see "The Maya," page 7.

MAYA NUMERALS The numbering system of the ancient Maya was composed primarily of dots and bars. Each dot represented the number one while a single bar represented the number five. Numbers one through four were represented by an increasing number of dots while the number five was represented by a single bar. The numbers six through nine were represented by an increasing number of dots accompanied by a single bar, the number ten was represented by two bars and the numbers eleven through nineteen were represented by an increasing number of dots associated with two bars. The chapters in this book follow these numbering conventions.

WAKAH-KAN The Mayan term for the archetypal World Tree, a central element in the spiritual worldview of the ancient and contemporary Maya. The World Tree, also referred to as the Cosmic Tree, *axis mundi,* or Sacred Tree of Life, has played a fundamental role in the sacred mythologies of the North American Indians, other indigenous Mesoamerican Indian peoples and other ancient cultures world-wide, including Egypt, India, Scandinavia, and the Middle East.

WAKAN TANKA The Lakota term for the Divine, typically translated as "Great Spirit" or "Great Mystery" and interpreted as the power or sacredness residing in all things.

YUWIPI The term for a traditional Lakota ceremony for physical and spiritual healing. During the yuwipi ceremony the Lakota healer, known as a yuwipi man, summons spirits from the non-physical spiritual realms to assist in healing the person(s) requesting the ceremony.

BIBLIOGRAPHY

MAYA INDIANS: GENERAL

Andrews, E Wyllys IV. *Balankanche, Throne of the Tiger Priest.* Publication 32. New Orleans, LA: Middle American Research Institute, Tulane University, 1970.

Agurcia, Fasquelle, Ricardo. "Rosalila, Temple of the Sun King." Ellen E. Bell, Marcello A. Canuto and Robert J. Sharer, eds. *Understanding Early Classic Copan.* Philadelphia, PA: University of Pennsylvania Museum of Archaeology and Anthropology, 2004.

Aveni, Anthony F. *Skywatchers of Ancient Mexico.* Austin, TX: University of Texas Press, 1980.

Aveni, Anthony F. *Stairway to the Stars.* New York, NY: John Wiley and Sons, 1997.

Bell, Ellen E., Marcello A. Canuto and Robert J. Sharer, eds. *Understanding Early Classic Copan.* Philadelphia, PA: University of Pennsylvania Museum of Archaeology and Anthropology, 2004.

Bricker, Victoria and Gabrielle Vail, eds. *Papers on the Madrid Codex*. New Orleans, LA: Middle American Research Institute, Tulane University, 1997.

Campa, Mario Perez and Laura Sotelo Santos. *The Mayas: The Splendor of a Great Culture*. Trans. David Castledine. Anzures, Mex: Monoclem Ediciones, 2006.

Coe, Michael D. *The Maya*. 8th ed. New York, NY: Thames and Hudson, 2011.

Demarest, Arthur. *Ancient Maya: The Rise and Fall of a Rainforest Civilization*. Cambridge, UK: Cambridge University Press, 2004.

Fash, Barbara W. *The Copan Sculpture Museum: Ancient Maya Artistry in Stucco and Stone*. Cambridge, MA: Peabody Museum Press, 2011.

Freidel, David, Linda Schele and Joy Parker. *Maya Cosmos, Three Thousand Years on the Shaman's Path*. New York, NY: William Morrow, 1993.

Foster, Lynn V. *Handbook to Life in the Ancient Maya World*. New York, NY: Oxford University Press, 2002.

Gallenkamp, Charles. *Maya: The Riddle and Rediscovery of a Lost Civilization*. New York, NY: Viking Penguin Inc., 1985.
Grube, Nikolai, ed. *Maya: Divine Kings of the Rain Forest*. Kóhn: Könemann, 2006.

Herrera, Antonio de. *General History of the Vast Continent and the Islands of America*. Vol. 4. Translated by Captain John Stevens IV. London: Printed for Jer. Batley, 1726.

Houston, Stephen D. and Takeshi Inomata. *The Classic Maya*. New York: Cambridge University Press, 2009.

Katz, Friedrich. *The Ancient American Civilizations*. New York, NY: Praeger, 1972.

Kelly, Joyce. *The Complete Visitor's Guide to Mesoamerican Ruins*. Norman, OK: University of Oklahoma Press, 1982.

Milbrath, Susan. *Star Gods of the Maya: Astronomy in Art, Folklore, and Calendars*. Austin, TX: University of Texas Press, 1999.

Miller, Arthur G. *On the Edge of the Sea: Mural Panting at Tancah-Tulum, Quintana Roo, Mexico*. Washington D.C.: Dumbarton Oaks, 1982.

Martin, Simon. "Cacao in Ancient Maya Religion: First fruit from the Maize Tree and Other Tales from the Underworld" in *Chocolate in Mesoamerica: A Cultural History of Cacao*. Cameron L. McNeil, ed. Gainesville, FL: University Press of Florida, 2006.

Martin, Simon and Nikolai Grube. *Chronicle of the Maya Kings and Queens: Deciphering the Dynasties of the Ancient Maya*. 2nd ed. London: Thames and Hudson, 2008.

Morley, Sylvanus G. *The Ancient Maya*. Stanford, CA: Stanford University Press, 1947.

Perera, Victor and Robert D. Bruce. *The Last Lords of Palenque.* Boston, MA: Little, Brown, 1982.

Robertson, Merle Greene. *The Sculpture of Palenque: Volume III: The Late Buildings of the Palace.* Princeton, NJ: Princeton University Press, 1985. 3 vols.

Roys, Ralph L. *The Book of Chilam Balam of Chumayel.* Washington, D.C.: Carnegie Institution of Washington, 1933.

Schele, Linda and David Freidel. *A Forest of Kings: The Untold Story of the Ancient Maya.* New York, NY: William Morrow, 1990.

Schele, Linda and Peter Mathews. *The Code of Kings: The Language of Seven Sacred Maya Temples and Tombs.* New York, N.Y: Scribner, 1998.

Schele, Linda and Mary Ellen Miller. *The Blood of Kings: Dynasty and Ritual in Maya Art.* Fort Worth, TX: Kimbell Art Museum, 1986.

Schmidt, Peter, Mercedes de la Garza, and Enrique Nalda, eds. *Maya Civilization.* London: Thames and Hudson, 1998.

Sharer, Robert J. and Loa P. Traxler. *The Ancient Maya.* 6th ed. Stanford, CA: Stanford University Press, 2006.

Stevens, John Lloyd. *Incidents of Travel in Central America, Chiapas and the Yucatan.* 2 vols. London: J. Murray, 1841.

Stuart, David. *The Inscriptions from Temple XIX at Palenque.* Lafayette, CA: The Pre-Columbian Art Research Institute, 2005.

Tate, Carolyn E. *Yaxchilan: The Design of a Maya Ceremonial City.* Austin, TX: University of Texas Press, 1992.

Thompson, Sir John Eric Sidney. *A Preliminary Study of the Ruins of Coba, Quintana Roo, Mexico.* Washington, DC: Carnegie Institution of Washington, 1932.

Tozzer, Alfred M. *Landa's Relación de las cosas de Yucatan: A Translation.* Papers of the Peabody Museum of American Archaeology and Ethnology. Cambridge, MA: Harvard University, 1941.

Webster, David. *The Fall of the Ancient Maya: Solving the Mystery of the Maya Collapse.* London: Thames and Hudson, 2002.

Wisdom, Charles. *The Chorti Indians of Guatemala.* Chicago, IL: University of Chicago Press, 1940.

MAYA INDIANS: CONQUEST

Carnegie Institution of Washington; Staff Members and Research Associates. *Cooperation in Research.* Washington, DC: The Carnegie Institution of Washington, 1938.

Casas, Bartolomé de las. *The Devastation of the Indies: A Brief Account.* Baltimore, MD: The Johns Hopkins University Press, 1992.

Clendinnen, Inga. *Ambivalent Conquests: Maya and Spaniard in Yucatan, 1517-1570.* 2nd ed. Cambridge: Cambridge University Press, 1987.

Conrad, Geoffery and Arthur Demarest. *Religion and Empire: The Dynamics of Aztec and Inca Expansionism*. Cambridge: Cambridge University Press, 1984.

Diamond, Jared. *Guns, Germs, and Steel*. New York: Norton & Company, 1997.

Elliott, J. H. *The Old World and the New 1492-1650*. London: Cambridge University Press, 1970.

Jennings, Francis. *The Invasion of America: Indians, Colonialism, and the Cant of Conquest*. Chapel Hill, NC: The University of North Carolina Press, 1975.

Mann, Charles C. *1491: New Revelations of the Americas Before Columbus*. New York: Alfred Knopf, 2005.

Scholes, France V and Eleanor B Adams. *Don Diego Quijada, alcalde mayor de Yucatán, 1561-1565*. 2 Vols. Mexico: Antigua librería Robredo, de J. Porrúa e hijos, 1938.

NORTH AMERICAN INDIANS

Amiotte, Arthur. "Our Other Selves." *I Become Part of It*. D.M. Dooling and Paul Jordan-Smith, eds. San Francisco, CA: Harper, 1992.

Albert White Hat Sr. Trans. *Lakota Ceremonial Songs*. Rosebud, SD: Sinte Gleska University, 1983.

Benedict, Ruth Fulton. *The Concept of the Guardian Spirit in North America*. Memoirs of the American Anthropological Association – No. 29. Menasha, WI: American Anthropological Association, 1923.

Brown, Joseph. *The Sacred Pipe*. Norman, OK: University of Oklahoma Press, 1953.

Bucko, Raymond. *The Lakota Ritual of the Sweat Lodge*. Lincoln, NB: University of Nebraska Press, 1999.

DeMallie, Raymond. *The Sixth Grandfather*. Lincoln, NB: University of Nebraska Press, 1984.

Fitzgerald, Michael. *Yellowtail, Seeker of Visions*. Norman, OK: University of Oklahoma Press, 1991.

Fewkes, Jesse Walter. *Hopi Snake Ceremonials*. Albuquerque, NM: Avanyu Publishing, 1986.

Hillerman, Tony. *The Boy Who Made Dragonfly*. New York, NY: Harper and Row, 1972.

Irwin, Lee. *The Dream Seekers: Native American Visionary Traditions of the Great Plains*. Norman, OK: University of Oklahoma Press, 1994.

Lame Deer, John Fire and Richard Erdoes. *Lame Deer Seeker of Visions*. New York, NY: Simon and Schuster, 1972.

Loeb, E. M. *The Blood Sacrifice Complex*. Memoirs of the American Anthropological Association – No. 30. Menasha, WI: American Anthropological Association, 1923.

Mails, Thomas. *Fools Crow*. Garden City, NY: Doubleday & Company, 1979.

Mails, Thomas. *Fools Crow: Wisdom and Power*. Tulsa, OK: Council Oak Books, 1991.

Mails, Thomas. *Hopi Survival Kit*. New York, NY: Stewart, Tabori, and Chang, 1997.

Mails, Thomas. *Secret Native American Pathways*. Tulsa, OK: Council Oak Books, 1988.

Mails, Thomas. *Sundancing at Rosebud and Pine Ridge*. Sioux Falls, SD: Center for Western Studies, 1978.

Miller, Jay. *Shamanic Odyssey: The Lushootseed Salish Journey to the Land of the Dead*. Menlo Park, CA: Ballena Press, 1988.

Mora, Joseph. *The Year of the Hopi*. New York, NY: Rizzoli International, 1982.

Neihardt, John. *Black Elk Speaks*. Lincoln, NB: University of Nebraska Press, 1988.

Parsons, Elsie Clews. *A Pueblo Indian Journal: 1920-1921*. American Anthropological Association, Memoirs no 3. Menasha, WI: The Collegiate Press, 1925.

Rice, Julian. *Black Elk's Story*. Albuquerque, NM: University of New Mexico Pres, 1991.

Schaafsma, Polly, ed. *Kachinas in the Pueblo World*. Albuquerque, NM: University of New Mexico Press, 1994.

Stolzman, William. *How to Take Part in Lakota Ceremonies.* Chamberlain, SD: Tipi Press, 1986.

Stolzman, William. *The Pipe and Christ.* Chamberlain, SD: Tipi Press, 1992.

Walker, James. *Lakota Belief and Ritual.* Lincoln NE: University of Nebraska Press, 1991.

Webb, William and Robert A. Weinstein. *Dwellers at the Source.* Albuquerque, NM: University of New Mexico Press, 1973.

Wright, Barton. *Hopi Material Culture.* Flagstaff AZ: The Heard Museum, 1979.

OTHER

Armstrong, Karen. *The Case for God.* New York, NY: Alfred A. Knopf, 2009.

Campbell, Joseph. *Historical Atlas of World Mythology Volume I: The Way of the Animal Powers.* New York, NY: Harper and Row, 1983.

Campbell, Joseph. *Historical Atlas of World Mythology Volume II: The Way of the Seeded Earth.* New York, NY: Harper and Row, 1988.

Chadwick, Henry. *The Church in Ancient Society – From Galilee to Gregory the Great.* Oxford, UK: Oxford University Press, 2001.

Danielou, Alain. *Shiva and Dionysus: The Religion of Nature and Eros*. New York, NY: Inner Traditions International, 1984.

Eliade, Mircea. *Shamanism: Archaic Techniques of Ecstasy.* Bollinger Series 76. New York, NY: Pantheon, 1964.

Long, A. A. *Epictetus: A Stoic and Socratic Guide to Life*. Oxford: Oxford University Press, 2002.

Pagels, Elaine. *The Gnostic Gospels*. New York, NY: Random House, 1979.

Pagels, Elaine. *Beyond Belief, The Secret gospel of Thomas*. New York, NY: Random House, 2003.

Plutarch. *Moralia, Volume V.* Translated by Frank Cole Babbitt. London, England: Harvard University Press, 1936.

Toynbee, Arnold. *Mankind and Mother Earth: A Narrative History of the World*. New York: Oxford University Press, 1976.

Toynbee, Arnold. *An Historian's Approach to Religion*. 2nd ed. Oxford: Oxford University Press, 1979.

Trigger, Bruce G. *Early Civilizations: Ancient Egypt in Context*. New York, NY: American University in Cairo Press, 1993.

Trigger, Bruce G. *Understanding Early Civilizations: A Comparative Study*. New York, NY: Cambridge University Press, 2003.

ACKNOWLEDGMENTS

*My gratitude for help and support in bringing this book
to life goes out to many people.*

To Joy Parker, a gifted editor, inspiring coach, brilliant teacher, and dear friend. This book would not have been possible without her insights and feedback based on her deep academic knowledge of the ancient Maya and personal experience from her own spiritual quest.

To Michael Harner for starting me on my shamanic odyssey, Joan Halifax for introducing me to my first Native American teachers and their ancestral lands, and Thomas Mails for introducing me to the hidden, esoteric spiritual wisdom of the indigenous cultures.

To my American Indian teachers: my adopted Grandfather, Marcellus "Bear Heart" Williams for his spiritual guidance, mentorship, patience, and kindness; Wallace Black Elk for teaching me the sacred Lakota ceremonial songs and providing the opportunity for me to dance and pierce in a traditional Plains Indian Sun Dance when he was the Intercessor; and Richard Moves Camp for his support and inspiration, and for teaching me, by the example he sets, the true meaning of the Lakota Values.

To my Maya Indian teachers: Hunbatz Men for introducing me to the world of Maya shamanism and guiding me on my journey with the Maya for twenty-five years, and Miguel Angel Vergara for continuing to help me deepen my experiences with the ancient and contemporary Maya.

To Fr. Thomas Keating for helping me understand my encounter with the Divine and introducing me to the parallels between indigenous spiritual practices and Christian mystical traditions.

To Shawn Randall for helping me deepen my connection to the Maya ancestors, and Molly Larkin for assisting me in creating workshops to share these teachings.

To my many friends who have shared this spiritual journey with me and to those who read and commented on earlier drafts of the manuscript.

To the staff of the Denison University Library who patiently assisted me with my research.

To my editors: Anne Dubuisson for helping me turn thirty-five years of field notes and journal entries into a coherent book outline and then expertly guiding me through the completion of the book; Lyn Robertson for her encouragement, thoughtful insights, and invaluable suggestions; and my copyeditor, Holly Thomas, for her support, professionalism, and attention to detail.

To the ancient Maya ancestors who left such a magnificent spiritual legacy and allowed me the honor and privilege of experiencing their wisdom through the visions they bestowed on me.

In Lak'Ech… A Lak'En

(I am you. You are me.)

ABOUT THE AUTHOR

Otto John Kralovec III began the study and practice of shamanism and the spiritual ceremonies of the indigenous cultures of North America in the early 1980s. In 1985 he traveled for the first time to the ceremonial sites of the ancient Maya Indians in Mexico where a series of profound mystical experiences changed his life forever.

Over the past thirty-five years, he has continued his in-depth studies with North American and Maya Indian spiritual leaders, learning their spiritual practices and ancient wisdom teachings. John has participated regularly in vision quests, purification lodges, yuwipi ceremonies and a Sundance. In 2007, he was initiated by Maya h-men Ildefonso Aké Cocom during a Fire Ceremony at the sacred site of Xoclán in Mexico. John is a Pipe Carrier and Purification Lodge leader and is also a gifted visionary and seer in the Maya Chilam tradition.

www.pathwaystothedivine.org
FB: Otto John Kralovec
T: @PathwaysDivine

61971523R00238

Made in the USA
Lexington, KY
25 March 2017